Writing to Deadline

The Journalist at Work

Also by Donald Murray

Crafting a Life in Essay, Story, Poem
0-86709-403-6 / 1996 / 166pp

Shoptalk
Learning to Write with Writers
0-86709-258-0 / 1990 / 207pp

Expecting the Unexpected
Teaching Myself—and Others—to Read and Write
0-86709-243-2 / 1989 / 276pp

Learning by Teaching
Selected Articles on Writing and Teaching
0-86709-025-1 / 1982 / 184pp

For more information or to place an order, visit our website:
www.heinemann.com

Writing to Deadline

The Journalist at Work

Donald M. Murray

HEINEMANN
Portsmouth, NH

Heinemann
A division of Reed Elsevier Inc.
361 Hanover Street
Portsmouth, NH 03801–3912
www.heinemann.com

Offices and agents throughout the world

Library of Congress Cataloging-in-Publication Data
Murray, Donald Morison, 1924–
Writing to deadline : the journalist at work / by Donald M. Murray.
p. cm.
Includes bibliographical references and index.
ISBN 0-325-00225-8
1. Journalism—Authorship—Handbooks, manuals, etc. I. Title.
PN4775.M84 2000
808′.06607—dc21 99-462112

Editors: Tom Newkirk, Leigh Peake
Cover design: Michael Leary
Manufacturing: Louise Richardson

Printed in the United States of America on acid-free paper
04 03 02 01 00 MV 1 2 3 4 5

This book is dedicated to
Christopher Scanlan,
master journalist,
caring teacher,
writing colleague,
constant friend.

Contents

Preface

This book, like all books, has a history. It began with a family that read newspapers morning, evening, and Sunday, stimulating my childhood imagination before I could read with the strange and interesting information they shared. I learned to read as much from newspapers as from books, working from the funnies to sports to "adult" news of murders, kidnappings, The Great Depression, politics, and wars in distant lands that I knew someday I would attend—and did.

When I was in the fourth grade, Miss Chapman looked down, pointed to me and commanded, "Donald! You are class editor." I had to learn to ask questions that produced answers, check the answers for accuracy, produce stories on deadline that could be understood, and master the mysteries of the purple ink and yellowish gelatin of the hectograph that produced the paper.

Each spring, bored, impatient to get on with real life, I dropped out of high school in the tenth, eleventh, and twelfth grades. I said I was twenty-one, then twenty-two, and finally twenty-three to work on the *Boston Record-American*. I don't know if they believed my age, but they knew I would work long hours for about four bucks a day. I didn't graduate from public high school, but I still made it to Tilton School and Tilton Junior College in New Hampshire to work in a dorm, play football, and serve as editor of *The Tiltonian*. After combat as a paratrooper in World War II, I went to the University of New Hampshire where I decided I was a poet and too talented to work on the college paper. But full-time jobs for poets were scarce, and weeks before graduation I got a job as a copy boy on the *Boston Herald*.

Years later, after practicing newspaper and magazine journalism, I was hired to revive the journalism program at the University of New Hampshire, and while I was doing that I served as writing coach at a number of newspapers including the *Providence Journal* and at *The Boston Globe*. Many newspapers had internal publications that publicized errors that had appeared in the paper. I was more interested in what worked—how did reporters and editors collect information, organize it in a clear, coherent, and often graceful style in a matter of hours, meeting impossible deadlines day after day, hour after hour?

My *Boston Globe* accounts of what worked and how were published in two editions of *Writing for Your Readers.* The second edition went out of print several years ago but this book is built on its foundation, using interviews with *Globe* writers and analyses of *Globe* stories and much of my commentary. But this new edition adds far more as it describes what I am still learning in an apprenticeship that began in the fourth grade when I was ten years old and continues at the age of seventy-five as I write my weekly "Over 60" column for *The Boston Globe.*

Writing to Deadline

The Journalist at Work

Chapter 1

The Journalist's Craft

A confession:

For decades, I was ashamed of my newspaper and magazine journalism. I had been an English major in college, where I was taught that poetry was the highest form of literature, drama was next, serious novels and some short stories were worthy of study, nonfiction in the eighteenth and early nineteenth century could become literature, but contemporary journalism was, well, journalism. It was not—and could not—be literature.

I bought into my professors' value system. After graduation I wrote journalism and dreamt literature. I was a professional writer but I was not literary. I published nonfiction in newspapers and magazines and books. I also published some poetry, a couple of short stories, and two novels, one under a pseudonym; but basically I was a journalist, not—I thought—a real writer. Even a Pulitzer—for journalism—could not change my feeling that I practiced a craft that could never become art.

And then one day, late in a life of writing, in answering a question after a public reading of an example of my nonfiction, I realized the obvious: Art is first craft, and I could take pride in the practice of my craft. More than that, I recognized that all I had written in every genre—fiction, poetry, nonfiction—was built upon the secure foundation of the journalist's craft. I reviewed, with a new pride, the assumptions of craft to which I had apprenticed myself so many years before and to which I am still—and now proudly—apprenticed.

The Craft of the Reporter

When I was a little boy my mother complained, "Donald can hear the grass grow." I was an expert at hearing what I was not supposed to hear. I listened to family stories—gossip—from the other room, behind the couch, under the dining room table, in the bushes beside the porch, below the open window, at the top of the stairs, beside the grates on the second floor that allowed the heat—and the stories—to rise.

I was a listener, a watcher, a spy, a sneak. I was driven by a continuous, hungry curiosity—and I still am. Part of the reason was that I was an only child in a home of four adults—grandmother, uncle, mother, father (in order of power and availability) and I needed to understand their complex relationship. If Grandmother criticized Mother about how she made the tea, Mother would complain to Dad when he got home from work that he should get a better job, and then Dad would beat me with his leather razor strap. I needed to learn the pattern, try to understand it—and hide.

My world was full of contradictions. We were strict Baptists and I was taught to respect the minister, but we always had "roast minister" for Sunday dinner, during which his sermons and private behavior were criticized. We were told to love thy neighbor as thyself and to hate the Irish Catholics who were most of our neighbors. I was told never to lie and then assigned to tell the landlord that my father was sick when he wasn't so we could avoid paying the rent. When I asked questions, the answers didn't clarify but increased the confusion. I became an investigative reporter before I knew the term.

An Instinct for Story

I developed an instinct for story, the dramatic interaction between people that moved forward with cause and effect. I was taught by listening to fundamental sermons that always had a clear moral, and by observation of family and neighborhood dramas in which the moral was far from clear. My Scots grandmother who ruled the family told stories. She came from a great oral tradition in which family history and the Great Truths were related by narrative. I not only listened to the stories of conflict, of loss and victory, health and sickness and death, in the family, but observed them. Dad got promoted, Dad got fired; Grandmother was the most powerful person in the world, Grandmother had a "shock" and was bedridden for life; I was told that if I turned the other cheek, Jesus would personally stay the hand of the bully; He did not. My life was full of conflict, contradiction, and mystery I needed to understand. I made up my own stories and even created a family of small people with whom I lived in the walls. If I could understand the stories, get them right, I could survive.

My need to know led me to the six reporter's questions that years later, when I was first working on a newspaper, I would count out on my fingers before returning to the paper and facing the fierce questioning of the city editor: Who? What? When? Where? How? Why?

Who? My mother would gossip about the people in church and then tell me not to judge Christianity by individual Christians. I disagreed. Practice authenticated the preaching. I developed the journalist's belief that people made events more than events made people—and even if events dominated, the story was about people—who did what to whom.

I listened to what was said and how it was said, inflection changing meaning. I learned to hear what was *not* said in a home where the greatest hurt was inflicted by silence. I was fascinated by the uncles who became boys when they visited their mother, my grandmother. I studied the Irish around me who were supposedly condemned to hell, were common, and who drank, and often found them kinder than my own kind. We moved to an orthodox Jewish neighborhood and I became a *shabbos goy,* earning a nickel to turn on the lights in Orthodox homes at Friday dusk. I found how different people were—and then I learned how much they were the same.

What? One of the few things my father and I did together was chase fire engines. Since we didn't own a car, our radius was short and it didn't happen very often, but we "enjoyed" the excitement of the fire, the terror of the victims, the bravery and skill of the firemen, the fire-fighting equipment—pumpers and ladder trucks, hoses, and axes. I had the reporter's questions long before I was a reporter—what happened, what caused it, was everyone saved, were any injured, how much property was lost, would it be rebuilt?

When? The reporter lives in the child's immediacy. Journalism, first of all, deals with the now. What happened overnight, this morning, tonight. Hour by hour, the world changes and journalism tries to keep up with it. Of course it is the continuing challenge of the journalist to put the present in the context of the past—and the future. What were the forces that came together in the moment? What will they produce in the future?

Where? The reporter wants to describe the setting—the presidential press conference on a golf course, the operating room, the alley where the shooting took place, the stock exchange, the playing field, the front stage and the back stage. Journalists focus first on people, but then must place the people in their world. The most effective reporters often write in dramatic scenes like a play or a movie, so that the readers witness the conflict between the characters in a setting.

How? When a classmate playing hockey fell through the ice and was rescued, part of me stood back asking questions: How was the boy saved when the ice broke? How did the ladders laid out on thin ice allow rescuers to reach him? My questions never stopped. How did the civil wars within our family hurt by silence, how could so much pain be caused by gesture? How could one policeman get a gang member to talk but not another? How did the fireman know this fire was set? How did the minority leader influence the legislative vote?

Why? Our children drive us crazy with their continuous *whys*. Why doesn't the sky fall? Why is grass green? Why does ice melt? Why is Dad mad? Why did he lose his job? Why did Uncle Joe refuse to let him borrow money? Why are you crying?

Most children learn not to ask why. It isn't polite. It makes people uncomfortable. And, of course, people don't really know why. Dad said he was fired because he wasn't a college man, but if sales had kept rising would the company bosses have cared?

Reporters are grown-ups who never stop asking why. And each answer leads to another question. Curiosity is a hunger that can never be satisfied. It is a way of life and, I think, a fine way of life because an unceasing wonder keeps the asker forever young, forever aware, forever seeking, gloriously unsatisfied.

The Craft of the Writer

My Uncle Don called me "a broadcaster" when I was a small boy, a Scottish term of insult for a gossip, someone who liked to tell stories, especially family stories, stories told in confidence, stories that connected what had been observed, overheard, discovered, and possibly imagined.

I loved to have stories read to me and told to me. I loved to read stories and to hear them on the radio—there was no television then—and I loved to tell stories that got better and better with the telling. While I was getting dressed, eating breakfast, walking to school, sitting in class, playing or working after school, eating, doing homework or avoiding homework, I was telling myself stories. Each night I put myself to sleep by telling stories. Stories explained the world, found cause and effect in confusion, sequence in contradiction, order in disorder. I was fascinated by stories, terrified by stories, comforted by stories, instructed by stories. I was a child of narrative, so I moved naturally from fourth-grade class editor to high-school editor to junior-college editor to copy boy to cub reporter, writing stories for the old *Boston Herald*—and getting paid for it. I began my full-time apprenticeship to the journalist's craft, which continues today.

Write with Information

I can remember the first green metal desk with the center well for the Royal typewriter to which I was assigned when I made it to the city staff of the *Herald*. I was on the aisle near the city editor, where he could educate me by public humiliation, ridicule, insult, and correction. This was not (and is not) my preferred method of instruction, but I had survived paratroop training in World War II so I survived this. I sat immediately behind Catherine Coyne, to my mind the best political reporter in the city and the only woman on the staff. Ahead of her was Don Fessenden on rewrite; just a few years later, I would sit beside him turning out forty to fifty stories a night with the two-finger, one-thumb typing technique I still use fifty-one years later. With their example and the city desk's direct instruction, I unlearned what my literature teachers had taught me. I was not to write with style but with information.

I had been rewarded at the university for writing backward, from literary theory to literary practice, from broad theme to specific material, from vision to word. Now I was commanded to write forward, seeing then reporting what I had seen—and, wonder of wonders, often discovering meaning I did not expect as I wrote.

I wrote with information: specific revealing details, concrete images, quotations, statistics, records, facts. Meaning came from connections between pieces of information, not from connections between words. The words were the symbols for information. Words allowed me to arrange the information so it had significance, order, logic, structure: meaning.

I resisted, of course. I was a secret poet desperate to go public, a novelist who was writing an experimental novel based on a theory, not on life. My novel was so significant that it had no individual characters with names, no dialogue, no scenes, no story—and fortunately, no publisher. I wanted to play solo before being a member of the band; I wanted to practice high style before learning the basic style of a delivery of specific information with clarity and grace. I did not know then that any high style I might achieve would be constructed on the firm base of reporting specific information with clarity and, eventually if I was lucky, grace.

I did not lose the love of words I still have today, but I discovered a new love—respect for the specific detail. I began to open my eyes at the fire, accident, election speech, even the news conference. I began to see the revealing detail and return to that third row desk where I tried to get out of the way of the information.

My breakthrough story came when I was assigned to follow Stan Eames, the paper's top reporter, to a nearby hotel where a man was on a ledge threatening to jump. Stan and I made it up to the room, but the story was his and so I went back down to the crowd that was chanting, "Jump! Jump! Jump!"

As I remember it, the man on the ledge crawled back into the room when an experienced police officer made a phone call to his room. Few of us can resist answering the phone even if we are on the way to killing ourselves. Since Stan was covering what was going on in the room while the potential jumper was on the ledge outside the room, I followed the specific detail—the terrifying chant of the crowd. I stood with the people who wanted him to jump and became increasingly angry when he did not. I wrote the story with information—specific, revealing details and direct quotations. I didn't attempt "great" writing, I just tried to get out of the way of the horrifying information. I had been on staff for at least a year by then, but I remember that this was the first story I wrote without fear of failure. I let the facts tell the story.

The crowd story had not been assigned, but I passed it in to the surprised city editor. It appeared in the classified section in the first edition of the paper, in the news section in the second, made page one in the last edition, and won an Associated Press Award not long afterward. And ever since, I have attempted to get out of the way of the information, to construct my stories with specific information.

Accuracy

I learned accuracy the way I had learned to march in the army—by loud, direct, specific instruction. Names spelled correctly, middle initials right, numbers and names of streets—or was it a road, a lane, an avenue, boulevard, circle? Ages of victims. Charges by police. Which police—city, county, state, public transportation police, attorney general's officers, FBI? Titles. Monsignors and rabbis and reverends and deacons. Doctors of medicine and dentistry and osteopathy and philosophy. I was told and then learned by public attack and embarrassment that it was worse to spell the name wrong than to charge a person with public lewdness. If you got the name of the street wrong, no one trusted anything in the story.

First, the Lede

We still used the spelling "l-e-d-e" for the word *lead* so it would stand out on the telegraphic printout—"NU LEDE"—to signal a new top for the stories that were almost always written in the inverted pyramid style, with the latest and most important information first. There are more variations on that story form than there used to be when I began, but the inverted pyramid with the most important information first, the next most important second, and so on, is still the basic news story format.

After wandering around in the discursive meadows of literary criticism, I was faced with an intellectual challenge: to put what was important first. I had to decide what was important. The city desk demanded a precision of thought that, at first, terrified me. I learned by trial and error, and in part what I learned were the newspaper clichés of vision at that time when newsboys still called out the latest on the street and first pages of the afternoon papers were replated—written new—every twenty minutes. Later on I would teach against this tradition, but first I had to know the tradition and practice it.

Catherine Coyne first told me the obvious: If I reworked the lede so that the information the reader needed appeared in the sequence in which the reader needed it, then retyped the first page neatly, the editors would edit the rest lightly. She was right.

The craft of the lead (its contemporary spelling) is still my obsession, although today most journalists spell the term "l-e-a-d." Note the two-word lead at the beginning of this chapter. I would confess the prejudice against journalistic writing that I once held and that my readers might hold, then introduce the craft I now admire and respect. The first few lines of a piece of writing establish the focus of the writing. Since I was going to write about a craft that is often scorned but that I have come to respect, the lead established the context of the chapter. It also established the relationship between writer and reader. It was a confession. Our relationship would be intimate, confiding, worthy of trust. The lead established the authority of the writer. I was secure enough in my craft to admit my limitations. The lead set the direction of the writing. I had to tell the reader what I was confessing and why I had changed my opinion. The lead established the voice, the music of the writing that reveals and supports the meaning: A book on journalism begins with a two-word, one-sentence, *journalistic* lead.

When I turned from newspaper journalism to magazine articles, I regularly—and compulsively—averaged seventy-five draft leads (yes, I counted) before I found the right one, which of course might be lead number three or number twenty-seven, but after writing the others I now knew it was the right one. The first-draft leads directed me to the focus of the article—what would be included, what would be left out; the direction and dimension of the article; the article's direction and pace—then, the later-draft leads would direct me to the voice.

Less Is More

In school I had been taught to write long. I have some papers I wrote in the third grade that are surprisingly close—strong verbs, specific nouns, short sentences—to how I write today. I did not get *A*s. But school taught me to use longer and longer words, to make great boa constrictor sentences constructed of multiple clauses. I was taught that length equals intelligence.

My teachers were right. I needed to learn to write with more complexity, to deal with complicated information and complex ideas, to connect clauses, to document and qualify, to build fully developed paragraphs. Then I had to unlearn these things so I could write with clarity, grace, and simplicity, varying the sentence length, using short sentences for emphasis, writing as simply as the subject allowed.

I was taught that a five-line paragraph in type became a ten-line paragraph when compressed into a newspaper column. My private rule was to worry about the length after five typewritten lines.

Verbs and Nouns

I learned a new respect for the verb, the engine that made the sentence go and could carry its own load of information. "The mayor came into the room," became, if accurate, "The mayor trotted," or stumbled or strolled or shuffled or strode. I realized the power of the noun to carry information, realized power of the basic English sentence: subject-verb-object. I realized that adjectives and adverbs, although necessary, could weaken—"very angry" was always less than "angry." I was learning my trade, how to hammer a nail straight, how to saw, how to plane.

Order

I moved from building sentences and paragraphs that carried meaning to constructing whole stories that made the reader continue to read. Why? Because I learned to deliver the information the reader needed or wanted when the reader wanted it. I remember telling myself that the reader needed a line that ran through the story that the reader could hold on to. If that line was there I might be able to add a bit of color. I learned the forms of stories: the inverted pyramid that gave the reader the essence of the story immediately and then explained it; the direct quote that plunged into the story immediately; the delayed lead that caught the reader's attention and then satisfied the reader's curiosity; the narrative; the interview that had one source and the profile that had many. Most of all, I learned that story had a form—some things were included, some were left out—and that I could extend and combine forms to contain the truth the reader needed.

Clarity

Finally, I began to learn the later lessons of the journalist's craft. I learned how to tell by revealing. I learned how to get out of the way of the story and allow the story to tell itself. And I began to trust the reader. I did not have to tell the reader what to think or how to feel, but simply give the reader the evidence and the reader would find the story.

Discovery

I also learned to trust the story, that I did not need to know in advance what I was going to write but that the drafts would instruct me. The act of writing would tell me what I thought and felt. The draft would reveal what it had to say and how it should be said. Writing was not the *result* of thought and feeling, but an *act* of thought and feeling. I began to write first for myself, to discover what I had to say and craft it so the reader could share my expedition into the unknown.

Voice

First: voice. The cry I made from the crib, the sounds I learned, the power of *I*. The grand ego from which all writers are bred. Discovering the power of your own voice, the delight in saying, the private joy of hearing what you say before it appears on the page. Then learning the other voices, the voice of the academy, the voice of the newspaper, and finally the discovery that you have not one voice but many. If you hear your own voice, you can adapt to the writing task and the music of the voice will instruct you. It will tell you if you are angry or sad, committed or distant, serious or humorous, and, as you write, the voice will change within the piece as you dance to what the voice of the text tells you that you have to say.

The Art of the Journalist

Art is a word most journalists fear. It seems pretentious, calling attention to yourself. It is something best said by others. And so we note that Camus and Hemingway were journalists and that the journalism of Addison, Steele, George Orwell, E. B. White, Marguerite Higgins, Meyer Berger, Rebecca West, Joseph Mitchell, Joan Didion, and all the rest through the centuries is art. But when they wrote their journalism, it was craft, a discipline of information and revelation.

❖ Journalist at Work ❖
DAVID MEHEGAN Interview

When I am at the *Globe*, I always enjoy stopping by David Mehegan's desk to chat about writing. Now the book editor at the *Globe*, he is articulate about our craft, and I learn from what he has to say about how effective writing is made.

David was born in Boston and grew up in the city and in Scituate. He earned a degree in English and journalism at Suffolk University and intended to go into broadcasting; but the opportunities came in print journalism, and he now realizes that he was better suited to that anyway. The story of his road to journalism may be instructive to those who want to find a job in hard times: the road is rarely clear or straight, but if you hone your talent through a variety of jobs, the break may come.

The first opportunity Mehegan had was as copy boy at the *Boston Herald-Traveler* while he was in college in the late sixties, ripping wire copy and getting coffee for writers and editors. David recalls,

> On that paper, an office boy (and we were all addressed as "boy," no matter how old we were) could get a tryout on the staff after a certain number of years. But the paper closed in March or April 1972 and I missed my chance. I was asked to write an inside story on the death of the *Herald* for *Boston Magazine* in June 1972, which brought me:
>
> (1) $250,
>
> (2) a plug in Frazier's column,
>
> (3) a million-dollar libel suit (settled out of court), and
>
> (4) by means too complicated to explain, a job as a college textbook editor at Houghton Mifflin Company.
>
> After two years of penury at Houghton Mifflin, editing books like *Fundamentals of Counseling* and *The Later Renaissance in England: Nondramatic Prose and Poetry, 1600–1660* and, believe it or not, a textbook on newswriting that is still in use, I went to the University of Massachusetts for more money and less stimulation as an assistant secretary to the Board of Trustees. During both of those jobs, I was working weekends at the *Globe* as a copyeditor.
>
> In 1976, Anne Wyman hired me to edit the letters column and do layout and copyediting on the editorial page. After three years and 35,000 letters, I became assistant magazine editor under Mike Janeway. Two years later, in 1981, Al Larkin went from magazine writer to magazine editor, succeeding Janeway, and I took his spot as writer. I was a staff magazine writer for three years, then went back to the night desk for one year. I went to the city desk as a general assignment reporter in 1985, then joined the suburban team, then went to the Business section in 1987 to cover the retailing beat, then became assistant book editor in 1991.

Q: *How do you prepare to interview someone?*

A: I need to know enough about what I'm writing about so that I don't ask questions that make me look foolish and so that I have a chance of understanding the person I'm talking to. But I do not worry about being ignorant because my theory is that we are all professional ignoramuses, it's our job not to know something and then to find out.

Q: *Do you have any special techniques for face-to-face interviews?*

A: No techniques, except to approach them with sensible curiosity, to treat people courteously, to show intense attention, and to try to respond deftly and intelligently with unprepared questions when the subject says surprising or unexpected things. Most people distrust and dislike reporters, but if they feel they can trust you, they will freely tell their story. I take notes and almost never use a tape. For me, every interview is a stumbling, mumbling thing.

Q: *How do you get people to answer questions they don't want to answer?*

A: Again I think trust is the key. Sometimes people can't answer a question, but more often they are afraid of what you're going to do to them in print. I give off-the-record assurances freely, probably more freely than most reporters, and always keep that commitment. What you lose in juicy quotes you often gain in deepened understanding, which is the much more important thing in the long run. You want to build a reputation for being a straight-shooter. If you prove trustworthy, they will be more talkative next time. Getting information from liars and other unsavory people is a separate problem.

Q: *How do you collect the revealing details that make a story clear and lively? What do you look for when reporting a story?*

A: Collecting details is not difficult; seeing them often is. One has to be alert to pick up anything that is funny, poignant, startling, or beautiful. Unexpected discoveries are the raw material of vitality in a story. I look for any detail that makes that story different from any other. William E. Homer, Jr. (*Herald* financial editor and my first journalism professor) used to repeat *ad nauseam*, "Individualize by specific detail."

Q: *When you have a complicated story, do you have any techniques that help you understand it?*

A: I just write it. That helps me understand it.

Q: *When you're covering the same beat over a period of time, as you are these days, how do you keep from going stale? It's my judgment that you haven't gone stale.*

A: I think I am extremely stale, but sometimes I think that may not be entirely a bad thing. In covering a beat, particularly a business beat, it is easy to become fascinated with a subject as you become more knowledgeable about it, and to begin to make the fatal supposition that everybody finds this stuff as interesting as you do. We've all encountered the guy at the party who drones on about the wholesale coat-hanger business.

I hate malls and stores and shopping, and I tend to think, "God, this is boring stuff, surely my readers think so, too. There must be something I can do to make this interesting." This leads to twists and variations and odd leads, which are all to the good.

An example that comes to mind at the moment was a recent story about Caldor, the department store, which I started by quoting Admiral Jellicoe at the Battle of Jutland. I don't know if that worked, but it came from my saying to myself, "There must be some new way to get people to read about this."

Q: *Do you outline, organize your notes, etcetera?*

A: No, I minimize rituals that delay the actual writing. I do push all the other crap out of the way. Sometimes I make a simple list of elements that must not be left out.

Q: *I've been concerned about lead writing recently. What do you try to do in a lead, how do you try to do it?*

A: I try to do in the lead [the post-hot metal spelling] what I try to do throughout a story, which is always to speak directly to the reader's desire for interest and enjoyment. I'll use any trick that will work, as long as it makes the reader go on to the next paragraph.

I try not to write the conventional "who-what-when-where" lead that we all learned in Journalism 101 because I believe that in most cases that lead makes dull, and sometimes difficult, reading. There isn't much point in cramming all that information in the first sentence if it produces an unreadable sentence. Sometimes you must write it that way, of course.

Q: *What do you concentrate on while you're drafting a story?*

A: I concentrate on continuous logical transition from one point to another, from lead to the end. A story should move well, like an actor on stage. Put another way, it should be a chain, rather than a stack, of facts. I also concentrate on writing strictly to length. I do not want my stories trimmed or bitten because I have overwritten. And I care about endings. I think a story should end and not simply stop.

Q: *Will you say something about voice? How do you hear and tune your voice?*

A: I don't know about hearing and tuning, but I would say that I try to write every story with such a voice and tone that the reader is aware that here is a person on this side of the keyboard. I want it to sound like me, to the degree that is possible.

It's easy to forget that newswriting is a convention-bound literary form with its own argot, and most stories read like they could have been written by a newswriting software package. Without being excessively colloquial, I try to tell the story as I would if I were telling it to someone standing next to me at a bar or at a party. We ought to remember that we are storytellers, not just researchers, and every storyteller must develop a voice. When people say of one of my stories, "I would have known that was you, even if it hadn't had your name on it," I feel that I am succeeding.

Clearly, though, I'm not talking about your "Pope shot" or "Plane crashes, 230 die" type stories, where the reader demands raw facts as fast and as clean as possible. When news happens at 5:00 P.M., who can think about voice?

Q: *What is the writer's task as you see it?*

A: After putting facts on the public record, I think our task is to help the reader find his or her way through the facts, to help the reader make sense of them. So the whole story, from first sentence to last—in the way we organize it, in the way we use faces and voices, in the tone we take, in the facts we use, in the overt analysis we venture to offer—should reflect our intelligent understanding, which we give to the reader.

I think we should be intelligent in our approach to what we do, not in the sense of braininess, but in the sense of espionage: the capacity to take in and interpret information.

I also think we should try to entertain whenever possible, to give good reading, using style and eyes for detail, without going so fatally overboard that we are attracting the reader's attention to us rather than to our story.

Q: *What are the three problems you face most frequently in writing? How do you solve them?*

A: First, getting started. Second, getting into the story everything I think should be there. Third, assembling the story so that it has integrity and logic. (A fourth problem is working conditions: the infernal racket and crowding in the newsroom, which may bother me more than most people.)

Number one: I get started by fiddling around and procrastinating so long that terror of failing to produce a story forces my fingers to start rattling away. I don't believe I have ever failed to produce a story that I was committed to, though each day I think, surely this will be the day.

Number two: I often make a list of points that must not be omitted no matter what, and I make space for those points.

As for number three, good assembly for me is largely a matter of revision.

Q: *What is your process of revision and editing? Do you have your own private checklist? If so, what is it?*

A: Revision is a grand term for the frantic process of fixing the mess, which is usually all there is time for. There's no checklist except for the "don't leave out" list. I just keep reading the story, first on the tube, then in paper form, usually standing up at a file cabinet far from my desk, tinkering and tinkering, shifting paragraphs around, throwing out words, shortening sentences, worrying and fretting, checking spellings and job titles and numbers. I try to look at the copy intensely, as I did when I was an editor, operating on the assumption that any mistake I miss will get in the paper. I never say, "So-and-so will catch it." So-and-so won't.

Q: *What advice do you have for beginning writers?*

A: With respect to writing, I guess it would be to write clear, straight, fresh, active sentences with as many aggressive verbs as possible, and to avoid conventional journalistic writing.

Q: *What are the three most destructive things that editors can do?*

A: I have never known a truly destructive editor. An editing change that alters the meaning in an important way or introduces an error (which has happened to me, though not in the Business section) would be a destructive change. But that does not happen if editors communicate with writers. You have to encourage them to do that by being responsive to their questions and telling them to call you at home. I like to be called at home and I thank editors for calling me with a question, no matter how the question is resolved.

Q: *What are the three most helpful things that editors can do?*

A: I suppose it would be to read closely and respond thoughtfully. Fix what is obviously wrong. Raise with me any concern or doubt so that we can eliminate problems.

Q: *What can a writer do to develop an effective relationship with an editor?*

A: You can encourage able editors to do their best work by treating them and the editing process with respect. As difficult as writing is, if an able editor can help, I can't imagine that anyone wouldn't want that help. Also, I think you should raise complaints or grievances directly with the editor, in a civilized way, if you think a principle is at stake. Some people would rather smolder and bitch to their neighbors.

Q: *What advice do you have for a beginning editor?*

A: Presumably a beginning editor would be a copyeditor. My advice to a copyeditor is to read it again, and one more time, if you can, and to ask questions fearlessly. Do not be intimidated when your questions are unwelcome, as they frequently will be, even by other editors. Also, remember the medical principle: "Above all, do no harm."

Q: *What books, authors, and publications have you found helpful as a writer that you would recommend to beginning journalists?*

A: It is the books *of* writing, rather than those *about* writing, that have meant the most to me. Paul Hemphill is a writer I admire, along with E. B. White's essays, most of the time. John Updike's critical writing is to me a model of fairness and clarity, although I don't like his fiction much. Tuchman's and Manchester's books. William Maxwell and William Trevor. Amos Elon. Flora Lewis.

Q: *Do you have favorite* Globe *writers?*

A: Not exactly favorites, but some I always read without restlessness. Alan Lupo for wit, clarity, toughness, compassion, and good reporting. Curtis Wilkie and Joan Vennochi for a good seamless blend of reporting and interpretation (and consistent high quality overall). Dick Knox for thoroughness, clarity, and dedication to quality. Susan Trausch, Richard Saltus, Dick Dyer, Bob Taylor, Dave Greenway, Dave Wilson. Many others.

Chapter 2

The Process of Newswriting

"If you want to write, why don't you?"

"I don't have the talent."

"How do you know?"

"I just know. I mean, I'm not especially creative. I was never, well, one of the creative ones. You know."

"I don't know. Let me see something you've written."

"Well, I don't, uh, have anything . . "

"Why don't you sit down and write something right now."

"What?"

"Anything. Try a news story about a meeting you've just attended. Or just get something off your mind, something you've been thinking about, something that irritates you, an event or a person or place you keep remembering."

"But I don't know where to start. I don't know how you do it. Writing's a mystery to me."

A Journalist's Process

But writing isn't a mystery. It is a process, a logical series of language acts than anyone who can write—and read what they have written—can perform.

If you ask professional journalists what they are doing at any stage of the reporting or writing process, they can tell you. They may be uncomfortable answering because many of them like to believe that writing is magic, but they can answer—and the better the writer, the clearer the answer.

This book demystifies journalism. It makes the craft accessible and it is constructed on one basic description of the writing process that has evolved from my study of how professional journalists and successful student journalists write, all tested against my own daily writing experience. I preach what I practice.

Writing to Deadline

When I give talks people ask, "How do you get the writing done?" My answer, "I have a deadline." But they ask, "How do you know a piece of writing is finished?" "When I get to the deadline." Writers write and they get the writing done because they have deadlines. I am told that the term comes from an actual line drawn outside of a prison's walls. When prisoners crossed the deadline they were shot. Dead. And that's the way I feel about deadlines. They must be met or I will face professional death.

Early in my career as a journalist, I worked on rewrite, taking information over the phone from reporters on the scene and writing thirty-five to forty-five stories to deadline each eight-hour shift. It was the most important—and most intense—training I could have experienced.

Today I write my columns on deadline—before lunch on Monday, a week before they are due. This way I protect myself and am sure to meet the real deadline. I write my nonfiction books and novels on deadline, breaking them down to daily tasks and then meeting those morning deadlines. When I have ghost-written for corporate or government officials, I have written to deadline. When I write articles or essays, I write to deadline. When I was in a poetry group and had a deadline every two weeks, I wrote poems. Now I do not have a deadline and I am not writing poetry. A deadline drives the writer to begin and—more important—to finish writing. Many want-to-be writers begin, but few finish. Publishing writers finish because they have to meet a deadline.

We put off the moment of writing—and for good reason. The writing has to develop. Virginia Woolf said, "As for my next book, I am going to hold myself from writing it till I have it impending in me: grown heavy in my mind like a ripe pear; pendant, gravid, asking to be cut or it will fall."

Here are some tips on writing to deadline.

Know the Limits

And accept them. When you are on deadline you need to know the prescribed length. Writing a seven hundred-word column as I do is different in every way from writing a three thousand-word chapter on the same subject of aging. A feature film is different in concept from a short subject from a thirty-second commercial. Besides length you need to know as much as you can about the purpose, the context, the audience.

Rehearse

The most important writing is done away from the writing desk, when your unconscious and subconscious are playing with the subject. When you have an assignment to deliver on deadline, take some time to sit back and think about the subject. I gave up smoking fifty years ago because I was lighting up a cigarette before writing a new story on rewrite. This was addiction to tobacco but it was also an excuse to sit back and think what I might write. One night I ran out of smokes and couldn't write. I gave up smoking but not sitting back and thinking first. If I had three hours to deadline, I'd rehearse for an hour and half, write for an hour, edit for half an hour; if I had an hour, I'd rehearse for thirty minutes, write for twenty, edit for ten.

Focus

Again I turn to Virginia Woolf, ". . . . if there is one gift more essential to a novelist than another it is the power of combination—the single vision." I would not limit it to the novel. The writer must find a way to bring all the elements in the story to be written together. I usually do it with a line, a fragment of language that contains a tension.

Select and Develop

One of the most important secrets of the professional journalist that is vital when writing to deadline is to select. The writer must write from an abundance of specific, interesting, significant information but the writer must also select the single point, perhaps two, maybe three if they are connected that can be made within the limits of time and space. Then, that point—or those few points—can be developed and documented with in the limits of length.

Order

On deadline the writer must find a clear line that carries the reader from beginning to end. The lead is vital and even on deadline I may write three, five, a dozen leads until I find one that contains the tension that will be released during the writing—and reading—of the piece. On deadline, it is a good idea of what the end will be. Often it is the second best lead. Once you know the lead and the end you may want scratch down a series of three to five details or points that will carry the reader from beginning to end.

Write Fast

Write with velocity to meet the deadline. The writing would flow, carrying the writer, then the reader, on a flood tide toward meaning. Fast writing also allows the writer to escape the censor that is always within us, and to write what we do not expect. Writing on deadline is thinking on deadline.

Write Out Loud

When writing on deadline it is especially important to listen to the voice of what is being written, the music that will reveal and support the meaning of what is being written.

Edit

Allow time to stand back and be your own first editor, answering the reader's questions, clarifying, cutting, correcting, and polishing the writing.

This is the process on which *Writing to Deadline* is built:

EXPLORE

FOCUS

REHEARSE

DRAFT

DEVELOP

CLARIFY

Your process will vary because of several elements:

- *Your own thinking style.* How your mind collects, organizes, and understands information.
- *The style of the publication.* The manner in which your publication—or your department within the publication—reports and writes the news.
- *Your experience with the writing task.* I find that the less familiar I am with the task, the more trial runs I have to make on the computer screen, the more instructive failures I have to print out and read, but when I am experienced I can survey the territory ahead and do more of the writing in my head before the first draft.

- *The writing task itself.* At the moment I have a contract for a book on aging that will have chapters at least three thousand words long. They will be written differently from the seven hundred-word drafts of my newspaper columns on the same subject, which I write in one sitting. A hard news story on deadline is a different task from a backgrounder, an interview different from a profile, a commentary different from an investigative report, a brief different from a series.

  But each writing task has a process.

How Process Helps the Writer

If the writing goes well, writer, editor, and reader share an equal delight in the story, then there's no need to know the process. But when the writer faces an unfamiliar or difficult task, when the story isn't working to the satisfaction of the writer or editor, then it helps to break the task down to a sequence of reporting and writing steps that can be examined in turn.

A writer, for example, may find the writing difficult because the reporting has not been done—or the writing may be hard because the writer has done *so much* reporting the writer is overwhelmed. The definition of the problem often reveals the solution. The writer may need to go back to the street and report, or may need to put the piles of notes and documents and taped interviews away and write the first draft without reference to the notes, so that what is important comes to mind and what is not important is forgotten.

If the writer records, mentally or in writing, his or her process, the writer may see where to concentrate on improving. As an English major, and a shy one at that, I first had to work on reporting, learning how to ask questions of people who didn't want to give answers and then how to ask questions that produced more than an unhelpful "No," "Yes," or "Maybe." As a police reporter I had to concentrate on the inverted pyramid, getting all the important facts in the lead. The end could fall away. It was simply the least important information. When I was assigned to write editorials, I had to learn how to write endings, the most important part of persuasive writing. To write magazine articles I needed to learn to write the anecdote, the brief story on which many journalistic magazine articles are built. I do not outline my weekly columns or novels, but I do outline nonfiction books such as this, building it up, chapter by chapter, writing the subheads before I write the text.

When I get into trouble writing, I return to process. Have I started to write too soon, have I delayed too long? Do I need more prewriting or discovery drafts or do I need complete revisions—a complete rethinking—or do I just need line-by-line editing?

A knowledge of process keeps me moving through the task. It tells me it is time to stop reporting and start planning, stop planning and start drafting, stop revising and begin final editing. It also is instrumental in planning my time—or the time the publication has given me. Recently I was asked about how I organized my time when I was free-lancing, feeding a wife, three daughters, and myself without a regular income and I wrote: "I'd better have a good idea of how much time I could afford to spend. On a major article at top fee: Four weeks max of research, one hundred fifty titles, seventy-five leads, a two-hour draft, and two weeks of revision." I knew my process in economic terms. It helped me put breakfast cereal in the bowls.

How the Process Helps the Editor

The biggest problems between writers and editors occur when the writer is at one stage of the process and the editor at another. This may happen when the writer is trying to find the order in which to tell the story and the editor responds line-by-line to spelling, mechanics, and grammar. It can also happen when the editor talks about the form of the story and the writer thinks the story is finished and just needs an editorial dust-up.

If the writer and editor can articulate the process approach, then the writer can tell the reading the writer needs *at that stage of the process:*

> "I don't have all the facts yet, can I have more time on the story?"
>
> "I don't have anything but the lead, will you look at that?"
>
> "I know the story is rough, but I want to get the order right. Would you read this story to the end?"
>
> "I've got the story blocked out. Will you see if there's any documentation you want?"
>
> "Since this is a follow-up story, I think it should be a narrative beginning. What do you think?"
>
> "I think I'm done, will you give a line-by-line reading?"

The editor can also look at a draft and suggest that the writer move back or ahead in the process:

> "I'd like to see you go back and try some other leads. You don't seem to have the story in your sights yet."
>
> "Enough planning already. Let's see a draft. I want to hear the voice of this story."

How to Discover Your Process

Remember that you don't have one process, but many variations on a basic process or even many processes. The process will change according to how you think, your publisher's tradition and style, your experience, and the task. The secret, however, to discovering your process, is to make notes on what you did *when the writing went well.*

We do not want to replicate failure but success. The faltering professional athlete looks at films taken when she was in championship form. She goes back to the habits, rituals, and practices that produced her best performance. You should do the same. Keep track of when the writing went well so you can put yourself through the same process when the writing doesn't go well.

That piece of good writing doesn't need to be the greatest story ever written, just a solid workmanlike job—or even less. I learned as a teacher and writing coach that all I needed to begin helping a writer was one element, one spark that might be on or off the page.

One beginning writer might have a good eye for detail, another a sense of story, a third an ability to organize complex material, and still another a powerful and effective voice. In each case the writer can begin to create a writing process by emphasizing that skill, the building backward and forward. Sometime the strength may not even be on the page. My first magazine stories were accepted because I had access to a story the magazines wanted. They worked with me so I could report the story, plan it, organize it, draft and redraft it until it was publishable, and in the reporting and writing I developed a process that I kept revising.

To demystify the journalist's craft, try this writing process and then change it to make it your own.

❖ Journalist at Work ❖
DAVID ARNOLD Interview

David Arnold, who now writes for the *Boston Globe Magazine,* describes the indirect career line that made him a *Globe* writer:

> I was graduated from Harvard in 1971, where I majored in photography, and I don't recall writing a paper after freshman year—such were the demands of a grade-yourself Ivy education in the late 1960s. I earned a master's degree in 1976 in design and photography at Yale, then worked as designer photographer for an architectural firm in Cambridge and then at WGBH television and radio before starting my own design studio. My freelance clients included the *Globe,* which offered me a full-time design position in 1978 too tasty for a starving entrepreneur to refuse.

From the beginning, I have been impressed by David's eye and ear and how he has grown until he is one of the most proficient and versatile writers on the *Globe,* ranging between hard news and features.

Q: *Your stories are full of powerful images and significant details. I imagine that comes in part from your experience as an artist/designer. Will you talk about what role your background in art plays in your work as a reporter and writer?*

A: When I think I'm a keen observer because of the art background, I discover I've just forgotten whether the guy I interviewed had a beard or mustache, and I end up grabbing a wet photograph from the photo lab to finish the story.

So I'm not sure where the art fits in, although I do catch myself staring at colors, textures, or the lines of facial profiles while I report. I'm a firm believer that I can bring the reader closer by subtly prodding at stimuli that might reach the nose, taste buds, ears, and eyes.

I honestly think theater would be wonderful training for journalism. So much of what we repackage for the reader condenses and distills characters, action, and drama, much as the playwright or screenwriter might do.

When I did layout and art directed the stories I wrote for sports, I sometimes worked totally backward and capitalized on the control.

The normal sequence is to report a story, then write and deliver it to an editor, then a designer chooses the appropriate artwork and fits the story to the available space on the page. I work in reverse.

First (sometimes before I report), I sketch a layout—a storybook, for example—on the pad of tracing paper I keep on my desk. I sketch hits on a tone I may have been unable to articulate. For instance, the storybook format may lead to a fairy-tale tone that delivers color and playfulness to the project I never would have envisioned had the process begun with words alone.

Design was a mission because I had been trained for it. It said, "You shalt not fail it because you have invested mightily in it."

But journalism is a grand experiment. It says, "Hey, have fun." I think I make a lot of editors nervous.

Q: *Why did you switch from design to writing?*

A: I returned to a Greek island ten years after spending a summer farming there to observe and photograph some pretty drastic changes that had settled in. Wealthy Germans had decided the island made a terrific nudist hideaway. The villagers, who had been devoutly religious, sold their scruples to the tourists.

Mike Janeway, then editor of the *Boston Globe Sunday Magazine,* needed a story fast and suggested I write up the trip. I whimpered about how a high-school teacher had told me English must have been my second language. Besides, I couldn't spell. Janeway said, "just show me your observations. I'll worry about the spelling."

So I wrote just as fast as possible. I had nothing to lose. In the end, Janeway got his story and I got the writing lesson of my life: Writing has more to do with an ability to observe than to spell. I don't think I've ever written a piece that was quite so fresh and uninhibited.

Q: *What were the most important things you had to learn?*

A: Not to overwrite, not to spend three paragraphs describing the clash of plaids in the living-room decor.

Q: *How did you learn that?*

A: I learned by trial and error. I must be one of the few staffers in history who has had to correct his own correction. You don't do this more than once.

Q: *Who helped you to learn and how did they help?*

A: Alas, the now-departed writing coaches, first Alan Richman, then Bill Miller. They were a constant resource, another ear, impartial observers, and always on my side.

I get very nervous when stories squirt out of the sausage machine here with hardly an editing change. And I'm kidding myself if I believe the prose is impeccable. The truth is that no one has the time to do more than tinker with the writing because, justly, their job is first to get it right and get it clear.

Q: *What do you know now that you wish you had known then?*

A: You can take chances, strive for similes and metaphors, be creative, dare to characterize. Take one of the most boring stories in the newsroom—the "day after bad weather" story—and do something different with it: Go sledding in the new snow, join a plowing crew, call Tromso, Norway, and find out just how bad a day folks north of the Arctic Circle had. If the story bombs, at least you won't be asked to do another one for a while.

Q: *You go to Russian missile cities, to the Canadian Rockies, to Central American reefs, through the sound barrier in an F-18 jet, and then do quick, daily, general-assignment stories. Will you talk a bit about the advantages and disadvantages of each type of assignment?*

A: I think general assignment is the most versatile, stimulating reporting slot on the paper—providing there's opportunity occasionally to wander into other departments for a change of pace. The people I meet on the street in general assignment usually are under tremendous stress; they teach me daily about myself and perhaps will be role models should fate deal me a bad hand. I don't understand the stigma general assignment has around here. It's the only position that allows a reporter to write his or her own ticket.

The daily hits obviously facilitate the writing of the longer pieces. I particularly enjoy breaking the unwritten journalism rule that says: Write it immediately after you report it. The *Adventure in Travel* magazine sometimes works a year in advance. If I'm lucky enough to sell it a story, I separate the reporting from the writing by months. This way I'm able to go powder-snow skiing in the summer and kayaking in the winter. I'd like to think a sense of yearning creeps into the writing that enriches the piece.

Q: *I've noticed you laughing while you seem to be writing and simultaneously listening to someone on your telephone headphones. What's going on?*

A: Telephone headphones are a terrific editor-avoidance mechanism. I wear them whether I'm on the telephone or not. I laugh when I write sometimes, not because I think I'm the next James Thurber, but because when I go fast enough, the words take me unintended places. The twists can be funny and are almost always worth polishing.

Q: *What is your writing process when you do a quick hit and are on deadline? What tricks of the trade do you use?*

A: Never look at notes. Draft first and quote from the best representatives of involved parties by the fourth or fifth paragraph. The easiest kicker is a quote. Be aware of my own prejudices, and give the last word to the side I personally disagree with.

Q: *Is your writing process different when you have more time? What are the significant differences in how you work? What tricks of the trade do you find helpful on those stories?*

A: Take the story down to the back room in the library and read it aloud. I also give it to Dave Morrow, to my mind the writer's editor most accessible on the news desk. Morrow thinks nothing of proposing an entirely different lead and then working it with me until we decide it's good or terrible. Kathy Everly in science and health also has an excellent eye, although she's smarter at avoiding work than Morrow. She doesn't rewrite, she just notes in boldface: "Doesn't work for me here, Babe."

Q: *Your endings are unusually good as well. Will you say something about how you work on endings? What do you look for as an effective ending?*

A: If the story is not controversial, I allow my own voice to creep into the ending to personalize it. Joe Kahn in the living department does this with diligence.

Q: *Do you have any rules or principles you try to follow when writing?*

A: Odd how the following rules have stuck. They could be argued to oblivion, but for me they work.

The first three are from Al Richman:

- There's always a story there somewhere.
- If you need to explain the humor, forget it.
- If the story's good, don't let the writing interfere.

Others are:

- Try for an action verb in the first sentence.
- Don't lead with a subordinate clause.
- Don't lead with a quote.
- If the story's about an individual, get the name in the first paragraph.
- You haven't got a newspaper story if the reader can't use the information.
- Don't end your best quotes with an attribution (put it within the quote, set off with commas).
- A feature about people needs descriptive detail about the people, which takes work. Reference to blonde hair is almost always sexist. The hands (actions, color, condition) can usually give a reader telling detail, as can the knickknacks on living-room mantles. Eyes have texture; eye contact is another descriptive tool. But mention of high cheek bones only proves you wasted too much time reading Ian Fleming.
- A story proposed by an editor should be championed by the editor.
- Judge your writing for fairness by whether or not you're willing to send the person you're worried about a clip.

Q: *How can an editor help you? How can an editor hinder?*

A: For every time an editor bums me by making phrasing more clunky to my ear, she or he saves me tenfold with points of accuracy.

Q: *What advice do you have for young reporters?*

A: Stretch and let the editor rein you in. One of my best experiments was a Christmas story where I followed undercover cops nabbing pick-pockets on the subway. My worst experiment came with some local, seemingly minor flooding. I decided to chart the city's history by "reading" the layers of strata exposed downtown as work crews excavated for pipe damage. Then I discovered some residents had suffered serious property damage. You can't mix cuteness with even minor suffering. It was twenty minutes before deadline and John Burke hadn't had time to rein me in. We ran a wire story. Burke wasn't pleased.

Q: *Are there books or writers you would recommend that we read to learn to write more effectively?*

A: Almost any good children's book. I recommend them not because I've read all the literary masterpieces and have worked my way into the library toddler wing. It's because, with two youngsters at home, I don't have time to read anything else. The experience has been an eye opener. Children's books often have complex themes, yet the writing is clear and condensed, the vocabulary elementary, the alliteration and rhythms of the words and phrasing playful and always audible, and the humor very funny.

It seems the essence of voice in these books is what's left out, not what's written. So I recommend *Mr. Popper's Penguins* by Florence and Richard Atwater, *Charlotte's Web* by E. B. White, *Amos and Boris* by William Steig, and *One Morning in Maine* by Robert McClosky. Look at it this way: You'll have four books under your belt in one sitting, with time to spare.

❖ Journalist at Work ❖ Analysis of Two DAVID ARNOLD Stories

David Arnold works general assignment, ready to handle any story that breaks. He is versatile and he is good. Here I put the magnifying glass on two of his stories so that I, and you, may learn.

On February 7, 1990, Arnold wrote a story that began:

The year Paul Tucker the football player made all-New England tackle was the year Paul Tucker the art student stood before one of a series of paintings by Claude Monet and wondered: "Wouldn't it be nice to reunite them someday."

This could have been a puff piece on a museum, a ho-hum opening, but Arnold gets a person in the lead and sets up dramatic tension: The student has a dream.

Tucker has done just that. His "Monet in the '90s" exhibition of series paintings, opening today at the Museum of Fine Arts, is one of the most significant compilations of French Impressionist work ever assembled, according to art historians.

The dream is fulfilled, but it wasn't easy. Arnold fills his story with anecdotes, quotes from Tucker and others, and specific information about the problems of building such an exhibition. He closes his piece with some reverse tension, a hunt that hasn't worked out—yet. Note the easy way Arnold uses narrative.

Some of his quests have been less successful. Take the search for one of Monet's 10 Creuse Valley paintings. It started four years ago with the incomplete records of a London auction house as Tucker attempted to trace the painting's whereabouts. Partial records sent him to a modest home outside Paris and a Madame Y, who sent him back to London—and then to a secretary for Elizabeth Taylor. Taylor, sources recalled, had purchased the painting.

And he weaves in details of Tucker's trade.

Tucker, governed by tools of his trade he calls "The 3 F's": Federal Express, FAXes, and "Fones," finally reached Taylor at her home outside Los Angeles via a string of acquaintances. Yes, she would loan her Monet.

He paces the story well.

Quickly, Tucker located a photographer in Los Angeles and dispatched him to Taylor's home so the painting could be photographed for the book, already at the printer, that accompanies the exhibit. Three days later, four years into the search, the photographer's 8"-by-10" transparency arrived in Tucker's office.

Arnold often combines longer paragraphs or sentences with short ones for emphasis as he does here.

It was the wrong Money.

"Nice picture, though," Tucker noted. But it was inappropriate for the series theme of the exhibit.

Tucker continues to look for the missing Creuse Valley canvas. He's been back to Paris, three weeks ago at Madame Y's door once again, and continues to chase down new leads in hopes of making the Chicago opening in May, or perhaps even the latter part of the Boston show.

"I'm not giving up," he said, his teeth seemingly ever so slightly clenched.

Reading that story, I appreciate the reporting that went into it, the asking of the right questions, the seeking and reseeking of the specific, revealing detail. Arnold's reporter eye (and ear) is apparent in a story that appeared two days later. This story would have been dismissed by many journalists. It isn't a *serious* story. But it is a story that made page one more lively and was read, I suspect, by more readers than most serious stories were that day.

> Lisa Lyles had researched the challenge and knew the demands. So she planned and trained—swimming laps for aerobic capacity and practicing yoga for mind control.
>
> But in the end it was a swatch of tacky cloth applied to the fingers that gave this compact, 130-pound Melrose resident the racer's edge yesterday.
>
> Sticky-fingered Lyles, with an ear for expensive opera, was able to snag 60 compact discs worth $2,054 during a two-minute dash through the aisles of Tower Records.

Again the story is packed with specifics. On February 19, 1990, in the health and science section, David Arnold pops up with a story about poverty in the 1800s that begins:

> Bailey Taft was a stone mason from Uxbridge 160 years ago, a man in the prime of life but so desperate for funds that he mortgaged his hand-hewn rocks for a loan he couldn't repay. In a subsequent loan, he lost the tools of his trade.
>
> Not even the labor of his five daughters in a nearby textile mill could keep Taft from landing in the local poorhouse shortly before he died in 1871.

Arnold's story goes on to report some surprising discoveries about poverty in the last century. It was however, in the February 11, 1990 *Globe* that David Arnold wrote a story in which he was both reporter and participant.

FERGUSON, British Columbia—We descend pitch after pitch, our turns blasting waist-deep powder snow overhead in terrain so wild and steep that our guide calls it "just this side of Tiger Country."

This is no delayed lead. Arnold puts us right on the slope with him.

Up here, they call unskiable terrain Tiger Country.

Now he defines that term and emphasizes it as he does.

But we are chomping at its edges, the fastest 10 of 44 skiers who had come to heli-ski a new wilderness pocket of the Canadian Rockies recently opened by Canadian Mountain Holidays. In our hearts we are an invincible platoon, leaping 15-foot cliffs with a yelp and then plummeting thousands of vertical feet with hardly a stop.

A neat context paragraph (nut graf, billboard, who ha, pick your own jargon) that locates the story. Note, however, that he includes their feelings in the last half of the paragraph, foreshadowing what is coming.

At the end of the day, one of us would be dead.

Bang! Dependent clause and straightforward sentence. Here is another case of using a shift from longer paragraph to short for emphasis.

Eric King, a 45-year-old resident of Santa Monica, Calif., died alone 12 days ago on a steep slope of a mountain called Hanging Gardens. He had more than 3 million vertical feet of heli-skiing to his record, an accumulation of wilderness skiing shared by perhaps two dozen Canadian Mountain Holiday veterans.

Now we need exposition and we get it. Arnold is answering the reader's questions as they are asked: Who died? What happened? Where?

"I like to ski fast, and I hate being last," he liked to say.

Again a short paragraph to emphasize the victim's attitude toward dangerous skiing.

His death was particular to this environment where seemingly bottomless power creates wind-blown hollows around tree trunks that can snare you like quicksand. King fell backwards into a hollow and suffocated, drowning in the powder snow we had come to dance in.

Now we get the technical details explained in clear terms.

. . . Here, the risk of avalanche is minimal, our guide, Danny Stoffel, tells us, just before the ground starts to move.

Later in the story Arnold brings himself into the experience. It documents the dangers they would face and their mixture of fear and innocence that was swinging toward fear. The reader is placed within the experience and this foreshadows the ending of the story. Notice how he sets up the tension between what they are told and what happens.

I hear the avalanche before I see it, a whoosh of snow, like sand from a dump truck.

It always helps when you can use another sense, in this case hearing.

"Avalanche!" shouts Jim Wolff, an emergency room physician at the Emerson Hospital in Concord. I'm close by, as is Peter Swift, an oncologist from Burlington, VT.

The slide is perhaps 80 feet wide and carries 300 feet downhill, leaving a fracture wall at its top about one foot high. Wolff's skis have cut the snow free; it misses me by feet but slips Swift on the opposite side. The boiling snow spits one of his skis 20 feet high, sending it shimmying like a hooked marlin. The ski knifes back into the snow and disappears.

Arnold works in names and personal details with grace and clearly describes what is happening.

Seconds later, the world is quiet except for bursts of muffled voices in the falling snow. Swift is uninjured but visibly shaken: as is Wolff.

Hearing is used again: "The world is quiet except for muffled bursts of snow."

Our guide, waiting for us below at the helicopter pickup site, had not seen the incident but seems awfully quick at assessing it as "sloughing." We should expect five, maybe six a day when it snows this hard, Stoffel says.

"Just ski them out on top," he says.

Easy to say.

Now a nice touch of humor. And the tone is right for the kind of people doing this skiing.

In the woods, it is hard to ski beside buddies. And they detract from the freedom we are here to celebrate in a world where we can descend seemingly vertical pitches as the powder brakes our speed. This is freefall in a dream, cliffs are followed by pillow-soft landings, the experience is narcotic.

Skiing the trees requires constant vigilance, charting the course as if steering through shoals with the throttle up. Can I make that slot? Is there room for two turns? Small clearing to the right . . . better line here, and time for nice turns . . . how many is there room for? Can't see a thing for a few turns, so much snow is flying overhead. Ouch, my legs hurt. But here comes a jump—so gentle. Elbows up, now tight trees ahead . . . I smell of balsam.

Arnold takes us inside the act of skiing with a brilliant action description. Observe how he builds it up and increases the fragments, the bursts of language, that are appropriate to the way the skier would think at that time. Arnold makes us experience the story as much as he can. Then there is that wonderful touch, using another sense: "I smell of balsam."

. . . Now we leap frog each other, one person always close behind the other, partners sharing the untracked snow. I will never know for sure if, midway down a tree-studded ridge called Hot Chili, this new buddy system saved my life. My partner is Ed Swift, a Carlisle resident, a reporter for *Sports Illustrated*, and no relation to my previous buddy Peter. My confidence is gone; I have become keenly aware of my feet, which are all over the place and are now leading me into a tree well.

Arnold describes the search for King, the result, and what follows in a disciplined manner that is more moving than melodrama. He documents the changed mood of the group and the more disciplined control exerted on the group. And then he takes us back out on the slope with him.

I fall facing up, my feet caught in a web of branches, my head under a veil of snow so translucent the air seems just inches beyond. The first split second passes smoothly—I think: drop the ski poles, clear the snow, stay calm. But the snow doesn't clear.

We are prepared for this surprise. Arnold will fall as King did.

The more I wipe the more snow falls in. My lungs are aching now—I had been panting hard going into this fall. Now I flail. So this is panic. Just a precious few inches to air, but I can't rise up. My arms are useless, nothing to push on. No control, lungs exploding. And then there's Swift's hand, clearing the snow from my face. "You seem to be somewhat covered up," Swift says.

Effective narrative pacing with revealing details.

He says I was close to the surface, I was just about clear of it and that I hadn't really needed his help.

I'll make a note of that, Ed.

Again, the touch of humor.

I quit for the day and later wonder: had King had a helping hand, would he be alive?

And now a more serious reflection.

By week's end, we have had more snow than guides recall ever falling in these mountain. We have had shoulder-deep powder. We have felt unprecedented exhilaration, shock, fear, and camaraderies. We have had death. I arrived cavalier about the trouble my ability might lead me into, I leave with realigned priorities. My family calls. I leave lucky.

Note the tension within his summary, the good and the bad.

Chapter 3

EXPLORE: Report for Surprise

The best writers seek surprise, delight in what they do not expect to find. They come to the story with a focus, an expectation, but they treasure the contradiction, the traitor fact, the quotation that goes against the grain, the unexpected that reveals.

Unfortunately, journalists—both editors and reporters—usually see what they expect to see even if it isn't there. The news appears to be predictable as you cover the flood of information that flows through the city room day after day. Patterns are discovered, and those patterns make it possible to control and communicate the flow, but it is easy to see patterns that are no longer there, or to see the patterns roiling below the surface of the flood, the ones that will dominate the future. We saw the all-powerful Russian menace when it was actually weak, collapsing in upon itself; we did not see the significance of AIDS, and then we attempted to relegate it to one narrow segment of our population despite clear evidence to the contrary.

In exploring the world, a writer should also look for what *isn't* there as much as what *is,* hear the unsaid as well as the said, imagine what might be. The best writers accept, even delight in the unexpected. E. L. Doctorow says, "Every time you compose a book your composition of yourself is at risk. You put yourself further away from whatever is comfortable to you or you feel at home with. Writing is a lifetime act of self-displacement." Graham Greene saw it as a responsibility. "Isn't disloyalty as much the writer's virtue as loyalty is the soldier's?"

The Writer's Ten Senses

To write with information, the writer has to pay attention to the world. What is, what isn't, what should be? What's going on and what does it mean? The writer makes use of every sense—and even develops a few new ones. The constant awareness of the working journalist is not a mystery. It is something that can be learned and practiced.

Work on one sense at a time, beginning with your strongest one, not your weakest. Find out what you can do with that effective sense, then move on to other ones. What I have done—and what I often had my students do—was to sit in one familiar place and, using just one sense, list fifty or one hundred specifics as quickly as possible.

Sight

Since I am a visual person, I would begin by using the sense of sight. I go to the supermarket where my wife usually shops—and where I wait on the bench facing the checkout lines. Here's my list:

1. Many people think they can pay for all the food when they can't.
2. How much food sent back.
3. Eggs one of first items you can buy. Gets in bottom of carriage. Many eggs broken.
4. Old ladies and their purses.
5. Feel they have to make exact change.
6. Unaware of holding up line.
7. Impatient husbands.
8. Impatient mothers.
9. How many kids take headers off carts.
10. What's the manager looking for when he hires a new checkout clerk.
11. Fat people and fat food.
12. Poor people and fancy food.
13. Hiding food on bottom of carriage to see if clerk will miss it.
14. How many use debit cards?
15. Elderly stop to chat with sale clerk.
16. Hunger for social contact.
17. *Young* with baby.
18. How good young father is with baby.
19. How many speak to bagger with Down Syndrome!
20. How best packer tosses groceries from grabbing hand to bagging hand.
21. Manager strut. Wouldn't want to work for him.
22. "Twenty-one." That must be the shoplifter alert. Assistant managers all go to aisle three.

23. One-way, see-out window in office over return and lottery counter.
24. Mirrors that can be seen from that window.
25. Where guard stands when bank service picks up cash for armored car at curb.
26. Who buys lottery tickets? Most appear poor.
27. What's stacked for impulse buying.
28. How customers are forced to weave through store.
29. It's January and they have the Easter bunny out.
30. Father Joe looks naked without his priest's collar.
31. He's trying to look anonymous.
32. That couple is heading for divorce.

And on and on. We look for what we catch out of the corner of our eye. What is being done and *not* being done. How it is being done. Actions and reactions. Gesture and expression. How people walk. The obvious process and what it reveals, the hidden process and what it reveals.

Hearing

Most of us are poor listeners. We hear what we expect to hear. When my mother-in-law lived with us, she'd ask polite questions but never listen to the answers.

"How was your lunch?"

"I ate an old lady. Live. With ketchup."

"That's nice."

I was always ashamed of myself when I spoke to her this way, but then a week or a month later I'd do it again. And she could have done it to me.

Effective journalists train themselves to listen. I used to practice taking notes listening to the radio in the dark and it came in handy many times when I was at the scene of a crime, covering a military exercise, interviewing a politician in the back of limousine at night.

I began my trade when tape recorders were large and heavy, and I rarely used them. Sometimes I will today but I also take notes. Why? For two reasons. Sometimes the tape recorder doesn't work. I also listen better and ask sharper questions when I make notes.

There were two principles approaches to the interview: attack dog or interrogation. Neither suited me. I wasn't bright enough, quick enough, frightening enough and I didn't see my colleagues who were all those things getting more and better answers than I was. I preferred the friendly chat approach. To do this, you have to appear contagiously relaxed, listening, nodding, responding with some language but with a great deal of understanding expressions and body language. (Note to men: Woman are much more likely than men to be good listeners. Go to a restaurant popular with women for lunch and observe how they listen to each other.)

It takes a great deal of energy to pay attention and listen well while appearing casual and relaxed. You have to listen to what is said and how it is said. Inflection, pauses, expressions, gestures may carry a meaning opposite to the one carried by the words alone. Listen for what is not said. Listen for the context of what is being said. Listen with empathy—how does the speaker hear what he or she is saying?

Listen to other sounds that reveal the place. In our favorite Czech restaurant, you can hear the food being prepared. The service is slow because each order is prepared individually. What are the sounds at a fire—of a roof collapsing, of a firefighter having a heart attack, of a business owner arriving to see the store on fire, of glass being broken, of bootsteps, of water gushing from a hose?

Touch

Touch is a sense seldom used by reporters, but as a reader I'd like to know what a football field with real grass feels like compared to artificial turf. I'd like a sports writer to put my hand on it, my foot on it. I'd like to know what the surgeon feels as she cuts, what she feels for, where the strength comes from—hand, wrist, shoulder, back. I'd like to know the heft of a popular handgun, how all the equipment hung on a police officer feels. I'd like to have the reader run my hand over the grain of the pine coffins Evan Hill of Newport, New Hampshire has made for his wife and himself. I'd like to feel what comes out of Wynton Marsalis's trumpet, the resistance of the keys in a concert-tuned grand piano.

Smell

One of the senses we depend on the most is one we discuss least and rarely report, but it can be a powerful sense to use if we can catch the odor of fear on death row, the artificial perfume of the funeral home when no flowers have been sent to honor the dead, the Saturday morning smell of fresh-cut grass, the smell of fresh bread before we find the bakery.

Taste

When I was in combat I often had the metallic taste of fear in my mouth. I once wrote a column about the tastes of childhood, paying tribute to the school lunch that was so much more exciting than the Scots Yankee food at home. I paid special attention to the greasy and exotic experience of American chop suey. If we can make the reader taste, smell, touch, hear, see our stories, the worlds of which we write will come alive for them.

Change

There are five other senses the reporter should work to develop. One is a sense of change. We should be aware of change. Little remains the same in our society. When I return to my home town, I see the basement of St. Ann's, where everyone worshipped in the Depression until, years later, a huge church was built above. I knew many people who lived in cellars for years before they could build a house. My old neighborhood, which turned from Protestant to Irish Catholic in my childhood, is now Asian. We can see wherever we go the memory of the past and the shadow of the future, and many stories are simply a record of change, the shutter snapped to catch a significant moment.

It is the reporter's job to catch, from the corner of the eye, the coming change, the hints of what will be in what is.

Effect

One of the failures of journalists is not to have a continuous sense of the effect of news on readers. A simple bus-route change may isolate hundreds of elderly citizens. Where are the victims of the fire, the plant closing, the race riot six months or a year later? How does the change in school funding affect the students—and the teachers? What are the side effects of a new drug—or a new postal regulation, a change in zoning, a tax increase?

Conflict

We live in a world in which forces are on collision courses. It is the job of the reporter to cover the collisions before they happen, when they occur, after they are over. The reporter needs to develop a sense of conflict, when the interests of one group will meet the contradictory interests of another group. There are few surprises for the reporter who is alert to the trajectories of self-interest.

Context

Another failure of journalism is to put the specific detail—the fact, the quotation, the profile, the event—in context. Few acts occur in isolation, they have causes and repercussions. Journalists are historians of the immediate. They should place the day's event—the vote, the game, the discovery—in the context of the past and the future. The detail gains its truth and significance when it is placed in context.

Self

I was taught to be objective as a reporter and writer, and that was good in that I was not allowed to make up truths. I need to report accurately and document what I said with authoritative evidence. But too many journalists go on to distance themselves from their experience, to deny their responses to the people and events they are covering. I learned that my experience in the military police didn't prejudice me as a police reporter but illuminated the experience, helping me understand so that my readers could understand. We need to bring ourselves to the challenge of reporting and writing, to admit our feelings and thoughts, then to temper them with an appropriate professional attitude.

Asking the *Reader's* Five Questions

It is amazing how often as a journalist I found that a story had five key questions. These were not the questions I wanted to ask or even the questions my editor told me to ask. They were the questions that the reader would ask and if I did not answer them the reader would be unsatisfied. Often they were the obvious questions, so obvious that other reporters overlooked them. And they were questions that need to be asked of every source, since the difference between the answer either became the story or led to the story.

I would take a minute before starting on a quick daily story, a six-week magazine story, or a year long book project to ask the five questions my readers would ask. I still do this. I have to keep learning.

On a story about an addition to a high school, the questions might be:

- What's it cost?
- Where's the money coming from?
- Why is the addition needed?
- How will it help students? Teachers?
- Is there a temporary alternative?

When I come to write the story, I order the questions in the sequence I think the reader will ask them. In some cases I type them into the copy, then cut them out in the final editing, although in a few complex financial or medical stories I have left the questions in as headings to give the reader a map of a complicated issue. Thus:

- What is the cost of a temporary solution?
- What is the cost of a permanent solution?
- Why is the addition required?
- How will it help students? Teachers?

The five questions became four. The next day they might be five or six, seven or three, but they would anticipate the information the reader needs *at the moment the reader needs it.* The effective story is a conversation with the reader in which the writer listens to the reader and responds.

I have also found the five questions to be an effective tool for writer and editor on a complex story. Ask the questions the reader will ask in the order he or she will ask them, and the obscure story can be reordered into clarity.

Seeing the Obvious

One problem editors and writers share is how to get ideas. The reader's appetite for fresh stories is never satisfied, and as soon as you get an idea, it's used up. Following are techniques for developing new ideas and a discussion of what to do with them.

A good way to measure the vigor of a newspaper is to count the number of good stories that were not produced by journalism routine: the calendar; the police radio; the competitor's newspaper; the publisher's second cousin; or the PR release.

Inventory the Obvious

An editor once said that a good reporter "is forever astonished at the obvious." Inventory the obvious. List what is happening to you: your feelings, satisfactions, worries, wants, anxieties, hobbies, needs. You are a reader as well as a writer. Look for story ideas among the things that are changing your world and the world of those about you. Where's the money going? Where's the time going? Where's the fat going? What makes people laugh or get mad? What are people buying or not buying? What do they do for fun? What changes are taking place or not taking place in your family and on your street?

Brainstorm

You can brainstorm alone or with a partner. You can do it with no goal in mind, just to see what ideas are dredged up, or with a goal such as how we should cover the election this year. The important thing is to suspend the censor, be willing to be silly, and just list specifics. For example:

- Crime.
- Jail.
- Bail.
- More bail jumpers in a time of prosperity?
- Different crimes in a prosperous period?
- Different crimes?
- Check 1928 and 1932 police records.
- Talk to retired detective.
- Interview Prohibition detective.
- Changes in bail business.
- Pot smugglers compared to Prohibition smugglers.
- Used to be illegal bootleggers in the city. Still?
- Women treated differently from men on bail?
- Who's buying yachts?
- $300,000-plus houses selling best in our town.
- How come? People paying cash.
- Why?
- Why are bankruptcies increasing in a period of prosperity?

That's just a quick start on a brainstorming list that goes off in several different directions and circles back through itself. It's the best way of telling you what story ideas you already have stored in your brain. Brainstorming mobilizes memory and the subconscious. Once you have a brainstorming list, look for items that surprise you and circle them. Then look for the items that connect and draw lines between them.

Mapping

Try mapping instead of brainstorming or outlining. Mapping is a technique used in British schools that allows many people to explore a subject more effectively than they can by traditional outlines. Those who are interested in right-hemisphere brain techniques believe this approach reproduces the way in which the more creative parts of the brain work. Put the topic in the center of the page in an oval, and then as quickly as possible draw lines out that follow the ideas that occur to you. Figure 3–1 on page 42 illustrates a page of a five-minute mapping on a common journalism subject.

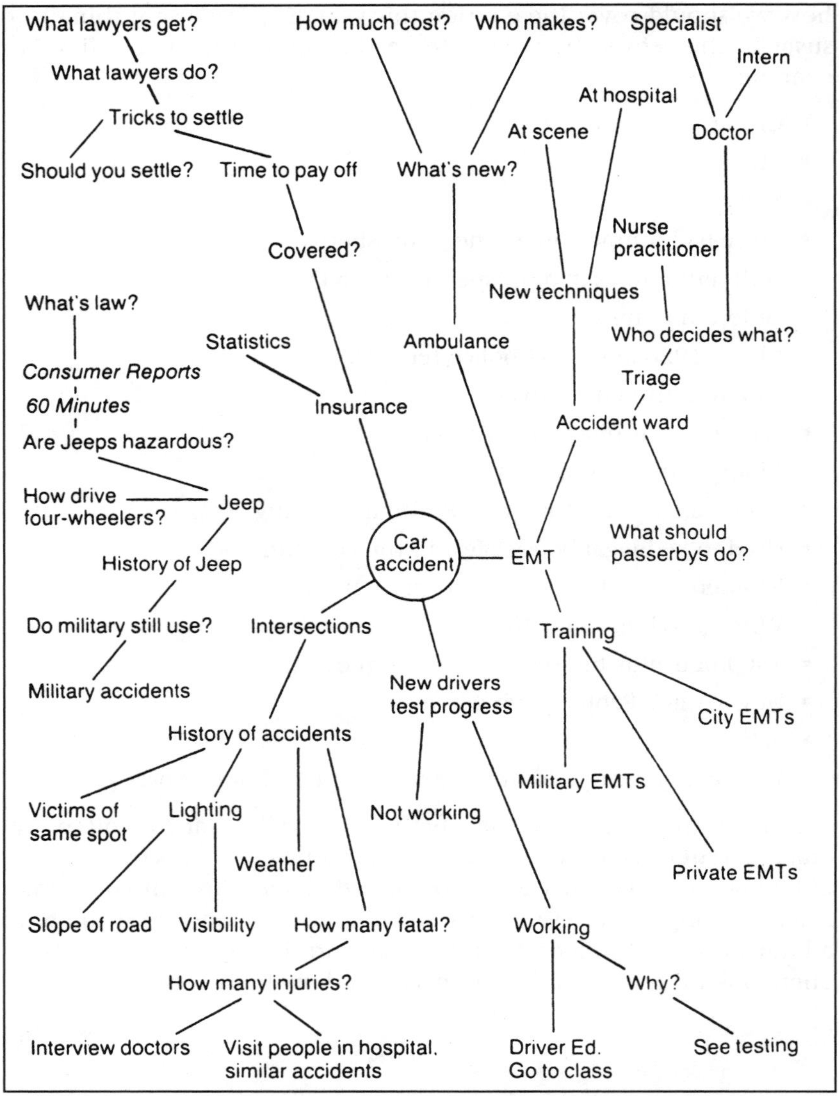

Figure 3–1

Five-minute mapping technique to explore a subject effectively

Change Your Point of View

Drive to work by a different route. Go to a familiar place at an hour when you're not usually there. Shop in a supermarket patronized by people on welfare—or one in the wealthiest neighborhood you can find. Stand in line at an unemployment office and listen to what people are saying. Sit in a waiting room at a hospital clinic. Watch the ball game from the bleachers. Study the point-of-view diagram in Figure 3–2.

Pursue a New Interest

Pursue an interest that forces you to see the world from a new point of view. Sketch, paint, take pictures. I draw, and to sketch an island I have to see that island more intensely than I have ever seen it before. I have to understand how that island was created and how trees manage to grow from the crevices in the rock. I have to know the bone structure within a face to reveal the face. I have to know how a chair is made to support the weight of the person sitting on it. I also find that when I am engaged in art, writing ideas come to me, for often good story ideas are not so much pursued as received when my mind is in a receptive state.

Keep a Notebook

Keep a notebook that you may call a journal, a log, or something else. When I called my notebook a journal, it evoked pretentious literary generalizations that embarrassed me. Now I call the notebook a daybook,

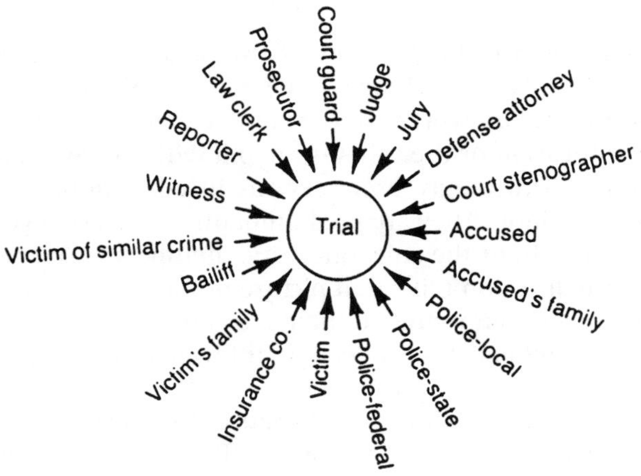

Figure 3–2
Point of view

and it has become a sort of traveling office in which I can scribble ideas, draft leads, brainstorm, map, record overheard conversations, list unexpected statistics, diagram pieces of writing, write drafts, and carry on a continuous conversation with myself about my work, how it is going, how it isn't going, and where it should go.

This notebook is with me all the time. It is the place where I work during those fragments of time that are otherwise wasted. I write sitting in the doctor's waiting room, during the traffic jam, while the commercials interrupt the ball game, or when I'm waiting for the meeting to start. I prefer a spiral-bound notebook that prevents gaps in the continuing chronological record of what I am doing and what I may do next. I keep a small tape recorder with me when I'm driving and make oral notes that I transfer to the daybook later. Starting a new notebook, about every two months, I go through the one just finished and list ideas that still interest me in the beginning of the new notebook.

Compost

Compost. Keep a file drawer of reports, brochures, handouts, speeches, magazine articles, newspaper clippings, photos, letters, drafts that didn't work—all sorts of stuff. Go through the file every few months and turn it over the way you would a compost pile; see what connects. You'll throw most of it away, but you'll also unearth material that you've been collecting on topics that can make good stories.

Role-Play

Make believe you are the prisoner or the person being arrested, the lobbyist or the legislator, the judge or the member of the jury, the waiter or the cook, the factory worker or the labor leader, the twenty-year-old without an education or the thirty-year-old with too much education. Journalists are disturbingly homogenous in educational background and economic position. They are predominantly white, college educated, living in the suburbs or the chic inner city, members of the professional class. But journalists don't like that picture of themselves. They imagine that they are rebels, but in this country they are very tame rebels, insiders in society, members of the 5 percent or fewer who imagine that they run things.

If that's who we are, it is our obligation to at least use our imaginations to extend the limits of our world. Role-playing is one way we can step out of the usual costumes and experience other lives so that we will know the questions to ask to get a fully documented story.

Read Magazines

Buy a different magazine each week. Buy a science magazine, such as *Nature* or *Discover*, this week; a literary magazine, such as the *Massachusetts Review*, next week. Try *Yankee, Backpacker, Money, Country Living, Mother Jones*. Almost every interest has its own publication. Read them, the ads as well as the text. Tear out the most interesting articles and carry a small file of those to read in spare moments so that you can extend your world.

Look for the Authorities

When you are on a story, look for the authorities other people seem to turn to, and interview them. In the accident ward, you will notice doctors deferring to one nurse; at the garage, one mechanic is called over for an expert diagnosis; at the fire, one firefighter is consulted to decide if the roof is safe; at the Senate hearings, the "names" will look to a staff member for direction. Newspapers will have better stories if we discover these hidden authorities and interview them.

Try Another Genre

The poet sees poems, the novelist novels, the dramatist plays. A good way to get new ideas for your writing is to look at the world through the lens of another genre. If you've been writing profiles, it may be good for you to write a straight news account or an editorial about something in your territory. If you've been writing editorials, it may be a good idea to do a profile. You may want to imagine your beat being covered by a screenwriter, a historian, a mystery writer, a *New Yorker* profile writer. Write a few pages in this new genre using the approach and the language to help you see the familiar anew. A few of these pieces may be publishable, but that's not their purpose. They help you use your craft to see the stories under your pen that you should cover.

Read Outside Your Interests

Always have at least one book in the briefcase or on the bed table outside your everyday interests. Read poetry, literary fiction and escape fiction, history and biography, popular science and nature books. Study essays and short stories and screen plays and novels to see how their craft may apply to your writing.

Free Write

Free write. Sit down and write as fast as you can for a few minutes. It is amazing how much you can write in four, six, ten, or fifteen minutes. Let the language lead you toward meaning. If you free write frequently you will be surprised how many ideas will come from these unplanned pages.

Think Like an Editor

Step back from your manuscript, the way an artist steps back from the easel, and look at what is there which may—surprise—be far different from what you hoped would be there and look for what isn't there that you thought would be. Skilled editors can read a manuscript at three levels simultaneously, but I find I need to step back and scan the draft to see what I have said and what I have not said. I look for the one, overall meaning. Then I step closer and look for a clear path of meaning from the lead through the main points to the end. Then I look for the documentation that supports each point, the proportion of the parts, and the pace of the writing. Finally I move in close, reading it line by line, tuning the voice or music that supports the meaning, asking and answering the reader's questions, adding what is missing, cutting what is unnecessary, and cleaning up errors in spelling, grammar, or mechanics unless they are essential to communicate my meaning.

I'm always shocked to see bored people in a city room. You expect to encounter bored people in post offices, legislatures, even on college campuses. The one thing that comforts me most as I travel far beyond middle age is that I shall never write all the stories I have to write. There will always be new ideas, forms I haven't yet attempted, voices I haven't mastered. Every morning at my desk I will find new and interesting ways to fail. In the writer's craft I have found the wisdom of the sculptor Henry Moore that stands within sight of my computer screen:

> The secret of life is to have a task, something you devote your whole life to, something you bring everything to, every minute of the day for your whole life. And the most important thing is—it must be something you cannot possibly do!

As reporters we are given license to pry, to be nosy, to be forever curious, to learn. Insatiable curiosity is the quality common to the famous editors I have known. Henry Luce, a founder of *Time*, was like a terrier with his questions. So was DeWitt Wallace, who created *Reader's Digest*. A retired editor who has this quality is Tom Winship, of the *Boston Globe*. I was on a trip to Alaska with him and he always encouraged the people he met to tell him more; he was excited by what he learned about oil wells, seals, ice, people. Once he heard me speak, and afterward he wanted to see my notes, how I made them, how they were covered in plastic, the kind of notebook I used. His hunger for detail was never satisfied.

I can hear the grumbles from the city room reporters: "So what if I have great ideas. The *Globe* [the *Blade*, the *News*, the *Times*] doesn't want 'em. " That depends. Some editors do encourage ideas from their staff, and some do not. But I think every writer can devise a strategy to deal with the problem. Here's the one I followed at the old *Boston Herald* when I was starting out:

- I'm in charge of my own career. It is my responsibility and in my best self-interest to come up with stories I want to pursue.
- Editors can't see the ideas in my head. I draft the lead I hope I will be able to write, list the major points (no more than five), point out why the story should be written, how the information will be gathered, and how much time and space it will take. If the story depends on tone—if it is a mood piece or humor—I write a draft and show it to the editor.
- I expect rejections. The more ideas I have, the more ideas I will have. And if the idea is really good and the paper I'm working for has been given a fair opportunity to see its importance and is not interested, then I query a magazine or book publisher and write the story on my own time. The paper needs your ideas, but even more than that, you need to be having ideas so that you are alive, aware of the world in which you live.

Avoiding the Clichés of Vision

The more professional we become, the greater the danger that we will see what we expect to see. Experience, of course, is an advantage; but it has a dark side. It may keep us from seeing the real story: the cause that does not fit the stereotype, the effect that is not predictable, the quote that we do not hear before our question is answered. The effective writer must always have an essential naiveté—skepticism must be balanced by innocence. The reporter must be capable of seeing what is new. Clichés of language are significant misdemeanors, but clichés of vision are felonies.

A young man has run amok in the neighborhood, killing eight and maiming fifteen. The man is described as quiet, studious, polite to the neighbors, good to his mother, neat, mild-mannered, and the last person in the world you would have expected to do anything like that. Carol McCabe laughs as she tells about the mother of one such young man, who said, "He never did anything like that before." He is the cliché killer, and the reporter is happy to find him. There's no problem writing the story; it's been written before. The neighbors all fall into the stereotype. They aren't lying, but they are shocked—they do like the mother—and they want to avoid responsibility for what they've overlooked the last twenty years. And besides, they know the journalistic stereotypes as well as the reporters do.

Some good, hard-edged reporting will discover that neighborhood pets have been disappearing for years; the nice young man was seen grilling pigeons when he was three years old; that he didn't play doctor, but instead the Nazi torturer; that the neighbors have called the police numerous times because they could hear him beating his mother; that his father, two brothers, and three sisters have refused to live at home with him; that the seemingly studious young man has the reading level of a nine-year-old; and that his mother has stonewalled any attempts at getting psychiatric help for him.

That story may lead to other stories: Poor kids get better counseling help than middle-class kids; early help for disturbed children is crucial; nearby agencies provide such help; there are danger signals that neighbors and teachers should pay attention to.

As journalists, we lose our sense of wonder and surprise. We leave the city room knowing what we'll find, and then, of course, we find it. This cliché often is compounded by editors who tell reporters what to find and give them a hard time when they don't fill in the blanks of the editor's stereotype.

Some of the stereotypes of vision are:

- The victim is always innocent.
- Corporation executives are workaholics.
- Bureaucrats are lazy.
- Housewives hate being housewives.
- Politicians are crooked.
- All gays cruise.
- It's lonely at the top.
- It's boring in the suburbs.
- It's exciting in the city.

There's never a peaceful evening on an urban ghetto street corner where good friends spend a few peaceful hours reminiscing and kidding each other; there's never a Friday evening in a New Hampshire country store marked by distrust, meanness, and potential violence.

The reporter has the challenge of getting the unexpected material into the notebook that will become a story with density, feeling, a point of view, and voice.

Here are reminders of what goes into the good reporter's notebook:

1. What isn't being said—significant pauses, distances, facial expressions, gestures, body actions and reactions.
2. The details of the environment that the news sources create. The gadgets on the desk, the books on the shelf, the pictures on the wall are usually calculated to reveal, but the person they reveal, sometimes, is not what they expect. Once I interviewed the leader of an organization working to control the birth rate around the world. His own desk was crowded with pictures of his large family. His double-standard answers were revealing in a way he did not intend.
3. Listen to what you're hearing, not what you expect to hear. On one story I found that a grandmother who took in a grandson and did a marvelous job of raising him was motivated not by grandmother love but by hatred of his other family. It was a stronger and a truer story.
4. Put the reader on the scene. A hearing isn't just testimony, it involves people, place, action, and reaction.
5. Don't just talk to members of Kiwanis. Many newspapers read as if their communities were composed entirely of lawyers, opticians, and realtors, who spend most of their time giving each other plaques. Make sure you talk to the old and the young, the housewife as well as the career woman, the building inspector as well as the mayor, the factory worker as well as the factory owner, the fire person as well as the police officer, the nonunion worker as well as the union member, the quiet as well as the loud, the contented as well as the discontented.
6. Look for stories that have no event. Many of the most significant developments in our society never come to trial and are never the subject of a press conference on television. Some stories that should be covered: the 100,000-mile cars that are repainted instead of being turned in; the shirt collars that are being turned; the thirty-five-year-old children who are still living at home; the additions that are being built on houses because people can't afford larger homes; the huge increase in home vegetable gardens; the increase in women sewing and tailoring for men as well as women, and sewing done by men.
7. Practice empathetic reporting. Get inside the skin of the judge on the bench, the prosecutor, the defender, the witness, the victim, the criminal, the parent, the wife, the child. Become each person for a moment so that you will know the questions to ask that reveal the point of view and the attitude of each participant.

Make your own list of the ways in which you can see the stories that aren't appearing in the daily paper—and should. For example, the elderly represent an increasingly large market for computers. Is e-mail keeping families in touch? Is e-mail reaching across generations—are grandparents and grandchildren in touch? Are doctors making e-mail "house calls"? Do patients ask doctors questions by e-mail? Is e-mail shopping helping the elderly this holiday season? How is an e-mail message different from a letter? Family reunions on e-mail? E-mail finds old college roommates, wartime buddies? How e-mail helps shut-ins? Elderly loneliness? Increase in genealogical research with e-mail and Internet?

What to Do When You Have to Write the Same Story Again and Again

Looking back I realize I played an important writing game when I worked at the rewrite desk on the old *Boston Herald*, zipping out twenty, thirty, forty stories a night. The game was simple: How could I do something different that would be true to the story and work within the limitations of space and deadline?

This game is one of the reasons that at seventy-four I am eager to write another column, draft another revision of one of my books, work over a poem, or return to the novel. I may say the same old thing, but I keep finding new ways of approaching the old subjects because of the game.

I do not, of course, play the game on every story, but I play it when there is a hint of repetition or a too-comfortable familiarity as I start to work. The new ways of saying the old thing do not have to be radical, but they have to give me a problem to solve.

Mihaly Csikszentmihalyi and Jacob W. Getzels wrote a book, *The Creative Vision*, which sits on the shelf across from my desk because it reports on a long-term study of artists documenting how the successful ones find problems to solve where others see no problems—a good lesson for all of us.

All stories, even those in the Bible, are old stories. But there are ways that we can make them new, for the moment, both for our readers and for ourselves. There are three particular areas where we can seek new challenges, new ways to tell old stories. We are not discovering a new planet, but we are assigning ourselves explorations of our craft that will make our work more interesting to ourselves and our readers.

Old Stories Seen in New Ways

Each story can be seen in many ways. Here are a few that may expose a new story within an old one:

- Change the angle of vision from the senator to the senator's aide, the view of the opponent, the voter, the lobbyist, the citizen affected by the vote. Most stories are told from a predictable angle of vision. Move the angle of vision just a bit and you may see a new story in an old one, a story that reveals the essence of the story more effectively.
- Focus on a single person: the suspects, the victim, the arresting officer, that officer's partner, a senior officer, a rookie, a member of the victim's family, the suspect's family, the officer's family, the district attorney, the police photographer, the ambulance driver, the trauma doctor, the trauma nurse. There may be a hundred different ways to view a single event. Choose the most significant, not the most traditional, one.
- Put the story in historical, social, or political perspective.
- Put the story in context. Show how it relates, how it influences and is influenced by the world around it.
- Look ahead and see what may happen because of the event.
- Describe the process of the story in detail, showing how the event evolved.
- Focus on the background instead of the foreground—the technology available, considered, rejected, and used in the trauma center.
- Focus on the conflict behind the scenes that caused the conflict within the story.
- Take the reader into the committee room, the police-dispatch center, or the company sales meeting so the reader is within the event taking place.

Old Stories in a New Form

There are a limited number of forms in traditional journalism, and we keep distorting the news (and boring our readers) by shoehorning all stories into those forms. We do what we are comfortable doing, and that's what is often wrong with stories: they are comfortable, familiar, ho-hummers. Instead, try something different:

- Tell the story as a story. Use narrative to reveal the beginning, middle, and end of the conflict ordered by time.

- Write the event through a profile.
- Tell the story with an interview with one or more people.
- Create a dialogue between contestants. Let them reveal the story.
- Reveal by a scene: characters, action, dialogue, conflict and resolution, setting.
- Write the story as a rhetorical form central to the story: a police report, a political speech, a company memo, a nursing report, a job application, a letter by a participant to a friend.
- Film the story in print, moving the camera in close and back, to reveal it to the reader in images and scenes.
- Use lists, parallel columns, charts, or other devices appropriate to the story to reveal its significance clearly to the reader.
- Select the central scene, conflict, personality, or issue in the story and write a forty-line story focusing in on it.

Old Stories Told in a New Voice

The voice (the style, the tone, the music) of the story provides an opportunity to make familiar stories lively and more effective. The tuning of the writer's voice to the message of the story is also a game of craft that can be satisfying to the writer and increase the writer's involvement in stories that have been written repeatedly.

- Look for the phrase that reveals the central issue of the story. One of my personal favorites was *The Boston Globe's* Brian Mooney's lead, "Dapper O'Neil was at home among strangers . . ."
- Match the tone of the story to the meaning of the story: controlled anger, nostalgia, humor, cynicism, historical recollection, grief, wonder.
- Use the tone of the people in the story—angry workers, fire victims, politicians, police, intellectuals, commuters, business consultants, doctors, lawyers.
- Throw a change-of-pace pitch at the reader. Relieve the pressure on the reader with a touch of humor in a serious piece, a touch of seriousness in a humorous piece, an anecdote in a factual report.
- Vary the documentation. Use what will help the reader, not what you are used to using in a particular story. Stories shouldn't be limited to one traditional form of documentation such as anecdotes, quotes, or statistics.
- Vary the length of sentences and paragraphs. Use shorter ones for the most important points.

- Set goals for your own writing. Decide you are going to work on one thing this month: writing shorts, trying humor, making people come alive on the page, learning to use statistics more effectively.
- Write aloud and read aloud, using the sound of the words and sentences (the beat, the pace, the rhythm) to reinforce the meaning of the story.
- Focus on one section of the writing this week, another next week: endings, leads, turning points, description, and so on.
- Take the clichés of journalism and put a twist on them:

"local businessmen"	"local and almost-local businesspersons"
"politicians"	"the elected and the self-elected"
"housewives"	"home managers"

- None of these are examples of great literature—and yours probably won't be either—but they are fun to write and fun to read.
- Stir in a bit of surprise. Use the unexpected word, phrase, line, or tone when it does a more effective job of revealing the story.
- Be selfish. Take command of your own stories. Make them fun. Risk. Try what you don't think you can do. Teach yourself in print. On each story set up a new challenge. Our craft is, after all, based on play, and we must never take it so seriously that we forget to play with what we see, how we order it, and how we tell it to ourselves and our readers.

❖ Journalist at Work ❖ STEVE KURKJIAN Interview

One of the most significant developments in contemporary journalism is the institutionalizing of investigative teams that have special financial support, extensive time and resources, independence from daily news operation, and particular skills.

Steve Kurkjian was an original member of the *Globe's* investigative unit, the Spotlight Team, and is exposing those who need to be revealed. He is known at the *Globe* for his ability to get people to talk who do not want to talk.

Q: *How do you prepare for an interview?*

A: People dread being mentioned in any investigative article, even if they are not the main focus of the story, and so it's no wonder that their first reaction on getting a call from a Spotlight reporter is to refuse an interview. No set formula works in dealing with a reluctant interviewee.

But before every interview I prepare a long list, a short list, and a "hello–goodbye" list of questions I will use depending on the person's reaction to my call.

Q: *How do you start the interview?*

A: The most crucial time is the first two minutes, during which you don't let the subject do too much talking because his first reaction is going to be negative. The things I try to impress on him during that period are written into my "patter." They include:

1. I already know most of what went on from other people I've interviewed.
2. Some of the people I've interviewed have mentioned his name as a person who could add one or two things and whose word can be trusted.
3. It is very important that I speak to as many people as possible because this is a vital story, with all sorts of social and political consequences, and I have to be absolutely sure of my facts. (This plays to his conscience—if he doesn't talk, then he is conspiring in the printing of a story that may be inaccurate.)
4. I am a good guy, who has worked like hell on this story; he is a good guy for not having gotten too deeply involved in the skulduggery, and we have a common body of interests and are really working the same side of the road.

Even if the person is the one and only source who can provide the whole story I don't let him think the entire article rests with him. It's too heavy a load for one person to bear to think that it's his word against someone else's. Few people want to become martyrs, and those who do have usually lost their perspective and objectivity and so aren't much help.

Q: *What do you do after the "patter" stage?*

A: The best way to proceed is to go for those one or two nuggets of information that you want this person to confirm, deny, or elaborate on right after you have finished your patter. If he's expansive after that, ask him to "step back" a little and go for more cosmic information, such as, "How could this have happened?" or "Why didn't official investigative bodies stop this right away?" If he opens up here all of a sudden, he's the expert and is leading you through the rocks and shoals of a complicated story. Foster that feeling in him, even if it's stuff you already know about.

Q: *Are there hazards in this approach?*

A: The only problem with such an approach is that the source begins to feel superior in his relationship with you, which means he feels he could lie to you about something to make himself look good. The best way of dealing with that, I've found, is to impress on him that you need accurate information all the way through, that if one middle initial is out of place, the whole story could be rebutted. If you find he continues to lie or exaggerate facts, confront him with it in a direct manner. But don't be offensive, because he could always hang up leaving you with nothing.

Q: *What conditions do you prefer for an interview?*

A: I like to call at the home of a background source I need to give me the substance of my story. He feels more comfortable at home, less a part of the corporate or government structure on which you are asking him to give damaging information. I tell him that I'm calling from my home, giving him the impression I am so thoroughly committed to the story that I will work day and night for it. If he gets a positive feeling about the person he is speaking with, he is more apt to talk honestly

Interview the principal of the story in his office. Ask to tape record the interview. It saves you from taking notes and mistaking a quote. If he's hesitant, we offer to provide him with a copy of the transcript of the interview.

Q: *What standards do you have for confirming information?*

A: I do not like to take anyone's word for anything unless I have a document supporting the contentions. Of course, we don't always have the time or the ability to get the documentation even if it exists. I've adopted an informal guide that I will not float an allegation of illegality against anyone unless hard documentation is in hand, or there are several supporting sources. I think it is wrong to hold a reporter to the standard of getting three confirming sources before publishing a story—some allegations should require half a dozen such sources, others just two.

❖ Journalist at Work ❖ Analysis of a TOM ASHBROOK Story

It is possible to report a story before it occurs. Tom Ashbrook, now a software venture capitalist, gathered the background information for this story and when it occurred he was ready to pounce.

GOODWINS MILLS, Maine—The cops came early and they got it all: heaps and bundles and lush green acres of prime Maine reefer, the best darn marijuana crop that Billy Carvell had ever seen.

This is a good example of vigorous lead writing with the added touch of hinting at the voice appropriate to the locale of the story. Too much would be hokey; the right amount adds appropriate liveliness to a story that would usually be greeted with a loud, "Ho-hum."

It was hanging from the barn rafters. It was leaping up ten feet behind the brush and cedars. It was tied down bushy and flat, hid between the corn rows and growing like crazy a stone's throw from the Hebron Community Church.

Notice how active this description is: hanging, leaping, hiding, growing. Then at the point in the paragraph of most emphasis, the end, we have the church.

But mentioning the church has a purpose, it demonstrates the point of the story that pot is being grown in the rural heartland of America, Republican, church-going, Norman Rockwell country. Too often we have nice touches that do nothing to advance the meaning of the story.

From the road, you never would have guessed it. The Carvell farm looks straight off a Maine travel poster. A red and white barn on a country road. A "pick your own" tomato patch every summer. Pumpkin on the lawn every fall.

Again, this paragraph puts the story in a context and reinforces the meaning being developed.

But when York County police moved in on the homestead Monday morning, they found more than $1 million worth of marijuana, about two hundred pounds cut and dried and ready to go, plus 1,300 thriving plants.

I don't like the term "delayed lead" because I think that Ashbrook's lead contained the news, but by the third or fourth paragraph of a story that depends on description and tone, the reader needs some hard facts. Here they are delivered in hard-edged specifics.

"If you know anything about marijuana, you'd be impressed with this," said one detective with grudging admiration after the raid, handling a thick cluster of succulent buds. "This is as good as it gets."

A nice time for a quote, an attribution, an authority other than the reporter speaking. There's a nice bit of action woven into the attribution as well.

Each paragraph—each sentence, each phrase, each word—should drive the story forward. The reader should receive a delivery of information that will satisfy the reader's hunger for information and increase the reader's appetite for more information.

Out on bail, Tuesday, alleged pot farmer William H. Carvell, 43, was more taciturn:

I'm not sure I understand who he is more taciturn than or even if that's the right word, but I need the facts in the paragraph and I like the way the quotation is set up.

"I'm just a country farmer who found out there was more money in pot than in corn," he said.

The effective writer anticipates the reader's questions and answers them. The reader asks how a Maine farmer would get in the pot trade. Ashbrook lets the farmer answer.

Indeed. And not only for Billy Carvell.

An important transition and made clear enough so that the reader sees the turn in the road. Ashbrook's reader will not get lost, the writer is unobtrusively but effectively in charge.

It is harvest time in the world's premier marijuana patch, the United States of America.

Just about the time the reader is getting tired of the story, the author raises the ante. It's a new game. I'd better stay in and read on.

Cocaine may grab the big headlines these days. Crack may send cities into turmoil. But deep in the coke trade's shadow, marijuana—the dowdy green matron of the drug scene—has become one of the largest cash crops in the United States. And America has earned a dubious distinction as home to the cream of world marijuana production.

Anticipation again. The reader's going to begin saying, so what? What about coke, what about crack? Ashbrook puts the pot trade into context and tells the reader how important this story is.

As recently as 1980, by federal estimates, just 7 percent of available pot in America was domestically produced. The vast majority and the best quality of marijuana came from Mexico, Columbia, and Caribbean and Southeast Asia.

You don't believe him? Well, step back a minute and let him give you a bit of history.

But by last year, America's homegrown portion of pot had nearly quadrupled, to account for 25 percent or more of the country's available marijuana. And the quality crown, judged on potency, had come home. "Americans now grow the best pot in the world," says Brian Murphy, a staff member at the National Organization for the Reform of Marijuana Laws, in Washington. "It's the Dom Perignon of the marijuana industry."

The writer should never forget that readers want to be informed. Readers want the Globe *to make them authorities; they want to be able to tell their coworkers, their neighbors, and their families something new. Ashbrook gives them surprising information they can use to surprise the people around them.*

Predicting that the United States might become a net exporter of marijuana in the 1990s, exasperated federal law officials agree.

And listen to this.

"We can grow it here," says Jack Short, acting chief of the federal Drug Enforcement Agency's marijuana section, "and we can produce the best."

And this.

Both these facts are well known to a growing circle of American pot producers. Estimates of the domestic pot crop's value now range from $10 billion to $30 billion. From cash-strapped farmers to highly organized criminal syndicates, the lucrative production of America's new moonshine has proven an irresistible lure.

Ashbrook wraps up the information he has delivered above and makes the transition back to who's growing it. By using the word moonshine *he gives the story an appropriate historical perspective, harkening back to another time when rural America was engaged in illicit activity.*

With domestic marijuana production reaching unprecedented levels, the summer has produced a raft of eye-opening pot tales. A sampling:

Once more, he lets the reader in on what his doing—"Hey, come over here and lookit this!"

• In Tucson, a Mecca for allergy sufferers where marijuana can not grow without careful cultivation, officials reported last month that pot pollen led all others in Tucson's daily pollen count, outranking Bermuda grass, salt cedar and ragweed. "I guess we aren't winning," said a local police officer. "We never do."

The writer uses an interesting variety of anecdotes.

Pot pollen; that's amazing, says the reader.

• In Fort Benton, Mont., a prominent farming family raised and sold more than $400,000 worth of marijuana in a failed attempt to save the farm from foreclosure. "It was either do this and save the ranch or there wasn't going to be any ranch," said a son-in-law.

An echo of what the Maine farmer said. His was not an isolate case.

• In Akron, Ohio, a major University of Akron area landlord was arrested this month after police shut down a sophisticated underground pot production chamber. Police said Albert Thrower owned 30 cars, 300 college rental properties, an airplane, six legal businesses—and a marijuana goldmine concealed behind a trapdoor in his barn floor.

A pet hate of mine is to use a word to qualify or define an area. GRRRRR.

But we have another form of pot production and, because the writer has earned our trust, we believe it is typical of a larger problem.

"If we didn't have such a big coke problem, we would be taking better care of our marijuana problem," said the DEA's Short, calling the 7.4 million pot plants eradicated last year only a fraction of the total crop. "The vast majority of our resources go to cocaine."

By now the reader's asking, why is something not being done about this problem? Again, Ashbrook anticipates the reader's questions, which is a matter of timing and pacing.

The careful grooming of prime strains and new hybrids has produced a level of pot potency largely unknown in the 1960s, when a rebellious generation of baby boom Americans turned on to cannabis. Recent crops of American pot have yielded record-breaking levels of

Once more, the writer recognizes when the reader will grow tired of the story and raises the ante: The new U.S. pot is especially powerful.

He also puts this in historical perspective by weaving in a reference to the 60s.

tetrahydrocannabinol, or THC, the psycho-active chemical in marijuana.

Note how quickly he explains a technical name. All the way through, he uses language in such a way that both the pot sophisticate and ignorant old-timer like myself can understand the story.

In 1986, the average THC content in sensimilla pot seized by the US enforcement agencies was 8.5 percent, almost triple what was once the norm and twice the potency of pot coming from Mexico and Colombia. Symbolic of pot's new hierarchy, Colombians have recently been reported smoking American marijuana on the streets of Bogota.

Good details with a lively touch at the end of the paragraph that picks the reader up and pushes him or her toward the next paragraph.

The stabilization of potent hybrids has brought a new sophistication to pot shopping. The talk of marijuana connoisseurs has begun to sound like the airy blurbs in a Macy's wine catalogue.

Effective bit of lively language.

Ed Rosenthal, a columnist for High Times magazine, recently described current favorites among premium pots in an interview:

Now the writer is going to document what he just said.

On Afghani Durban—"A dense, fragrant smoke. Not sweet, more musky. It has a very soaring high. It's light."

On Skunk No. 1—"An odor a lot like skunk, but a very smooth taste, a very up high. Heavy yielding."

Amusing examples, but they aren't used just to entertain; they testify to the popularity of pot in a time when coke, crack, etcetera dominate the news, and they speak to the potency of the present marijuana, a major point in the story.

On Northern Lights—"Perhaps the most potent pot there is. An Afghani sativa. Very strong, but lacks personality. Like vodka. Usually crossed with something to give it more character."

It always helps to allow the reader to hear other voices within the story, especially when the voice supports a major thesis of the article as this voice does. Ashbrook gets out of the way and let this authority speak.

And the price? Good grades run from $150 to $300 per ounce and up across the country, with Boston-area smokers of the illegal weed paying at the high end.

Put the reader's questions right in the story. The answer supports the reason why so much is grown: It is a cash crop.

Officials warn that pot smoking—especially of America's potent new product—can cost a user more than money.

We've been having fun. It all seems silly and harmless. So the writer turns the story level up again. This transition paragraph announces to the reader that important information is on the way. You'd better keep reading.

A recent survey of more than 1,000 emergency patients at Maryland hospital's shock/trauma units found that 35 percent had used marijuana within four hours of the injury that landed them in the emergency ward. Thirty-three percent had used alcohol. Sixteen percent had used both.

Good, solid, hard news.

"The unspoken fact of American life is that marijuana kills," says Robert S. Wiener, a spokesman for the House Select Committee on Narcotics. "The reality is that it's very, very harmful."

He puts that limited study in a broader context.

Law enforcement officials say that the trend in recent years has been toward scattered cultivation in many small, less easily detected plots and toward indoor growing under artificial light.

Now the story is going to achieve closure. It won't just drift off, but will echo the beginning so that the reader will see the original pot raid from a new and significant perspective.

Oregon, California and Hawaii usually lead in pot production. Massachusetts ranked 34th among the 50 states in a 1987 National Organization for the Reform of Marijuana Laws survey of marijuana crops. But indoor production knows no bounds, with national trade magazines hawking everything from seeds and growing kits to Kentucky bat guano fertilizer.

Authoritative details with a nice kicker at the end: bat guano, indeed.

Other favorite production spots from pot farmers weary of having their own land seized in an arrest are US national parks and forests. The National Forest Service estimates that last year alone it destroyed $1 billion worth of marijuana on public lands, and it found less than half of what was there.

Another unexpected site.

In York County, Maine, detective Michael McAlevey estimates that even with the big bust of Billy Carvell this week, his department is detecting only 10 percent of the marijuana grown in Maine's southernmost county.

Now we return to York County, after having seen the dimensions and significance of the problem.

"We have hearsay that there are doctors out there doing it, lawyers doing it, businessmen doing it," said McAlevey, who grew up a mile down the road from the Carvell farm and went to school with Billy.

"Plus, there's a Yankee attitude that you mind your own business—that what somebody else is doing behind their barn is their own business."

And it isn't just the farmers.

Nice touch that increases McAlevey's stature as an authority. He's a native who knows what's going on.

Out along the Maine backroads, where handwritten signs advertise the legal bounty of the land—sod, rabbits, hardy mums—neighbors said knowingly that Billy Carvell's bust was not the end of the local harvest of moonshine marijuana.

Back to Norma Rockwell country. This story is shaped like a diamond. Many of us, myself included, think it can be helpful to visualize the shape of a story. I even draw such shapes in planning a complex story, something that John Updike has done for some of his novels. Ashbrook's story starts with a specific raid on a specific farm, then shows the significance in many ways.

He puts it in several economic perspectives, even in a perspective of world trade. He introduces us to the new and powerful pot, considers law enforcement problems, points out the health dangers involved, and then, once we have the information we need to understand the significance of what Billy Carvell was doing on his farm, brings us right back there.

"Let's put it this way," said one, stuffing a wad of tobacco into his cheek and glancing into the woods. "There's a lot more out there to be picked."

Chapter 4

FOCUS: Find the Tension

The experienced writer sees the world through the lens of language, and that lens captures the tension between forces in the world that will produce a story. That tension may be between one individual and another; between a new idea and an old one; between an individual and society; between a belief and a newly discovered fact; between what is said and unsaid, seen and unseen; between the writer and the world; between what is being done and what should be done; between cause and effect; between reality and illusion. The writer seeks the drama in the world.

The starting point is in conflict. It is not that bad news is good news, although any responsible newswriter or editor must carry a burden of guilt about that. The writer stands, notebook or tape recorder in hand, at the crossroads where the forces of the world may collide.

It is at these crossroads that the world changes, and it is the job of the newswriter to observe, document, relate, and connect, to tell those affected by the collision that it is coming, that it is happening, that it has happened; to describe and predict the chain of action and reaction that results from each collision; and to reveal the individuals who are involved and how they cause change or are changed.

The dramatic interaction of people and forces is caught by the writer in a word, a phrase, a sentence, a paragraph. The writer selects and narrows so that language, the writer's lens, makes what is at first only glimpsed come clear. Focus identifies and isolates a central tension or conflict so that it can be explored in writing. The vision is held and then developed, as idea becomes draft and draft becomes published story.

Finding the Line

Writing my regular "Over Sixty" column for *The Boston Globe* has made me realize there is a moment when I know have a column. That always-surprising moment arrives when I hear "the line."

Although I recognize this crucial point in my writing process while writing my column, I find that I have been depending on the line while writing articles, difficult letters, talks, poems, and books of fiction and nonfiction. The line is a fragment of language—sometimes a single word, often a phrase or series of words, rarely a sentence—that makes me follow it. It might be described as a question that demands an answer, an experiment that I must perform, an itch I must scratch, a path I must follow, a hint, a clue, or a vague shape I cannot yet make out but must try anyway.

Elements in a Line

The elements that exist (most of the time) in this linguistic trigger mechanism include:

Tension. A sense of forces on the move headed for a collision or being driven apart.

Conflict. The forces are engaged in a battle that needs coverage, explanation or resolution.

Irony. The dramatic difference between what should be and what is.

Energy. A force that will be released by the writing of the story.

Play. The possibility of surprise or contradiction.

Discovery. A sense that the writing of the draft will teach me something I do not know I know.

Music. The voice of the text.

Form. A hint of the shape of the piece; its length, pace, proportions.

Ease. The illusion of ease, which may be false but often is not when I have found the line and follow it.

All of those elements are usually in the line, and they are so important for me that I will not start a draft, even on deadline, until I have found the line, the path of possibility. That is my starting point.

The Form of the Line

The line comes to me in many forms. Often it arrives in my head when I least expect it, but almost immediately it is written down in my daybook, a spiral notebook I keep near me most of the time, or on the three-by-five cards that I keep in a leather folder in my shirt pocket. Other times it comes as I scribble in my daybook, more consciously thinking about what I may write. In either case, the scribbling is vital: Writing the line usually changes it in small but crucial ways that are constructive, and it starts to grow its own meaning. Writing the line preserves it; last week's line becomes this week's column.

I am going to share some of the lines that have worked for me because of their very ordinariness. The lines I share with you will not impress you. This is private language, private notation. I hear the mystery and the music and the potential meaning in what is meaningless to others. If I am successful, I will turn it into public language and during the process I, the writer, and others, the readers, may experience the magic, the music, and the meaning.

But first I have to be able to hear and see what is not yet there. I have to be able to catch the vague shape of possible meaning, the hesitant, quiet sounds that may grow strong. The line appears to me in many forms.

Word. The word *playground* keeps appearing in my daybook. That single word contains significant tension for me because my family religion, combined with my inherent cowardice, made the playground a place of terror, testing, and failure. I will explore that word in a column that may explore the underside of childhood—and cause my readers to explore their own childhoods.

Fragment. A fragment is not a sentence, often not even a clause, but simply a few words that have potential meaning among them. This is the most common way the line appears to my ear or my eye. I read "ordinary war" on my daybook page and started to pursue a novel. Obviously, the horror of war is what becomes ordinary.

Image. In one unexpected moment I saw the way my mother kept the three places always set at the kitchen table ("the places at the kitchen table were always set"), although father was rarely home for supper, and in a poem I recaptured the lonely silence of our suppers.

List. The list is a powerful thinking tool. When young children start making lists, we know they have made an enormous stride forward. My line is often a list:

touch
old
holding hands in middle of Monday night football
parents' marriage bed

That led to a column on touching—and more. All the elements on the list were in the column, although in a very different order. It was not an outline but a confusion of items that were significant to me and became ordered and meaningful through their writing.

Lead. I do not try to force a marriage between the line and the lead, but that relationship often does develop. The line is the starting point for my written exploration. "I am not going to write a column about my daughter Hannah's wedding" became the lead from which the column grew. Many lines are shaped and developed in my head, in my daybook, or on my word processor until they become the lead. I am one of those writers who must have the lead before I go on, and I have come to realize that it is usually the line that gives me the lead.

Those are the most frequent forms of the line that come to me, but there are others, such as a quotation. A surgeon told me he was going to sit by the pool and write when he retired. I got back at him in a column. He said he was going to "take up" writing when he retired. I said I would "take up" surgery. Often a fact, or the illusion of fact, in a statistic or a report will contain the acorn of a piece of writing. A revealing detail—the colonel who ordered one of our regiments to attack another was promoted to general and sent back to safety in England—may lead to an article, a story, an essay or a book.

Pursuing the line. Making use of the line is, for me, a strange form of pursuit that has taken me years to perfect and to grow comfortable using. It is not a chase. That's the first lesson.

I may have to force myself to my writing desk, but once there I have to relax, to become receptive to language, to write easily. I do not pursue the line as much as put a tail on it. I am the private eye following a suspect who may saunter through a shopping mall or race along a mountain road. My job is to stay in sight, out of sight. I follow language to see where it will take me, influencing the text as little as possible.

I write my first draft quickly and uncritically, allowing the text to tell me what it will say. I am stenographer more than maker. Then, once I have a draft, I cut and add, shape, form, polish, and clarify. But it all begins with the line. That is where the text begins. I write as I draw, by following the line.

Finding the Design

When I read years ago that the novelist John Updike said, "I really begin with some kind of solid, coherent image, some notion of the shape of the book and even of its texture. *The Poorhouse Fair* was meant to have a sort of *Y* shape. *Rabbit, Run* was a kind of zig-zag. *The Centaur* was sort of a sandwich." I shouted, "YES!" He had said what I had sensed, that I often visualized the shape of a story, a sort of map of the territory ahead or a way through the territory ahead.

My first novel looked like a stock-market chart with story lines rising, falling, and colliding. My first book on teaching writing was a stone dropped into a pond with each succeeding chapter an increasing circle. I often play with shapes in my notebook before beginning to write.

All journalists are familiar with the inverted pyramid, where the most important news comes at the top.

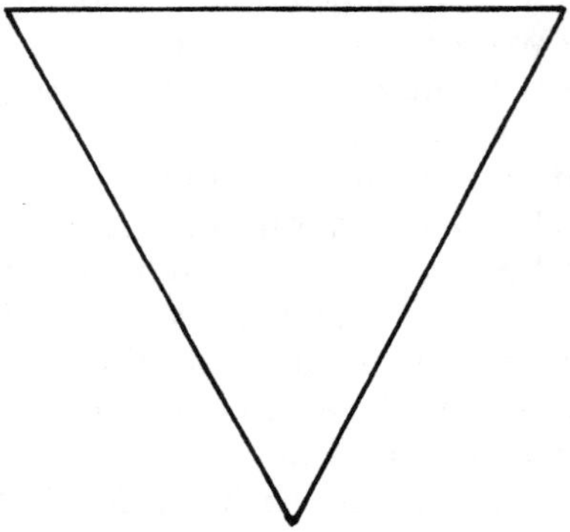

Then, when I wrote editorials, I had to write pyramids with the most important information coming at the end.

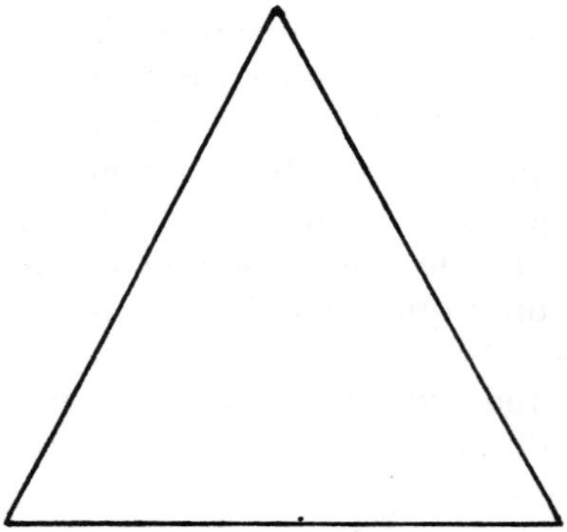

Some feature stories were crosses with an anecdote lead, a context paragraph, then the story.

Other stories I saw as boxes. This chapter is an example. I'm writing this section ahead of the ones that will come before and after it. I see the chapter as a series of boxes.

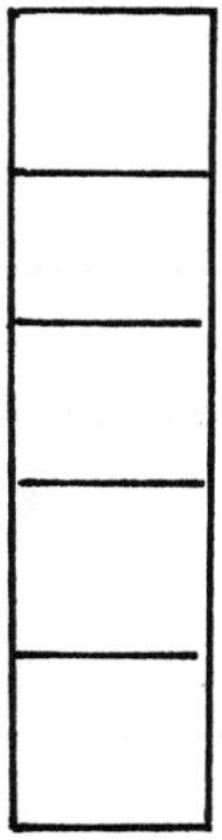

Other pieces of writing may be a meandering river as long as the current is strong enough to carry the reader forward.

I have written many mountain peak stories or a series of mountain ridges.

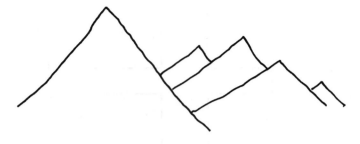

Some stories are a horizontal *H*, with important information at the beginning, then a narrative that leads to a restatement of the important information at the end.

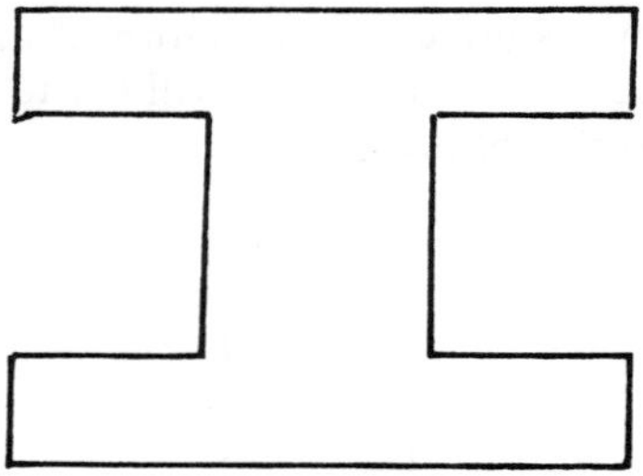

Often I think of an arrow that carries the reader straight to a destination.

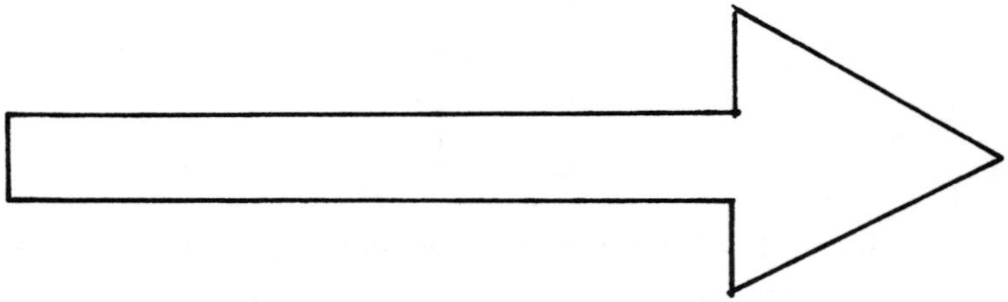

The shapes will change, combine, shrink, expand, but the shape of story is a good way to visualize what you may write.

The Qualities of a Good Story

The good writer is forever a student of writing, extending the writer's voice, learning the techniques of craft, and attempting experiments in meaning. It is a solitary business, but not a lonely one. Writers need colleagues, test readers, editors, and sometimes a writing coach who, like the opera star's coach, does less teaching than reminding.

The old definitions of hard news—the story that has to be printed today—and the feature—the story that can wait until tomorrow—do not cover the diversity of stories printed in today's daily newsmagazine. But whatever the form or the subject, any good story has at least seven elements.

Information

Information, not language, is the raw material from which effective writing is built. I have said this before, but it needs to be said again. The writer must collect specific, accurate pieces of information to be able to write effective prose. Too many stories and columns are written instead of reported; they are created by tricks of rhetoric when they should be constructed from a pattern of concrete detail. The revealing details that mark an exceptional story rarely come from competitors' stories, the telephone, or staring thoughtfully across the city room. Information that reveals is collected by pounding the pavement.

Significance

Good stories affect the reader. They challenge the reader's life, health, wealth, or sense of values. They give information the reader needs to know. They tell what has happened, what is happening, and what may happen. We should not, however, confuse significance with notoriety, doing stories on the rich, the famous, the powerful, and no one else. It is our duty to show the significance in material that at first appears insignificant.

Focus

The stories that newspaper writers usually take the most pride in are long, and often appear in a series. The newswriter is a territorial animal with a primitive instinct to use up as much newsprint as possible. But the stories that survive are usually short, precisely limited, and clearly focused. Most good stories say one thing. They tell not of a battle, but of a soldier, they talk not about governance, but about a deal, they discuss not a socioeconomic group, but a person and a life.

Context

The effective story is put into perspective so the reader knows where the story has come from, where it is going, and how widespread or how typical it is. Sometimes the writer who is not very skilled delivers the context in a big, hard-to-swallow capsule in about, say, the third paragraph. The more skilled writer weaves the context through the story.

Faces

We should never forget that people like to read about people. Journalism presents ideas by introducing the reader to the people who are creating the ideas or by showing the people who are affected by them. For ideas read laws, trends, scientific discoveries, judicial opinions, economic developments, international crises. News stories work best when the writer has the skill to get out of the way and allow the reader to meet and hear the people in the story.

Form

An effective story has a shape that both contains and expresses the story. A narrative will work if it has all the information the reader needs and if the story can be revealed in a chronological pattern of action and reaction. The writer must find a form that gives the reader a satisfying sense of completion, a feeling that everything in the story flows toward an inevitable conclusion.

Voice

Memorable news stories create the illusion of an individual writer speaking aloud to an individual listener. A good newspaper is filled with fascinating conversations. But the writer must remember to keep the voice appropriate to the story. We all know writers who use the same voice every time they write. There is always an Uncle Elmer who bellows in the same way at a football game, wake, Thanksgiving dinner, and in a hospital room. The good writer seeks a voice that is consistent throughout the story but varies its volume and rhythm to the meaning. And we should never forget that even in an age of mass communication, the act of reading is private, one writer speaking to one reader.

The Conditions That Encourage Writing

We are taught that we learn to write by the elimination of error. That is the second half of the story. The first half is that learning comes from identifying our effective writing and repeating it. Part of the repetition comes from knowing the conditions that make effective writing possible and encouraging those conditions on future stories.

Need

The most recent distant war calls up my own war memories—and guilts—which I must confront in writing. A story works best for me if I have a personal need to explore the subject, and I will try to turn an assignment so that I can learn something a reader will also need to know.

Habit

Nulla dies sine linea. "Never a day without a line." This saying stands in my office where I cannot avoid looking at it. I do not wake, singing, "To writing, to writing, I will go." I drag my rump to the desk by habit. Most of the time I like being there, but I never like *going* there.

Tools

I just started my 106th daybook, in which I make notes and practice some of the writing that must come before writing. I also found as I lived out of town for a month just how dependent I have become on my computer, my software, my hard disk.

Attitude

If it isn't fun, I won't do it. Fortunately the writer, even the staff writer on deadline, has considerable control over the writing or how the writing is done. I make a game of writing: I'll try this one without looking at my notes; I'll see if I can write the crazy way the editor suggested; I'll write the end first; I'll try to write faster than usual, or more slowly. Writing is too serious a business to be taken seriously. Good writing is the product of play.

Limitations

I am stimulated by a deadline and I set the deadline ahead of need—my *Globe* column is delivered the Monday of the week before it will be published. And I play daily deadline games: "I'll finish this section of the book before lunch." I also need space limitations (a seven hundred-word column, an eighty thousand-word novel, a twelve-line poem) to plan as well as pace my draft.

Experiment

I have a private experiment on each writing project. I'll try the present tense, or emphasize visual images, or depend on dialogue that keeps me interested in a type of story I have written many times before. It clarifies the meaning in a way it is not usually clarified and sharpens my writing skills.

❖ Journalist at Work ❖ RICHARD SALTUS Interview

As a reader who staggered through biology, chemistry, and physics at North Quincy High School, learning little and retaining less, I am impressed when writers can make such material interesting and clear. As a writer who did some magazine medical reporting, I know how hard that task can be. I have been impressed by Richard Saltus, a master science writer, and have interviewed him so that we can all learn how he works.

Q: *Where do you get story ideas?*

A: From journal articles, news releases, and meetings about various areas of science. From scientists whom I'm interviewing about something else. Occasionally from editors who suggest we expand on a previous story or work up a series on a broader aspect of areas we've covered. Often, by looking back at two or three stories I've written on a particular subject and seeing a pattern or logical follow-up.

The best ideas sometimes spring up in conversations with people entirely outside of science, readers, for example, who are curious about something, who have a friend or relative working on an interesting project, or who think we have missed the boat on a story that's already been in the paper and needs another angle. And, as on every other beat, there are natural stories: when shuttles are launched, Nobel Prizes won, nuclear accidents, new species discovered.

Q: *How do you make assignments your own?*

A: This is usually a problem only when it's a story that has already been done by another paper, magazine, or network. Aside from the unconscious, personal selection of subject matter that every reporter does, I usually ask myself, do I feel there is some level of accuracy or truth that seemed missing in the previous treatment? Have there been new developments? Was there an obvious bias? And, perhaps most important, after dipping into the reporting for awhile, are there aspects that speak to me in a way that didn't get much attention before?

Q: *What clues tell you that you have a good idea?*

A: When I look into the story and it opens up farther and deeper, rather than seeming to exhaust itself quickly, I feel I'm on the right track. The best feeling is seeing a number of pieces of a story converge into something coherent, and looking in the clips and the *Readers' Guide*, and finding almost nothing on it. I am less influenced than I used to be by what other reporters or editors think, although I don't discount it because in retrospect some of the best stories have been ones that I only had a hint of (and other people no idea at all) until I had done a fair amount of reporting.

Q: *What reporting techniques have you developed that you wish you had known when you began reporting?*

A: At the Associated Press, editors used to say that if you were any good, you could go report on something without having read a word on it. I didn't really believe it then, but now I'm even more aware of how important it is to know the lay of the land, to be as prepared as you can, before doing important interviews. On the other hand, there is something to be said for plunging in and starting to talk to a few people right away. But you can be sorry you weren't better informed if you interview crucial sources while you're still learning the background of a story.

In the past, I sometimes avoided the most obvious or oft-quoted sources because I suspected they would be unavailable, wouldn't talk, or wouldn't have anything new to say. I have since learned that often there is a good reason why certain people are quoted over and over. Not only are some people inherently more quotable, but there are sources who simply are always better informed, keep up with developments, and understand how to communicate with the press—and often they are easier to reach than you'd think.

Q: *What interviewing techniques have you developed? How do you prepare for an interview? What climate do you attempt to establish? How do you take notes? What are your favorite questions?*

A: I'm not conscious of many techniques as such. I suppose I try to get a sense of whether a subject is one who has his *spiel* already composed and just needs you to get out of the way, let him tell it, and then go back after particular questions. Some subjects need to be drawn out in dialogue form. I prepare by trying to know at least what has been written about the source or story in the mass media, or maybe in specialized places, too. If the person is exceptionally busy, or if I'm more than usually uninformed about the subject, I will write down some questions to make sure the interview is efficient.

With scientists, it's important to establish how up-to-speed I am on a topic, because that influences the entire shape of the interview. For me, the trick is to be as well informed as possible but to be in a frame of mind that more closely resembles the casual reader. That way, I hope to avoid missing the obvious big questions. One difficulty in establishing a climate is allowing your natural curiosity and fascination with a story to interfere with the detachment, even suspicion, that sometimes is necessary. If I fail at this, sometimes I'll be sorry later on because I may have been taken in or duped.

I don't have many favorite questions, but I admired one reporter who always posed everything in superlatives—"What's the biggest, best, worst, most important," and so forth—which can elicit good quotes. I usually ask scientists why they got interested in whatever it is they're doing. This is often important to the story and sometimes reveals something interesting about the person.

Q: *What kind of information do you try to get in your notebook that will make the writing go well?*

A: If there's time, I try to fill in around quotes and notes things that remind me of the context, so that if sentences are fragmented or illegible, I have a chance of reconstructing them. If the interview is for a profile or a scientist-in-the-workplace type of story, I look around and jot down anything about the environment that helps create a sense of the person: things written on a blackboard, items relating to the subject's life away from the office, clothing, notes from associates, it's all fair game. When a strong or unexpected emotion accompanies a quote, I'll try to get that down. I also try to jot little subheads or summaries of where we are in the interview if there's time, so I can find things more quickly; this also helps with the aforementioned illegible notes, of which I have more than my share.

Q: *What kind of rehearsing or preparation for writing do you do during the reporting, or between the reporting and the writing?*

A: Depends on the magnitude of the story. When I have gathered a lot of material for a big piece, I sometimes talk the story through with a friend (or stranger), who very often asks logical questions I have neglected to answer.

Many times I am surprised at what other people find more or less interesting in something I've been working on, and that may influence how I order the elements of the piece. From time to time I will try out leads in a spare moment, or nut graphs, or second graphs—just pieces of things that help me to know if I'm ready to write or still floundering. Occasionally, when the story is one that reminds me of the work of a writer I admire, I'll dip into his or her writing to remind me about the tone that person used, writing tricks that seemed to fit well with that subject.

Q: *How do you prepare to write? What do you do with your notes? Do you outline, and if so, how?*

A: I have no regular method of overcoming the resistance to getting started. I don't always clean up my desk and pay the bills first, but sometimes it's part of the process. Usually I read over all my notes and underline things I plan to use. Sometimes I start a laundry list on a file in the VDT (video display terminal) of things I want to be sure not to leave out. Then I put all my notes on a clipboard (I used to use file folders, but they inevitably ended up all over my desk and the floor).

On a story of any size, I'll try to outline by putting down single sentences, each with one idea (they tend to run into more if I don't watch out) that get me through at least half the story. It's rare that I can outline an entire story before losing patience and plunging in, but if I can get the top organized, I'm relatively happy. I've read about outline systems where people jot down ideas at random positions on a piece of paper and connect them in all kinds of different ways, but that's never really worked for me. Often, I'll write, say, the first 25 percent of a story and then print it out and use that as the beginning of an outline, to sort of hurl me along in some direction with enough momentum to outline the rest of it.

Q: *How do you find the lead? What do you look for in a lead?*

A: That's very difficult to do or to describe. The most important thing in the first lead I settle on is that it have the tone (or voice, if you prefer) that I'm aiming for. That's more important than the right content or the right idea, even. It has to evoke the effect I want the story to have—formal, conversational, dramatic, technical, skeptical, humorous, flippant, apocalyptic, heart rending, whatever. That may come through an appropriate quote, a summing up, or a setup for suspense. Many times a visual image is where I start, whether it's the ambiance of a laboratory, the main subject's gesture, or the look of a piece of technology.

More often than not, though, the lead I come up with this way doesn't survive revision, especially if it's a long and complex story, because by the time I get to the end the lead isn't right anymore.

Q: *How do you write? Slow? Fast? Do you listen to the text?*

A: The pace depends a lot on the mood of the moment. On one story I have to extract every word out of nowhere, going back again and again; on another, I may write almost as fast as I can type until I hit a slow spot. The latter is usually best, by far, even if it takes a lot of revision. Even when I have outlined, getting the organization to work requires a lot of tailoring to get the transitions smooth, and I tend to do that as I go along. So, the bottom line is probably that I write slowly, unless I'm on deadline.

Listening is very, very important to me, especially in leads, but all the way through. If the cadence isn't right, it's hard for me to go on. I don't consciously read aloud and listen, but the sentences ring in my ear.

There's a tendency for sentences to get monotonously similar in a long story if I don't take time to break them up as I go along. It depends on what I've been reading, too: A writer who effectively uses simple, short sentences will get me trying to do that. At other times, I'll be enamored of long sentences with phrases that unroll this way and that and paragraphs made up of a nicely balanced combination of fluid and punchy sentences.

Q: *What are your three greatest writing problems and their solutions?*

A: Organization. This just takes constant work, trial and error. I naturally prefer a more magazine-like organization where the material flows logically, building up and letting down but always with a leaning toward the end. Newspapers, though, call for front loading the story with the best stuff. Editors like everything mentioned or teased up high, then explained at greater length later on. This tends to be hard to do without confusing the reader because of switching back and forth among different elements; as the story goes on, you have to pick up the teased points and weave them in. I think this is really difficult, but editors and readers don't seem to have the patience for the other method. About the only solution is revision. Once in a while I find an organizational scheme in someone else's writing and try to apply it to mine.

Being natural. Newswriting has its boilerplate and its clichés, and science writing has another whole set of stock phrases on top of that. You have to keep being aware of worn-out wordage and fight, all the time, against the lazy approach.

The last third of the story. For some reason there's often a point where the energy of the beginning and middle expends itself but there is more to say. Probably because of having written so much in pyramid style, I think my stories tend to get out of control or lose focus toward the end, instead of gathering themselves for a final push that carries the reader to a strong conclusion. I suppose one remedy is trying to write this part first, but I can't say that I have put this into practice very often.

Q: *What do you do when you get stuck?*

A: I have to avoid the temptation to take it from the top again, though sometimes this can vault me over the trouble spot. On an important or long story, there's usually time to pack it in for the night and try the next day. Being stuck on a lead is the worst, because I don't like to go out and then return, no matter what the advice books say. If I can get a "good enough" lead, though, that will allow me to continue and then improve the lead later.

Q: *How do you read your own draft? How do you revise? How do you edit?*

A: Over the years, I've come to accept the truth that I rarely can get a good draft in one try. The more I revise, usually, the better it gets—and by a lot, not a little. In fact, I've come to like revising. After a day of sitting with your nose a foot from the tube in intense concentration, I am amazed at what things I see after dinner, and maybe after a glass of wine, when I pick up that printout and give it a fresh look. Obvious bad organizational choices jump out, transitions that make no sense, things that worked well—everything seems much clearer then. I like to go over the draft then, marking sections that need to go up or down or out. It's a good time to show the piece to someone else, if possible.

Then, in the morning, I make the changes in the VDT text but try to keep from doing major rewriting at that point, especially if the story isn't finished.

No matter at what point I turn in a story, my editor usually has a lot of ideas for changes or cuts. We happen to work well together: If we have a fair amount of time and the story is a major one, he'll edit my writing and add some of his own, and then I'll rewrite his rewriting and add some of my own, and after a few cycles of this, including some arguments, we tend to be in good agreement.

Q: *How has your writing changed recently?*

A: I'm not sure that my writing has changed all that much in the past few years, but I have a sense that it has become a little easier. As in many things, it may be that relaxing one's standards of what is acceptable quiets the harsh self-editor somewhat. This makes it easier to go on to the next paragraph, and the next one, without getting stuck. I'm sure I have benefited from the idea of getting something down and then revising it rather than insisting on a close-to-publishable text the first time.

On the other hand, I think I am more cautious about an off-the-wall lead that seems catchy but may be embarrassing when I look back at it later. If this means I am less experimental, that's not good. It probably means I get more stories done, though. I hope that in writing science stories I've become a little more conversational, because I have made an effort to replace jargon words with phrases that are more explanatory and helpful to the nonscientist.

Q: *How can an editor help you? How can an editor hurt you?*

A: It's a delicate balance, without question. A good editor can tell you when an organizational strategy doesn't work, but of course this doesn't mean you will always agree with him or her. At an earlier stage in putting a story together, an editor can help a writer to focus his inchoate ideas. It's a bad idea to become too dependent on this, however, both because it can make the writer lazy and because it erodes the writer's independence of thought. After all, the focus may be the wrong one. It's a rare editor, but a welcome one, who can point out problems of wording, style, organization, etcetera and yet trust the writer to revise the text himself. Some editors have a hard time keeping their own writing out of the story. They may in fact have good substitutes for the original wording, but I think the story should be told as much in the writer's language as possible.

This is where a good editor can become bad. A writer who has every lead rewritten, every unconventional approach turned down and every story reorganized will lose confidence and become resentful. In my opinion, better to let some stories go without drastic editing (as long as they are in decent shape and accurate) than to destroy the writer's belief that he or she can produce a piece that is satisfactory.

At the same time, a bad editor is one who lets every story by a writer go through without engaging it in terms of content and style. When a writer gets used to having no editing, it can either make him careless or feel that he has no one helping him improve, no one to differentiate between what he's doing well and what needs work. This is a bad thing.

Q: *What advice do you have for a beginning reporter/writer?*

A: Write for different editors and sections when you have the opportunity. Don't let one editor, if you should be having trouble, get you down. Be willing to listen to and go along with suggestions, though, because there are many people here who have a lot to offer.

Take as much initiative as you can. Always be thinking of stories to do, angles of running stories to take off on.

Be aware of the fact that although there is some competition with other media in Boston, the *Globe* stands apart, and for that reason you may not get much feedback. In other words, you may not frequently be asked why you did something the way you did, how you could have done it better, or what you think about the way reporter X or Y did it at newspaper Z? Supply your own stimulation in that respect or get colleagues to give you feedback.

Remember that the *Globe* has many places where a writer/reporter can fit in. If the current assignment or beat is causing you a lot of grief, keep in mind that people shift around a lot and a better match may be down the road.

Q: *Which books on writing have you found helpful? Which writers do you admire and learn from?*

A: I can't say that many "how-to" books are much good, unless one needs help with proper usage. One exception is *Writing with Power* by Peter Elbow, which contains a lot of good exercises and hints on organizing, dividing your time, getting looser, etcetera. I keep in my desk a folder with a bunch of examples of writing given to me by someone years ago who had it in a class. It has commentary about how they do what they do. I find it good to peruse when I'm stuck.

Writers I look to for inspiration or models include Didion, McPhee, Halberstam, Jeremy Bernstein, Lewis Thomas, the *Time* institutional style, *The New York Times* institutional style, or whoever had a good piece in the *Globe* today.

❖ Journalist at Work ❖ SUSAN TRAUSCH Interview

Susan Trausch has the ability to be witty on deadline. She has worked just about every beat in journalism, distinguishing herself in the Business section, as a member of the Washington Bureau, as an Op Ed-page columnist, and now as an editorial writer.

Q: *How do you get ideas?*

A: Pray.

Actually, ideas come from just living and doing the daily battle standing in line at the bank and always being in the wrong one; spending a day trying to get the funny noise out of the car and discovering its a tube of lipstick under the seat; living in an apartment with cardboard walls; having your credit card rejected in front of your fellow man. I write about the little annoyances that are big pains, and those are everywhere.

Q: *How do you decide which ideas to use?*

A: I carry a notebook at all times, except when I really need one, and put ideas and experiences in it. When there's a bunch collected on a subject, say, embarrassing moments, or funny things people do at farm stands—I might write it. Then again I might not. This is a very mystical process, deciding what to use and when, and I don't know how I do it. Sometimes a news story will kick off an idea. Sometimes an idea I haven't thought about for five years will resurface and seem relevant and writable. I like to pick something that has roots attached to it and says something about human nature or the way we live. The key is wanting to write it. The idea has to come easily or it's not the right one.

Q: *How do you recognize when an idea is working or not working?*

A: Sometimes I do. Sometimes I don't. The best thing is to get away from it and come back fresh. I usually write a draft on Monday and then put it away until Thursday or Friday morning. There's nothing like the sinking feeling of picking up a dud on Thursday.

It's a dud when the rhythm is off or the central idea doesn't hold together or it's loaded with clichés. The hardest part of writing a humor column is hitting the right rhythm. If one word is off in a sentence it clunks, and so I have to keep listening for the beat, starting at the top and reading and rereading. When I jump into the middle or work on one paragraph too long, I lose the timing. A paragraph can hang together just fine by itself and have perfect grammar, but it can louse up the whole flow of the piece if it moves too slowly or too quickly.

Writing a column is very different from writing a story. A story I can work on into the wee hours or do quickly on deadline. But if someone said to me, "Give me a column by three o'clock," I couldn't do it. I wouldn't trust what came out. I need those days away from it.

Q: *What process do you go through in writing the column?*

A: It helps if I have the lead and tone before I start, but even then it's never easy. By nighttime I'm more exhausted than on any other day of the week. It's a whole day of going inside yourself, playing with intangibles, roping in feelings, and trying to make it all dance on paper. I love doing it, but I sweat it.

Q: *Are you aware of your voice when you write?*

A: I'm very much aware of voice and try to write the way I talk. But at the same time I'm trying to keep myself out of it. It's a constant battle of the *I's*. The temptation is to keep starting sentences with "I," but the best writing talks about "you" and "us."

Q: *What do you do to find a good ending?*

A: The ending is as important as the lead in a humor column. It has to be a line that echoes the theme of the piece and ties it together.

Q: *What's the worst problem you face? How do you try to solve it?*

A: Getting stuck or not being able to start. I try to solve it by writing fragments, phrases, anything, just as long as something is going on the paper, or the screen as we say in VDT land. Eventually a fragment turns into a sentence that turns into a paragraph.

Q: *Besides writing the column, you did business stories. Do you have any advice for beginning reporters who are assigned to write in a specialized field?*

A: Ask dumb questions. Better to make a fool of yourself in front of the boys at the First National Bank than to do it for the world in print. You just look the man in the eye and say, "Tell me, what exactly is the GNP anyway?"

Q: *You had a year off to look at the press from a distance. What worries you?*

A: I think we should fight the "boys-on-the-bus" syndrome and not immediately cover something just because the *Times* or the *Post* did it. We should remember not to get carried away with our own power. The phrase "media star" should be a contradiction in terms. We should be nonentities, Columbos in ratty raincoats, just asking a few questions—"if you wouldn't mind, ma'am."

Q: *What is the best advice on writing you've received?*

A: It comes from O. Henry: "Write what makes you happy."

Chapter 5

REHEARSE: Writing Before Writing

When I first became a newspaper-writing coach, I found that most of the reporters went out and covered a story, came back to the office, sat down and started to write the story. Sounds logical, doesn't it? But I had been familiar with Donald Graves's research into the writing processes of young children and he discovered that the best writers rehearsed what they were going to write before they began. I found this was also true of the best writers on newspapers. They had been writing the story in their head—and often in their reporter's notebook—before they went out on the story, while they were reporting, and all the way back to their desks. They were rehearsing what they might write the way we all rehearse a marriage proposal, a request for a raise, an interview for a new job.

The other day a writer asked me how long it took me to write my weekly seven hundred-word columns. Even though he has published several books, he was surprised—even angry—when I answered, "thirty to forty minutes or so." That's the time I usually spend at the computer on Monday morning, but it might have been more accurate to say, "A week's worth of hours." As soon as I finish one column, I know I'm going to be writing the next one and most of the writing will already be done—especially the writing I don't know I've done—when I arrive at my desk next Monday morning.

How to Write Without Writing

To write without writing, you have to rid yourself of the popular idea that writing word by word, sentence by sentence, paragraph by paragraph is painful. Books are full of quotations from writers on the terrible, "pity me" pain of writing. The great sportswriter Red Smith is reported to have said, "There's nothing to writing. All you do is sit down at the typewriter and open a vein." But I follow the counsel of William Stafford: "It's *easy* to write." It should be and it can be.

Of course there are times when the writing is hard, usually because you've been forced to write before rehearsal or because you have standards higher than William Shakespeare who, I believe, just wanted to produce a show before opening night. "Perfect is the enemy of good," says John Jerome. My writing teachers—who did not write—preached that easy writing makes hard reading. Baloney. Good writing is the product of fluency, it flows across the page with ease. The reader should not feel the strain.

In any craft, spontaneity is the product of practice. I used to write at least one-hundred-fifty titles for each magazine article, seventy-five leads, and revise each of three drafts ten times. Now I revise far less because I have learned to be fluent, to allow the writing to flow, to follow Stafford's counsel to lower my standards at least to get a first draft.

Giving Assignments to the Subconscious

I have learned to give writing tasks to my subconscious—which may, in turn, pass the assignment on to my unconscious. I try to leave my writing desk knowing the task that will face me the next morning. The assignment is not what I will say but the writing problem I will face. I knew yesterday that I would start today by layering—writing over—the lead to Chapter 5 and go on to write about rehearsal. What would I say about rehearsal? That was a job for my subconscious.

Often when I go to sleep at night, take a nap, start on the treadmill or begin to lift weights, I will remind my subconscious of the current assignment. When Dr. Carol Berkenkotter of Michigan Tech studied my writing processes by having me keep a running protocol or dictated record of what I was doing, she found there were interruptions and that problems were solved when I was away from the tape recorder. The researchers finally figured out the obvious and called these moments "bathroom epiphanies." Driving the car, sitting on the pot, shopping, watching TV, reading, talking on the phone, answering e-mail, lifting weights, having supper with my wife, even writing something else, I will realize I've also been writing. James Thurber, the great *New Yorker* writer said, "I never quite know when I'm writing. Sometimes my wife comes up to me at a party and says, 'Damnit, Thurber, stop writing.' She usually catches me in the middle of a paragraph."

When I become aware my subconscious is slaving away in the engine room below decks, I try to ignore it. I may make a note, mental or with pen and paper, but I am wise if I don't interfere. What I need to write will be ready in its own time. Edward Albee the playwright says, "I try to let the unconscious do as much work as possible, since I find that's the more efficient part of my mind."

Listening and Looking

More writing takes place in the heightened awareness of a writing project. The topic becomes a magnet for what you hear and see. I just took a break from writing this section and sat down to read the paper. One of my other projects is a book on the connection between writing and drawing, which I think are both visual arts. In an interview with Michael Cunningham, who just won the Pulitzer for fiction, I discovered he is another writer who considered a career as an artist.

The writer is a spy, perhaps even a sneak. I listen to the conversation in the next booth at the restaurant, slow down when I walk by a lighted window at night, pay most attention to what I catch out of the corner of my eye, listen to what is not said, watch what is not done.

Talking to Yourself

As a writer I do a strange sort of talking to myself. It is not a conversation, certainly not a Q-and-A interrogation, not a narrative, it is most like taking a long walk with an old friend or a long trip in a car with a life partner in which topics come up and fall away in a kind of shorthand—a word, a phrase, a scene, a memory, a quotation, an unexpected connection.

This is word play and idea play and image play, connecting and disconnecting facts and details and fragments of language, allowing patterns to emerge and break apart, narratives to begin and stop and begin again. All this is wonderful defense against boredom. Sitting in the car at the bottom of the driveway waiting for my wife or sitting on a bench at the supermarket, I am not bored. I am writing—or rather allowing the writing to happen, delighted at what I may hear appearing on my page the next morning in one form or another.

Day Dream and Night Dream

I don't think dreaming is a requirement for writing—everyone dreams—but Ernest Hartmann's *The Nightmare—The Psychology and Biology of Terrifying Dreams* (Basic Books, New York, 1984) indicates that artists and other creative people are more likely to have lowered boundaries that allow them to be aware of their dreams. In my case, I dream asleep and awake. I'm not always sure of the difference between night dreams and daydreams, the almost continuous mental cinema of fantasy that passes through my mind. Often I'll mention to my wife something I am dreaming as I drop off to sleep that I think is happening, and she'll growl, "You're dreaming again."

I do think it is part of being a writer to be aware of your own thoughts and feelings, your own fantasies and imaginings even if they are unpleasant, especially if they are uncomfortable and run counter to what you or society thinks should be in your mind. Anton Chekhov said, "When men ask me how I know so much about men, they get a simple answer: Everything I know about men, I've learned from me." You are not the only one having these thoughts. It is in being open to the full range of human reactions to life that we can empathize with those who we are writing about, those to whom we are writing. *Movies in the Mind*, the title of a book on writing short stories by Colleen Mariah Rae, describes what is going on: The writing is being done, making itself ready to be harvested at the writing desk.

Active Reading

I am often writing when I am reading. The content of the reading makes me stop and think about the topic I'm working on. Sometimes that means marking the book, making notes, scanning a paragraph or even pages into my computer. Most of the time, however, it just stimulates a kind of shadow narrative that runs alongside my reading the way a coyote kept pace with our car in Yellowstone during one visit. We each knew the other was there, but we kept our distance. The story I'm reading stimulates the story that is being written in my subconscious while I'm away from the writing desk.

I also read consciously and subconsciously for craft, seeing how other writers have solved the problems I will meet on the page. Some of this reading is added to my mental toolbox, some is stored away unknowingly, and it will be remembered when I need it.

Making Notes

If I am recording notes on research or observation, they are made carefully, but many of the notes for my other writing are mental. I consciously assign them to memory, confident I will become aware of them if they are needed during the writing. I do not have a good memory in the quiz-show sense, but I do have a good writer's memory, a memory that comes from context and fluency. I can't sit down and list the details of a parachute jump I made in the army in 1944, but if I write a narrative of a jump, the technical words come back to me in the context of the narrative.

I am never without special three-by-five cards in a leather holder in my shirt pocket and never without three or four pens. I make notes on those cards and in the daybook I always carry in my briefcase, up to the TV room, back down to my office, but most of the notes are purposely unfinished: phrases, fragments of sentences, paragraphs that trail off. I want them to be incomplete, signals to that subconscious writer who is working behind the scenes, and most of the time I do not look back at the notes until I have finished a draft, believing that what I remember is what should be remembered, most of what is forgotten should be forgotten. After the draft is done I can check to see if that is true.

Outlines

If I make outlines they are fragmentary. No careful Roman numerals, large letters and small letters, numbers carefully indented. I love making such outlines. I am compulsive obsessive and got an *A* in accounting in junior college. I was the geeky kid who loved making outlines in school, but I found that formal outlines were prisons that restricted thought and discovery. They imposed a conscious organization that suppressed the subconscious text where the real writing is done. Sometimes I do make notes of sequences, what may follow, but these are always tentative, usually marked by question marks fore and aft.

Incomplete Drafts

At times the subconscious will demand attention. I will become aware of chunks of writing that tell me they must be written down, and I will write them as if I were taking dictation, careful to pay no attention to the spelling, the punctuation, the formal structure of grammar and rhetoric. I am only catching a voice, a flow of meaning, a *possible* way the writing may be done when I get to my writing desk. The subconscious writer works best in secret, without supervision, needing room, distance, respect.

When I study my own writing process and the writing process of other experienced writers, I discover that 60 to 80 percent of the writing process is completed before the first draft. As C. S. Forester, the author of the famous Hornblower historical novels, said, "The work is with me when I wake up in the morning; it is with me while I eat my breakfast in bed and run through the newspaper, while I shave and bathe and dress. It is the coming day's work which is occupying my thoughts; the undemanding routine activities permit—encourage—my mind to work on the approaching difficulties, to solve the tactical problems which arise in the execution of the strategic plan. So, the day's work is clear, usually, in my mind as I stand screwing up my resolution to begin again. Then I find myself in my workroom, uncapping my fountain pen and pulling my pad towards me and glancing down the paragraphs written yesterday, and instantly I am swept away into composition." Experienced writers rehearse what they may say, turning over the specific information from which an effective story may be built, connecting that information in many patterns of potential meaning, listening for the voice of what they may write.

Leading with the Lead

Readers make the decision to read or not to read after a sentence, two sentences, a paragraph, or two paragraphs. It's all over in a matter of seconds.

Listen to what the masters, and mistresses, of our craft say about the importance of the lead to the writer:

Raymond Carver

> I have that opening line and then everything seems to radiate out from that line.

Joan Didion

> What's so hard about the first sentence is that you're stuck with it. Everything else is going to flow out of that sentence. And by the time you've laid down the first TWO sentences, your options are all gone.

Paul Horgan

> The most important sentence in a good book is the first one: It will contain the organic seed from which all that follows will grow.

Elie Wiesel

> The first line sets the tone, the melody. If I hear the tone, the melody, then I have the book.

The beginnings—the first few lines that will capture or turn off a reader—in most newspapers are poorly written and poorly read. Readers move to other stories or to radio and television.

Some of the most common problems with news leads are:

- *Cluttered.* The reader has no time to breathe. These leads read as if they were written to cover every possible base; no editor can say the writer left anything out. Leads can be only one sentence long.

Some material can be put in the second paragraph or even the third.

- *Flabby.* I don't know what the story is about and if the writer is this confused, I don't care.
- *Dull.* Ho-hum. There is no tension, no energy that drives the writing forward. If the writer is bored, so am I.
- *Mechanical.* There is no human voice, no music, just another hamburger.
- *Closed.* This is private conversation between people who speak the same jargon. Stay away, you don't know enough to read this story.
- *Predictable.* I know what will be said and how it will be said. It is written in "journalese," the words and phrases that are the clichés of our craft. There are no surprises of language, no words and phrases that are unexpected and thus delight us as they capture and clarify a news event.

How the Lead Serves the Reader

An effective lead makes a promise to the reader. If the lead promises information the reader needs or wants, the reader continues. If the promise is attractive, readers who do not know they want or need the information will continue anyway.

Readers are in a hurry and have many distractions, and we have seconds in which to catch and hold their attention. Readers are selfish. They flip through the paper asking, "What's in this story for me?" or "Why should I read about another housing scandal?"

We have to say what's in the story for them, why they should read this story, and do it in a line, three lines, or five at the most. And those aren't the lines you are typing on the screen. They are column lines. We should tell ourselves that we have half a line on the screen, a line and a half, or two-and-a-half lines to capture the reader, no more.

The lead promises specific, accurate information the reader wants or needs. The good lead entices; it promises clarity, grace, and delight, something more than the reader expects. The lead promises to satisfy the reader's expectations: A news story delivers something new, a profile reveals a person, a narrative tells a story, an exposé exposes, an analysis goes below the surface. The lead provides a tension that produces the energy that drives the story forward. And the lead promises a closing, a sense of completion by the last lines of the article.

The writer must be aware of the promises made in the lead if they are to be fulfilled. And therein lies the importance of the lead for the writer.

How the Lead Serves the Writer

The lead tells the writer how to write the story. It focuses, orders, shapes the message, and establishes the story's voice. An effective lead solves most of the problems the writer will face in the first draft and solves them efficiently, ahead of time, when the writer is not trapped in a tangle of prose.

Let's examine the problems that can be solved by the lead.

Focus. The lead establishes the central tension of the story. Everything in the story will support and advance the significance of that tension.

Context. The lead places the central tension of the story in context. The story exists in a particular world that has its own history, its possible futures, and its relationship to the reader.

Form. In the first lines the reader, and therefore the writer, is told what the form of the story will be: narrative, profile, exposé, backgrounder, feature, news event.

Evidence. The effective lead often provides a sample of the type of evidence on which the story rests (statistics, quotations, observation, anecdote, and so on) and implies the abundance of the evidence that will be delivered to the reader.

Voice. Each text has its own voice, the voice of the writer tuned to the material. That heard quality in the story plays an important role as background music in a movie. The voice of the story is established in the first line, often in the first few words. The voice supports the material, tells the reader the significance of the material, instructs the reader how to respond to the story, and becomes the human element in the story, creating a compelling personal conversation between writer and individual reader.

Authority. Authority must be established in the lead if the reader is to believe the information in the article and respect its significance.

Audience. Each effective story is targeted for a specific reader in the lead.

Length. The lead implies the length of the story: a news bulletin, a takeout, a reconstruction, a single interview, or a roundup.

Pace. The lead establishes the pace at which the story is to be written, whether the story is a quick, hard-hitting series of actions and reactions;

a leisurely walk through; a street corner, on-the-scene interview; or a reflective conversation about a past event.

Order. The lead often predicts the order of the story: chronological, inverted pyramid, or cause-and-effect.

End. The lead usually implies the nature of the ending, since the last few lines may echo the lead in content or style, may answer the question raised in the lead, or may reveal a situation that was set up by the lead but is now more clearly understood because of the information in the story.

Complicated? Darn right. But time spent on the lead is worthwhile because it controls and predicts everything that follows.

How Lead Writing Speeds Up Writing

The secret to productivity is the lead. It would appear that careful attention to writing and rewriting leads would result in writers who stay in the batter's box and never march up to the plate. That can happen, but most of us who write fast do so because we concentrate on getting the lead right before we move on. Each lead I draft in my head and on the screen is a minidraft of the entire piece; the lead allows me to see problems ahead and to avoid or solve them before they bog down the draft.

Because of a trip to Europe followed by illness and a death in the family, I was jammed up to deadline a few years ago. I had to write half of a new edition of a book in one week. I wrote 235 pages in seven days, an average of 33.5 pages a day, an average of twenty of them new, the rest revised. How did I do it? By getting the lead to each chapter and to each section right and then writing fast, the way everyone on a newspaper should be able to write.

The closer the deadline, the more time I spend on the lead. Not hours, but minutes. It takes a couple of minutes, one minute, seconds even, to draft a possible first line. Five, ten, fifteen first lines, each with a different approach, and I find myself homing in on one. It is more a matter of this is right, this will work, than these are wrong, those will not work. I do more first lines, perhaps first paragraphs, polishing, fitting, and shaping, and I am off.

When I am lucky, this process takes place during the reporting and thinking stages of writing. It is a matter of five minutes here, three minutes there while I am waiting to see someone, driving the car, watching television, taking my morning walk, sitting in a parking lot, reading, or even writing another article or chapter. When I am on deadline, it is a matter of doing this in the first fifteen minutes, give or take five minutes, of the writing.

Qualities of an Effective Lead

The leads that attract readers and lure them into reading the story usually have similar qualities.

- *Focus.* The lead makes a specific promise to the reader. That promise is contained in a tension that will be released and resolved by the reading of the story.
- *Context.* The promise of the lead exists in a world that involves the reader. It has clear, immediate significance for the reader.
- *Form.* The lead implies a form (design, structure, pattern) that will help the reader understand the meaning of the information in the story.
- *Information.* Statistics, quotations, revealing details, and description whet the reader's hunger for information and promise it will be satisfied in the story.
- *Voice.* This is an individual, human voice tuned to the purpose of the story, a voice that provides the music to support the meaning of what is being read.
- *Surprise.* The promise of something new, something that will give the reader the opportunity to become an authority on the subject and surprise those with whom the reader works and lives.

Forms of Effective Leads

Take a piece of paper and list the leads you have in your toolbox. Most of us have many more ways of beginning a piece of writing than we realize. And writing such a list reminds us of leads we have read and those we might invent. Some of the leads in my toolbox are:

- *News.* Tells the reader what the reader needs to know in the order the reader needs to know it: who, what, when, where, why.
- *Anecdote.* A brief story that reveals the essence of your subject.
- *Quotation.* A quote lead can give additional authority and a fresh voice to a story.
- *Umbrella.* Covers several equal elements in the story.
- *Descriptive.* Sets the scene for the story.

- *Voice.* Voice establishes the tone of the story.
- *Announcement.* Tells the reader what you are going to say.
- *Tension.* Reveals the forces in the story and sets them in motion.
- *Problem.* Establishes the problem that will be solved in the article.
- *Background.* Provides the background so that the reader will understand the importance of the story.
- *Historical.* Places the story in a historical context.
- *Narrative.* Establishes the story as the form of the article.
- *Question.* Involves the reader in the fundamental issue of the story.
- *Point of view.* Establishes the position from which the reader will be shown the subject.
- *Reader identification.* Shows readers how the story relates to them.
- *Face.* Gives the reader a person with whom to identify during the reading of the story.
- *Scene.* Sets up an action between participants in the story that reveals the central meaning of the article.
- *Dialogue.* Allows the story's meaning to come from the interaction of principal people in the story.
- *Process.* Involves the reader in a process central to the meaning of the story.

These are only a few of the ways to write leads. Each has advantages and disadvantages. The anecdote or quote lead may pull the reader away from the true focus of the story; the backgrounder may delay the real beginning so long that the reader will move on to another story; the question lead might appear to be patronizing, so we should look to see which lead will best reveal each story and attract readers to that story.

Thirty Questions to Ask to Produce Effective Leads

The more experienced the writer, the more the writer delights in discovering new ways to find the lead. Sometimes writers turn to editors or colleagues and tell them the story so that they can "hear" the lead the writer has not seen. At other times writers make outlines or diagrams to find the focal point—a potential lead. Some writers find it helpful to look back at a collection of good leads they've saved.

Look around the city room and you will see writers waiting for the gift of a good lead from the muse. Some writers hope to find the lead in a coffee cup, the restroom, a candy bar. All writers know that good leads come through the window, and so writers stare out of windows.

In many city rooms, the top editors have offices with indoor windows and they stare at the empty expression on the faces of lead searchers staring back at them.

If staring out of imaginary windows, sipping stale coffee, and looking at blank faces doesn't work, however, here is an emergency checklist of thirty questions you may ask yourself.

In each case I have given an example of a lead I might write as I cover my aging beat.

1. What one thing does the reader need to know more than any other? The most common problem, even for experienced writers, is focus. The story simply does not have one dominant point; but in almost any story one issue, situation, or action should dominate. Step back and think a minute. Limit yourself to one quick note, and you may come up with "rule vote," "inquest set," or "effect on patients." Such a code phrase may help you to see where to start building a lead.

If one thing doesn't come to mind, it may help to list the three, four, or five most important elements in the story, and then number them in the order of their importance. When the story is stripped down to its basics you can usually see what is most important.

Example

We look old but we do not feel old. I am that old coot in the stands who shuffles over to his seat but knows he could go in a right tackle if the coach gave him the nod.

2. What would make the reader turn and say, "Now listen to this, Ira . . ."? Make your reader an authority, and you will have a vigorous, well-read paper. Readers want information that they can share with others. That information makes them important. They can broadcast your news. You may be able to predict which information they need to make them broadcasters if you stand back and look at the subject from the reader's point of view; if you were a reader, what information would you want to tell someone else?

Example

My wife and I spend $15,000 a year, $1,250 a month, $288.46 a week, $41.09 cents a day on prescriptions and I don't get anything back from my health insurance. I'm over the limit.

3. What surprised me when I was reporting the story? Anything that surprised you will usually surprise, interest, and inform the reader. It often helps to take a few moments to reconstruct what you thought the story would be before you went out and did your reporting and then to compare that with what you learned. What you learned is often what the reader needs to learn in the lead.

Example

Many patients in nursing homes told me they had feared the nursing home but liked it because they need the care and the companionship. They felt safe and not alone.

4. Can you find an anecdote that captures the essence of the story? Once I had a magazine editor tell me to write the way the Bible is written, in parables. I laughed at the time. Yes, he was an ordained minister, and yes, he was a *Reader's Digest* editor. But it's not bad advice. Readers often see a story most clearly in brief anecdotes that include all the elements of narrative: character, setting, dialogue, action, and reaction. Anecdotes capture and persuade the reader because they show instead of tell. They get the writer out of the way and put the reader on the scene.

Remember, however, that an anecdote lead is so powerful it may force the direction of the story. A marvelous anecdote that is just a bit off course will drag the whole piece in the wrong direction. The anecdote in the lead must clarify the main issue in the story.

Example

When I started lifting weights at seventy-three I felt old. Now I am older but feel younger. Yesterday I got on the leg press after a grunting, hairy, tattooed youth and raised the weights from his 145 to my 235 and did three reps of 12, lifting 8,450 pounds.

5. Have you an image that reveals the meaning of the story? Often one detail that the writer can make the reader see will capture the meaning. We can show the reader the shoe on the highway after the ambulance has driven away, the tails of the rats the children have killed in the tenement, the limp handshake of the political candidates just off the debate stage. A revealing image may not only give the writer a good lead but it may be something that can be woven through the whole story, repeated once or twice or three times, so that it helps hold a complicated story together.

Example

My wife is a few weeks short of eighty years old. She is bent over with osteoporosis and shuffles from Parkinson's Disease but three times a week or more she staggers over to the weight-lifting machines at our health club and takes on aging in hand-to-hand combat.

6. Where is the conflict? Good stories are often dramatic, and they can be told best by illustrating the actions and reactions of conflicting people or forces. It may help to play movie director and look for the center of dramatic conflict, so that you can reveal it to the reader in the lead.

Sometimes we can discover that center of conflict by diagramming the forces at work on scrap paper. If we draw circles around the territories of the participants in the story, we may see where they intersect. Sometimes arrows showing where the forces are headed will lead to the intersection where the story should begin.

Example
When you see yourself as young and others see you as old, their caring concern and offers to help may bring surprise and even anger.

7. How will this news affect my readers? Too often, we write a story without letting our readers know how the story affects them, particularly in political stories or technical stories written by specialists. We get so close to those stories and work so hard to make their complexities clear that we forget to tell our readers what the story means to them. A good lead can answer this question.

Example
If you are lucky you will become old but you won't feel old. You'll face the world through young eyes with young dreams and be surprised when a child, still a child in your eyes, says, "I think I need to take the car keys now."

8. What's going on? It may help to stand back for a moment to see the flow of events that is producing the story. Occasionally, a lead can place the reader in the flow to be carried along on the campaign trail, in the investigation, out of the dressing room, onto the field. Such a lead allows the reader to understand the story by experiencing it.

Example
Her husband sat beside his wife as she backed down the driveway for the first time in years. He could not tell just what she saw after her eye operations, did now know how much her Parkinson's, which made her live in slow motion, had affected her reaction time but he'd soon find out.

9. Why should anyone read the story? This is an essential question to ask yourself, especially at newspapers where projects go on long enough to have a life of their own. The reader may be forgotten during weeks of extensive reporting, writing, editing, and rewriting. Ask yourself why the reader should read the story, and you may recover the purpose and direction that the story has lost, and find a pertinent lead as well.

Example
When you see an old duffer behind the wheel, remember your town has no bus service, no train, no subway, no taxi. Without a license that driver would be imprisoned at home.

10. Is there a metaphor to capture the story? Our language gets much of its vigor from metaphors, and the right metaphor may focus a diffuse story. But metaphors are dangerous. A metaphor that is clever but not true forms a dishonest lead and a dishonest story.

Example
For retired men, the car keys are his varsity jersey. With them he is still in the game.

11. Where does the story take place? Readers in a television age especially like to see where the story takes place. A writer can top the stock television shots that usually fill our screen.

In writing a descriptive scene, be aware of the dominant impression you wish to convey. Descriptions are not written effectively if they move from left to right or top to bottom. The details should lead someplace. You can make the reader see the pol, the cigar, the face, the belly, the left hand on one person's shoulder, the right hand grabbing another person's hand, the eyes focused on a third person. Everything in that description should reveal the dominant impression of the politician as a superficial gladhander.

Effective description will include, when it is appropriate, all the senses. The reader, through the writer, should not only be able to see the story, but also hear it, feel it, smell it, and taste it.

Example
After pulling the elderly driver over, the police officer watches as he uses his left hand to lift his left leg out of the car, then to lift his right leg out. Then he grabs the steering wheel to hitch himself up on the seat, swivels around, reaches for the car roof, and hauls himself out of the car, staggering as he stands. The driver, embarrassed, explains, "The pills. It's the pills that make me sleepy. I'm not a drinking man."

12. What is the appropriate voice for this story? Voice, the way the story sounds, is the distinctive element in the story that gives the illusion of individual writer speaking to individual reader. It is the element of the story that carries its emotional force. The story may be detached, angry, humorous, caring, sarcastic, ironic, sad, amused. The whole range of human emotions is available to the writer using voice.

Journalism once attempted to achieve a single voice as if an institution were speaking. Today journalism not only allows increasingly diverse voices, it encourages them so that the reader hears writers speaking. It is our responsibility as writers to develop a range of voices with which we feel comfortable, and then to try them out by drafting leads to see which one will work best on a story. If we discover the voice then we usually have the lead.

Example

His daughter watched as her father, once a proud US Marine, later the busiest contractor in town, slowly eased himself out of the car and looked at the squashed tricycle. She didn't have to ask, didn't even have to hold out her hand. He gave her the car keys trying, she could tell, to make a joke of it but said nothing as he started up the back steps to the house.

13. Can we put a face on the story? We all know that readers like to read about people, yet we appear to forget this truism in writing a lead. If we can get a person at center stage in the first paragraph, we can get the reader's attention to a complicated and otherwise unreadable story.

Putting a face on the story, however, doesn't mean just a name, age, address, occupation. We have to reveal that person in action in a place, so that the reader can visualize and believe the person's story.

Example

Twelve elderly people in town gave up their driving permits last year but their story is best told by seeing what has happened to Ruth Storer, who lived six miles out of town at the end of a long dirt road.

14. Where is the tension in the story? Many stories are best told by depicting tension between forces. This approach is significantly different from conflict, in which forces attack each other. Dramatic tension is created when two forces try to pull apart and yet can't free themselves from each other—a description that fits many marriages. If we can discover that such tension is vital to our story, then we may find a lead that has insight and drama.

Example

His wife didn't want to tell him, neither did his son or his daughter, or his best friend, or the family doctor, but someone had to and so his grandson did it. "Gramps. I love you so much, I'm going to ask you for the car keys. You know and I know you shouldn't be on the road."

15. Is there a quote that tells the story? The effective quotation lead allows the writer to get out of the way and let someone in the story reveal the primary issue in his or her own language. The quote that is attributed to someone else can make a statement that the objective reporter cannot make. And the quote lead allows the reader to hear another voice.

The danger, of course, is that the writer will use a dramatic quotation that is not vital to the story; the quote will send the reader off on a false scent. The quote lead is such a powerful device that the writer must be sure it is honest and on target.

Example
"I didn't know I was old—never felt old—until they took my care keys away. Then I knew I was old."

16. Which elements in the story connect? And how? It is a principal responsibility of the artist and the journalist to make connections. The best leads often come to us when we explore the significant relationships within the story. To see these relationships in a complicated story, it often helps to list the people, institutions, ideas, issues, and facts in a story, and then draw arrows and lines connecting them until you see a significant pattern of relationships.

Example
Seven years ago he had sat on grandfather's lap and driven his first vehicle, the old farm pickup. Now he was the one by default who had to ask grandfather for those same keys and tell him he should drive no more.

17. What is the shape of the story? One nonfiction book I wrote had me stuck for weeks until I saw the book as a series of concentric circles. I visualized these circles moving away from a center, as they would if you tossed a stone into a still pond. Once I saw that, I tossed the stone—my lead—and the book was begun. A novel of mine didn't work until I saw it as a series of interacting fever charts and, therefore, understood how the paths of the characters crossed. I have written articles that are stairsteps, cones growing out from a point or drawing everything into a point, ladders, or a stack of boxes. Once you see the design you may be able to recognize the point where the reader can enter it, and you have the lead.

Example
Eric felt he was watching a film being run backward. Instead of looking ahead to taking over grandfather's farm at least as a summer place, he

saw the summers when his grandfather was the strongest man he'd ever seen, pitching bales of hay high on the truck, laughing louder than the wind, not the small man waiting on the porch steps for his grandson to drive him to the hospital.

18. What generalization can be made about the story? John Steinbeck used a three-by-five-inch card to set down what his novel was about. Sometimes when I hunt for a lead I find it helpful to do the same thing, to write a simple précis, a sentence or two stating what the story will say. Occasionally, particularly if I'm writing an interpretive or analytic piece, that sentence or two becomes the lead. But more often it is a generalization that helps me focus the story, and when I have the focus I have the lead.

Example

When we are young, we are impatient to escape our parents' control but as we age in the lockstep of generations, the day comes when we are parents to our parents and find the moment said, perhaps hearing our children's steps behind us.

19. What key questions must be answered in the story? Usually fewer than five questions have to be answered in the story. We can predict which question the reader will ask first, and the answer to that question may become the lead.

Most of the time we don't give the reader the question—the question is in the reader's mind—we just deliver the answer. Occasionally, however, the question or questions can be the lead. Dick Stewart used this technique in the *Globe* on August 21, 1980, to start a very complicated legal story.

> How was Levy Hart shot?
>
> And how did he suffer a massive skull fracture?
>
> These two central questions into the death of the 14-year-old Roxbury youth remain unanswered in the four volumes of inquest transcript released yesterday.

Example

The story is simple, grandfather ran off the road, but the results are complicated. Who will take over the farm? Who will care for him? Where will he be sent? How many lives will change because a deer vaulted into the road and grandfather slid into the ditch?

20. What is the best form for this story? Form can be a lens through which we see a story. Sometimes it helps to change lenses and look at the subject in a different way. What if this hard news story were written as narrative? What if this soft-lead story had a hard-news lead? What if the story were told in the first person? When we have found the proper lens—the form—we may discover the lead.

Example
As reporters, we keep our distance, telling your story, but this story is mine—it is the story of love and responsibility and pain. Last weekend I had to take the keys away from the grandfather who, so few years ago, first allowed me, sitting in his lap, to drive.

21. How can I summarize this story? Some stories need to fit under an umbrella, a sentence or two of summary that includes all the diverse aspects of the story. The umbrella lead is often an introduction to a quick, bulleted list of the key ideas in the story.

Example
We are an automobile society: without a driver's license you are a kid or old, very old.

22. Do you have a specific or two that reveals the significance of the story? To find a good lead, we should search our notes for the concrete detail, the fact, or the statistic that contains the essence of the story. If we find such a detail then we should give it to the reader in the lead; it will catch the reader's attention, and we can use the story to document its significance.

Example
Without his car keys he listed his couldn'ts. Couldn't go to the doctor, the grocery, the library, the post office, bank, to the Friday night poker game, to church, to the garage, to visit neighbors, friends, or family.

23. What is the story's history? Journalists are historians without the advantage of hindsight. Good leads often come when we put an event into its proper historical framework, something print journalism can do that electronic journalism rarely attempts. The historical approach often works well when our readers know from radio or television what has happened but don't know where the event fits into a historical context. That point may be a good lead.

Example
His father never owned a car, didn't need one, but the trolley doesn't run, no train to Boston, no bus, no taxi. In one lifetime. Just one lifetime.

24. What point of view should the story be told from? Point of view does *not* mean opinion. Think of the writer standing beside the reader and pointing out the story. The point of view is the place from which the reader can most effectively see the story. It may be on the street corner, in the police car, before the judicial bench, in the cell, beside the victim at the hospital, at the funeral home, in the parents' kitchen. Each story can be seen from many points of view, and when we are lead-hunting, we should circle the story in our mind's eye, clicking off quick pictures until we find the one that helps our reader see the importance of the story. And that's our lead.

Example
I see my grandson getting out of his car and stopping shock, stilling, before looking up at where I wait. He's grown tall and I've shrunk. He's a good boy, doesn't want to hurt me but I imagine his hand out waiting for the keys. I toss them to him as he approaches and I see his relief.

25. What are the problems to be solved in writing the story? Studies of the creative process have shown that the creative person is identified not so much by the ability to see solutions as the ability to see problems. It often helps to look for the problems that have to be solved by writing the story. These technical problems may be how to show the lasting price of rape without exposing the victim to a kind of journalistic rape, how to make clear a complex fiscal report's effect on the reader; how to reveal the lobbyist's part in getting a bill passed. If we define the problem clearly, we may discover the lead. Sometimes the definition of the problem is itself the lead.

Example
Grandfather was not a talking man. He never talked of his war, of his wives he had buried, the son he had lost, the bypass, the day when they said his office was closed, and I knew that whatever happened when I came to take his car keys away, it wouldn't be done with words.

26. What is the central event in the story? In covering a series of events that take place during a story, we may forget that one event—the speech at the Attleboro Rotary, the reverse on the nine-yard line—may be more important than any other. When we can find the key event, we may have found the lead.

Example
The keys seemed so lightly to leave his hand when he tossed them to me but when I caught them, they were heavy. I felt I had his whole life in my hand.

27. What is my opinion of the story? It often helps to have your own opinion about what you are covering, even if it is not an opinion story. This does not mean a lack of objectivity in writing the story; just the opposite. We must know our own prejudices to be able to write fairly. The way we feel about the story, however, may reveal the story's significance to us and, therefore, reveal the lead.

Example
The police, the courts, the department of motor vehicles should have taken action but they left it up to family to tell my grandfather, who had driven since he was a farm boy, he could no longer have the keys to his own truck.

28. Should I tell the story? Rarely should you use the first-person voice in a news story, for the danger is that you will get between the story and the reader, and the reader will learn more about you than about the subject. But there are still times when doing this will give the story special authority and put the reader on the scene.

Example
This is my story but it will become yours if you live long enough to have your grandchildren become your parents.

29. Why did this story happen? Who, what, where, when, why? It is the "why" that increasingly matters in newspapers. The "why" is what we give the readers that radio or television fails to give. In more and more stories, the "why" provides the lead.

Example
His strength was his independence but as he aged, a heroic individualism became denial, then stubbornness, finally irresponsibility.

30. What is the process? Most best-selling novels give the readers an enormous serving of process. They tell the readers how social climbers climb, how spies spy, how Hollywood works backstage, how airports, hotels, or factories function. If we look at the essential process that took place in the story we will often find a lead that will attract and hold readers.

Example
When the first neighbor called, we called the police in grandfather's home town but they said he had to go and turn in his license. And since he hung up when he suggested it, asking how he'd drive home, I was elected—being his favorite grandson—to make the trip to New Hampshire and return with the keys.

The Lead-Writer's Checklist

After you have written your final lead and finished the draft of the entire story, read the lead again to make sure it is:

- *Quick.* The reader will decide to read on, or not to read on, in a matter of seconds.
- *Specific.* Use concrete details, precise quotes, or revealing facts.
- *Accurate.* The reader who spots even a tiny error will refuse to believe anything you write.
- *Appropriate.* Does this lead fit the story you have written, not the one you hoped to write?
- *Simple.* Cut back the underbrush. Use proper nouns, active verbs, and concrete details.
- *Heard.* Does the reader hear an individual writer speaking directly to the reader?
- *Honest.* Can you deliver what you promise?

Lively Writing

Lively writing should be built on accurate, perceptive reporting. We attract and hold readers when we collect and deliver reliable information they need in a manner that reveals its importance to them.

A few editors place liveliness ahead of significance, others act as if lively writing is a sin. Neither is true, for nothing is as lively as an accurate, revealing fact. Lively writing doesn't have to be superficial, glib, or constructed with tricks to fool the reader. Liveliness that wears well is simple, clear, and appropriate to the subject. It follows George Orwell's counsel, "Good writing is like a windowpane."

City room traditionalists, who often haul as much theology to work as members of the Curia, talk as if lively writing were a sin. They place reporting far over on the right and writing equally far to the left. If the two meet, they are in conflict—"Just give me the facts, Ma'am."

Lively writing, like all effective writing, depends directly on skillful and plentiful reporting. You can't write nothing, although many of us have tried. The writer depends on the careful selection of information from an abundant inventory collected by the reporter.

The reporter/writer needn't be schizophrenic. There shouldn't be reporting and then writing. The two activities should be integrated, with the reporter writing in the mind and on the screen while reporting and continuing to report while writing. The emphasis moves from one to the other, but they are not separate tasks.

Each city room has reporters who are not effective writers, but the really effective writers over the years are always good reporters. Their writing depends on specific, interesting, accurate information, and, in fact, their awareness of what the text will need gives focus to their reporting. They ask the reader's questions before the draft is written.

Vision

Lively writing begins with the way in which the reporter/writer sees the world. Writing depends on our making the effort to see the story we are covering in a different light. But not for difference's sake. We move to a different angle of vision to see the story more clearly, more accurately, and to understand better what we see so that we can make our reader understand.

Wonder at the commonplace. Our job as journalists is to see the significant in what appears insignificant or commonplace to others. Some writing I've done about World War II began when I wrote, "I had an ordinary war." When I remembered what becomes ordinary in combat, I had significant writing to do.

We need to try to protect ourselves from the cynicism that so often blinds the journalist. We have to be open to experience, to record and call attention to what our readers are passing by every day. When we do that, they are surprised and delighted. We help them to see their world with new eyes.

Circle the subject. It is our responsibility to circle the story; not just to wrap it in a journalistic cliché, but to move around to see what's really happening. It may be a straight news story of a mugging, but that straight news story may be best told from the point of view of the victim, the mugger, the police, the victim's family, the mugger's family, the passerby, the social worker, the sociology professor, the district or defense attorney, and so on.

We may understand the story better if we put ourselves, for a moment, in the mind of each of the people involved. We might play with time, for example, and find a way to report on how muggers plan, how they arm themselves, and how they identify a victim; or we might leap ahead and see what they do with a stolen wallet or purse, or how a mugging changes the life of a victim.

We are on a continual search for the way we can best serve our readers. Where is the story that will reveal the information that they need to know?

Use a zoom lens. One writer always tells the human story, focusing on one mugging, one victim. Another writer steps back and reports each mugging the same way, always telling it as a traditional news story, with detachment, complete with a hard news lead or a delayed lead followed quickly by a nut graph. A third writer always goes for the big picture, reporting on violence in western civilization, past, present, and future. We fall into habits of vision. We take close-ups, or stay at a middle distance, or always go for the long shot.

A good way to get out of such a bad habit (which can be an institutional habit of the paper or a department on the paper) is to imagine a zoom lens and to move in quickly, then back, to see where this particular story lies. There is no right way to tell a story; each story demands its own telling.

Where's the fight? Lively writing often results from finding the point at which the people or the issues in the story are in conflict. The problem is that we all too quickly learn the stereotype for the court story, the press conference, the profile, the game story, the feature, the editorial, or the column. We look for the information that fits the stereotype and forget to search for the moment of tension at which the particular energy of this story is released.

If we search for the true point of conflict, we will serve our readers better, and we will have readers, for they will want to see what happens. There is nothing like a good fight to attract our attention. We shouldn't start fights or make them up, but if we see forces, or people, heading for each other, we should position ourselves to cover the collision.

What's the context? It's quite possible to produce a dull story filled with potentially interesting information, if we don't put the story into context.

Many stories float right off the page. There's nothing wrong with them; in fact, some can be almost technically perfect, but they do not connect with the world of the reader. It is our task not just to report information, but to put it into a context that reveals its significance.

Make them walk. Yes, readers want to read about people, and so many newspapers, our own included, fill stories with names that pop up like targets on an FBI shooting range. Readers need names and ages and professions and addresses, but they need much more than that. Readers want to meet people on the page who can be seen.

We should try to reveal the characters in a story in action and remember when we do that the action should relate to the story and advance the reader's understanding.

Hear them talk. Newspapers are filled with "quotetalk." It has quotation marks around it and is connected to the text with a "he said" or "she said," but it is a language no one has ever heard. And it is the same for all characters in all stories, despite their differences in age, education, social background, racial heritage, or regional location.

We must listen to those we quote and then capture their speech so that our pages are filled with the music of different voices, a music that is lively but, more than that, reveals what is being said and how it is being said.

Information

We will attract readers if we give people the information that will make them authorities. When a reader gets a specific piece of information the reader delights in passing that information along. The reader becomes, in a Scottish term for gossip, a broadcaster.

Accuracy of fact and context. Facts must be accurate. If we deliver the wrong information to the reader, and the reader uses it to establish his or her authority and then finds the fact is wrong, the reader is humiliated, and eventually we lose that reader.

The scholar's authority comes from footnotes, and in many cases our authority comes from attribution. In many stories our authority comes from the reader when we articulate a feeling or concern the reader has, and that reader says, "Yes, that's right."

Accuracy is not only a matter of fact, but of context. The context must ring true to the readers.

Revealing details. Too often writers, in an effort to lighten up, will spray their stories with specifics. Every profile subject puffs on a cigarette; every action is described in a specific, statistical manner; each face has a quote. I try to test the specifics from which I build my story by looking for revealing details, the concrete material that, piece by piece, reveals the story. The key word is *reveals*. Each detail should show the reader a bit more of the story.

The pressure to process information and publish it in the paper is enormous. One way we accomplish this task is to pour the information, like concrete, into preconstructed forms. We are often assigned to write a form such as a profile, a wrap-up, a hard news story, or a feature. The system works. In fact, it works too well. We often see what is going on in terms of the story it will fit. All writers can cite cases in which they have had to struggle to make a story fit an editor's preconceived form. They are not aware, however, how many times they see only what they need to see to produce a certain type of story.

On deadline, it may be necessary to fit the story to a familiar form. But the paper that is written and edited in a lively way will encourage writers when they have the time to allow the form of the story to arise from its facts.

Form is meaning. We should not overlook the fact that form is meaning. The form itself communicates a message. The inverted pyramid says that there is immediate information the reader needs to know; the profile speaks to the importance of a single person in making the news; and the event story presupposes a significant event.

If we look at the world with honest eyes, we may see stories that have been invisible to us before, and by writing them in a form that is appropriate to the information we have to communicate, we will share an important meaning with our readers.

The reader, of course, does not put a name on the form of the story being read. But the reader will sense a discomfort if the form of the story does not fit the facts. And the reader, on the other hand, will believe and delight in a story in which the form illuminates a significant meaning.

Short or long? As short as possible. Readers want stories that are short, but filled with an adequate serving of information. The length of the story should come from the amount of information the reader needs and the space it takes to put that information into an accurate and appropriate context.

Getting from here to there. Lively writing allows the reader to participate in the story. The reader has a sense of discovery. At each point in the story, the reader has a question answered, but a new question grows out of that: Will they meet? Will they see each other again? Will they move in together? Will they marry? Will they have children? Each story has its own sequence.

We should use the natural organization of the story. We may, for example, tell the story as a story, using narrative to guide the reader through a series of confrontations. A story may be organized by time, by geography, by cause and effect, or by problem and solution. We should look for the sequence that serves the reader best.

If the story is complicated or the form different from what the reader expects, then we may serve the reader by telling the reader what we are doing and why: "This is the story of a complex series of bureaucratic decisions in which good people are doing good and causing harm." Sometimes this can be done by using the reader's questions as subheads and then answering them. Other times we can have the clock ticking right in the story or use any other device that helps the reader through the information so that they will understand the significant relationships that build to a final meaning.

Voice

Lively writing ultimately depends on voice. When we think about voice, we usually think of an individual writer's voice, because those writers who are most successful have developed a distinctive voice, a way of speaking that is natural for them, hopefully appropriate to the subject they are writing about, and interesting to a reader.

This emphasis on the individual voice or style can be dangerous. The writer can be a prisoner of a distinctive voice, and a beginning writer can reach for a voice that isn't natural or appropriate. And yet, the quality of voice is central to lively writing. Readers hear the stories they read; they like the heard quality of writing, the sense of a personal conversation with the writer.

The voice of the text. I have come to believe that the best way to think about voice is not to emphasize the personal voice of the writer or the institutional voice of the publication, but to focus on the voice of the story. If we think of the voice that is appropriate to the story, then we can blend the personal or natural voice of the writer and the institutional or professional voice of the paper to produce a voice that reinforces the meaning of the story.

Talking with the reader. Not *at* the reader, not *to* the reader, but *with* the reader, conversationally, using the pace and emphasis and music that is appropriate to the information we are sharing. To make writing more lively, it may be helpful to turn off the computer monitor so that you are forced to hear what you are writing. The ear is our most effective editor. But more than that, if we want writing to be heard by our readers, we need to put that aural element into the writing.

Voice as meaning. What was true of form—that the shape of the piece communicates a meaning—is just as true of voice. The voice of a text is what causes (most of the time) the reader to believe the text, to understand the importance of what is being said. After all, writing is music to communicate, to reveal meaning.

We should also remember that the voice of the draft often reveals the meaning of the story or its importance to the writer. I listen carefully to what I am saying and how I am saying it. If I sound detached, for example, when I should be involved, or involved when I should be detached, I believe that the text is trying to tell me something. As I write, my concern, my anger, my unhappiness, and my sense of humor are all unleashed by my voice. I must harness and use them to serve the reader.

Voice, form, information, and vision are all used to produce lively writing. We should, however, remember what Hemingway told us: "Prose is architecture, not interior decoration." Our business is not entertainment, although it's no crime to be entertaining; our business is to reveal the world to the reader. Lively writing will produce the specific information, the appropriate forms, the interesting voices that will reveal what is wrong, what is right, what has happened, what will happen, what needs to be changed, and why and how.

Let's Get Organized

What do you do when you've got one-hundred-seventy-two separate notes, twenty-seven interviews, two-hundred-twenty-three clips, fourteen pamphlets, twenty-two speeches, eight charts, three-hundred-thirty-eight press releases, thirteen reports, eight memos from the editor, and a draft that rides off in nine directions at once? Here are some techniques that may help.

Say One Thing

The greatest problem in news writing is the story that lacks focus. The writer tries to say too many things of equal importance. An effective news story has one dominant meaning. The writer, the editor, and the reader have to know that meaning.

To discover the meaning you have to get disentangled from all your notes and clips. I like to take a note pad and sit in a comfortable chair where I can't even see the notes and try to write down the one thing the story must say. I try to do it in a sentence, but sometimes it doesn't need to be a sentence. It can simply be a phrase: "more taxes." Once I have that sentence or phrase, I have a North Star to guide me.

I still do not return to my notes. I list the most important points that document or develop the main point of the article. When I have that point, I put the supporting points in order and draft the piece from this outline, not going back to my notes until I have a draft done. You have to stand back from the clutter and see the points that are significant to a reader.

Saul Pett, who was one of the Associated Press's best writers, spent days putting his notes in piles to accomplish the same purpose. I think most expert writers of long pieces find the time spent stacking and restacking notes, clips, releases, and so on valuable in solving organizational problems before they create a draft that looks like a train wreck.

If the train wreck has occurred, it may be helpful to make a printout and cut it apart paragraph by paragraph. Then play solitaire with the paragraphs, rearranging the cards until they support the main point.

But you can't do anything until you've found the North Star, the one dominant point you want to make in the draft.

Draft Many Leads—or Last Lines

Another way to find the focus of a piece of writing is to write as many leads or last lines as you can, as quickly as possible: twenty, thirty, forty, sixty. Sixty is about normal for me on an article. I may use the third one, but after sixty I know the third one is good.

Each lead explores a direction, a focus, a voice that may work. Each lead—or last line—is a draft or sketch of the entire piece, in a sense. The experienced writer can see in those few lines the whole.

Drafting leads or last lines can be a good technique for meeting a deadline. The time invested to draft just a half a dozen leads pays good returns if you find the right lead instead of stumbling through a piece following the false directions of a bad lead.

Ask the Reader's Questions

Every good story is a conversation with an individual reader. The reader asks questions that do not appear in the text. Your text is an answer to those questions.

Again, if you have a complicated story, get away from the notes and list the five or so questions the reader will ask. They should not be the questions you *hope* the reader will ask, but the ones, like it or not, the reader *will* ask. Once you have those questions, you can anticipate the order in which they will be asked: How much will the transit authority's fare increase be? When? Why? How else can I travel to work? Any way I can start a repeal movement?

If you have to rewrite or edit a draft that is incoherent or confused, you can use the same technique to stand back and look at what is important to the reader. If you have problems standing back and getting outside your own perspective it may help to role-play a reader. Imagine yourself as a specific person, someone who is reasonably intelligent but who does not know the subject.

Seek a Natural Order

Today, many stories do not fit the inverted pyramid in which the order is of decreasing importance to the reader. That order, first news first, second news second, third news third, can still work, but many other choices are available to the writer.

The natural order is the one in which the story can best be told. The reader is carried along easily from point to point. There is no need for transitions, a device meant to make it possible to wrench information out of the natural order and present it to the reader. Transitions are always clumsy; try to find an order that makes them unnecessary.

Here are some forms of natural order that can be used in newspapers today.

Chronology. Time is the thread that holds the story together. Events are recreated following the order in which they occurred, and the reader is allowed to have the feeling of time passing—years, months, weeks, days, hours, seconds—whatever is appropriate to the story.

The trip. Many stories can be organized by taking the reader along on a trip with the news source. This may be a campaign spin, a walk through a prison, a visit to a neighborhood, anywhere with a natural movement across territory. The reader is carried along by this movement, and the information readers need is hung along the clothesline of action.

The search. We are carried along on the search for a suspect, a new product, a vote. The exposition is inserted where we need it to understand the search.

Problem and solution. The reader shares the problem of the scientist, the engineer, the field commander, or the coach and then takes part in the attempt to find a solution.

Narrative. The writer uses the ancient skills of telling a story to allow a series of meaningful events to unfold. The story moves forward along with the action and reaction of the participants.

❖ Journalist at Work ❖
BOB RYAN Interview

The Sports section of *The Boston Globe* has often been called the best in the country. As a sports nut who also travels a great deal, I find that to be true. The sports pages inform on a broad spectrum of sports. They combine feature and news, opinion and background, humor and technical information. These pages have shown that there is a place for the newspaper even when we have already seen the event on television. We still need good sports writers to tell us what we've seen. And one of the best of the best is Bob Ryan.

Q: *What techniques do you have for rehearsing or thinking about what you're going to write before you start writing?*

A: I do a lot of structuring while driving. I think out line after line, and I've even been known to jot down a phrase or story line in my notebook, which is generally within reach on the front seat. I really get psyched up for major stories, and I work hard on my leads and endings beforehand. I seldom sit down to write anything important not having thought about it for days. Incidentally, I usually assume that any clever phrasing in the body of the story will come by itself. It's leads and endings I worry about.

Q: *Do you rewrite?*

A: I'm starting to rethink my position on rewriting. I used to be doctrinaire and cocky: What I wrote I wrote, and that was it. I would edit, sure, but rewrite? Never. Obviously I knew this was dangerous. Pure laziness accounted for much of it. I've written four books with a minimum of rewrite. Could I have improved them? Certainly.

Q: *How do you organize a complicated story?*

A: God bless a) parochial school and b) prep school. Eight years of the former and five years of the latter gave me an irreplaceable background in the basics. I learned to outline in both places, and although I may not formally outline every major piece, I do outline most of them in at least a semistructured way. You've got to list major areas of your general subject matter; you simply cannot rely on memory. You need your lead, of course, and somewhere up high you've got to make a case for the story being written at all. What makes him/her/them/it special? Why now instead of last year? The reader deserves to know.

Q: *I never cease to be amazed that I can watch a game on television, fall asleep late, and find an account of the game in the* Globe *delivered to my house in New Hampshire before 6:30 in the morning. I'd be interested in some of your tricks in writing to deadline.*

A: This is what I do best, he said, with no hint of modesty. The most important thing isn't a trick. If you don't know the game you can't write a great sports game story. I could finesse my way to a smooth hockey game story but the aficionado of that sport will know I faked it, just the way basketball junkies know that, polysyllabic impressions aside, John Powers wasn't a real basketball man.

The most important aspect of writing game stories is access to information. A writer must have a comprehensible system of scorekeeping. Next, a writer must have a decent note-taking system, preferably one involving a spiral notebook that fits into an inside breast pocket (this may be the best reason to dress properly). The aim is to start writing with quick access to as much information as possible.

I start thinking about leads as soon as the game starts. Contingency leads can occasionally be formulated before the game starts, if a situation calls for it. I was sitting on a line for weeks prior to the seventh and final game of the 1974 Milwaukee–Boston NBA finals. I had occasionally envisioned it as the lead. Instead, I used it as the ending. It was, "How's the view from Olympus, boys?" There is a one-time-only line.

In an ideal situation, I have the basis of the lead ready by the time the game ends. Sometimes, however, it comes from postgame conversations in the locker room and sometimes from an overheard remark of another writer or a passerby. If nothing materializes prior to writing time, I sit and think awhile. If nothing clever comes then, I write a fairly standard wire-service type of lead and hope I can spice the story up with humor or profound technological insight.

It's nice if the ending ties in with the lead, but that doesn't happen all the time. About all that I ask of the ending is that it not be too contrived.

What I'm trying to do in a game story is to be informative, entertaining, and opinionated as hell. The old "five *W*s" are passé. I try to get the score in no later than the fourth paragraph. I editorialize, because if the *Globe* didn't want a point of view they'd rip the wire-service version from the wire. I want to impress both solid sports fans and just plain literate people. With the constrictions of a deadline it's a tremendous challenge to produce such a piece, and I am very proud of what I do.

Q: *What do you think of sportswriting compared to other newspaper writing?*

A: The beauty of today's sportswriting is the freedom granted writers by newspapers, such as the *Globe*. The reason why the best overall writing done at the *Globe* is done in the sports pages (an opinion I would defend to the death) is that we get good space, aren't as worried about offending people, and aren't as knotted up with "propriety" Creativity is stifled elsewhere in the name of "taste." Yecch.

I'll tell you something else. Too much attention cannot be paid to the basics of grammar and rhetoric. I'm shocked at some things I see in our paper. Where are the desk men, I wonder? It scares me.

❖ Journalist at Work ❖
Analysis of a MICHAEL KRANISH Story

To learn how to organize my stories, I pasted up a printed version of the story on the left-hand side of the page and wrote down by each paragraph how it contributed, or did not contribute, to the growth of the story.

I also did the same thing to stories I admired, trying to find out why and how they worked. This is what I have done to a fine story by Michael Kranish of the *Globe's* Washington Bureau.

ALEXANDRIA, Va.—On a desolate dead-end street, sandwiched between the National Linen Service and the Wild and Wooly Needlepoint store, the Nixon Presidential Materials Project is buried in a nondescript warehouse, an ignoble monument to the president who resigned in disgrace 15 years ago today.

A fine lead that is built from revealing specifics and puts the story in context. It is a long sentence for a newspaper, but it flows clearly and gracefully. I hear the writer speaking. Kranish promises me more interesting information if I read on. I did.

"So," said an archivist pleasantly, "do you want to listen to the 'smoking gun' tape?"

Notice how quickly Kranish sets a tone of casualness, unexpected by the reader for such a place. And how quickly we move to the central issue. Kranish has anticipated the reader's question, "Will I be able to hear THE tape?" and answered it immediately.

This is the only place in the world where the Watergate tapes can be heard, where The Voice, that raspy Nixon voice, conspires and curses until his presidency collapses. *"I want you to stonewall it, let them plead the Fifth Amendment, cover up or anything else . . ."*

Kranish moves back and puts the place in context and then makes you HEAR the voice on the tape. He delivers the quote. That line, "conspires and curses until his presidency collapses," is one I wish I had written. It is active and covers a whole period in history in a few well-chosen words.

In this era of Nixon comeback, of grand presidential libraries in spectacular settings, this is history's revenge. Congress did not trust the Nixon presidential materials to anyone but the National Archives, so the Nixon Annex on Pickett Street, costing $800,000 per year, was born. Congress decided that Nixon's own library, under construction in California, will have none of the tapes, papers or momentoes, which means that the Nixon there will be far different from the Nixon here.

I am impressed by how much information he packs into three clear, running sentences. He gives us specific information ($800,000), delights us with a meaningful phrase ("history's revenge"), and makes the significance of what he has told us clear at the end of the paragraph, the point of greatest emphasis.

This is the sole government storehouse of 40 million pages of Nixon presidential material, such a massive collection that the 23 bureaucrats here have only sorted through about 10 percent of it. Nixon, perhaps, still obsessed with secrecy, has kept much of the material from public view and is seeking to keep more of it private.

Specifics and news combined. Each word counts.

Yesterday, a few visitors sat in the archives' Listening Room, dominated by a large, black-and-white portrait of a smiling Nixon, and listened.

Now he sets the scene.

Marie Pierce, 21, a British tourist who read about the archives in a travel guide called *Let's Go: USA*, pulled on a pair of headphones and heard John Dean tell Nixon, *"We have a cancer within, close to the presidency, that is growing."*

Wonderful. We hear the tapes through the ears of someone from another country who is too young to have listened to the hearings. And we are given a sample quote.

"This cancer-on-the-presidency is the best tape so far," Pierce said, marveling at a conversation that changed the course of American history.

I learn from the way he adjusts the distance of his text, moving in close to give the story immediacy, moving back to put it in context. Too often we keep the camera at the same distance all the time.

Indeed, the political surreal is the rule here at "The Nixon Project," as it is called. In room after room, thousands of files labeled "John Dean" and "John Ehrlichman" are stored in special acid-free boxes. The archivists are ever alert to the possibility of, pardon the expression, a break-in. Security guards man the building 24 hours a day; the alarm is so sensitive it has been set off by a fly. No one wants a third-rate burglary.

And there is much to tempt the uninvited. If the storage of the tapes and papers is little known, then it is a vital secret that the 30,000 gifts to Nixon during his presidency are also stored in a back room that is not open to the public. There is the exquisite box with a portrait of Nixon and his wife, Pat, that was given to the president by a Soviet leader; the magnificent diamond and emeralds given by a Saudi prince; and the plastic, glow-in-the-dark set of hands clasped in prayer. From the extravagant to the odd, it is all here under the supervision of curator Wally Owen, who puts on white gloves before he touches any of the treasured items.

Notice how he orders his list from the expected to the surprisingly tacky. And the gloves are a nice touch. There is almost always a nice tension in each paragraph, such as the tackiness of the treasures and the respect with which they are treated.

"It is really a shame that there is no museum for this," Owen said, as he caressed a baseball glove that was signed, "Richard Nixon."

Kranish could have been heavy handed here, but he gets out of the way and lets Owen self-destruct. Nice verb "caressed."

But in truth, few people come here for the tapes, the transcripts or the treasures. The majority want Elvis. The Nixon Presidential Material Project so far has sold 12,000 copies of photos showing Presley, wearing a giant belt buckle and shirt open halfway to his navel, shaking hands with Nixon. No other item comes close in popularity.

Surprise is at the center of lively writing. Not tricky, hokey, made-up surprise but reported and revealed surprise put in a context that gives it meaning. Kranish doesn't write this paragraph. He follows Orwell's counsel and does not call attention to himself but becomes a "windowpane" and lets us see the story.

The archives forget nothing. At that meeting Presley gave Nixon a .45 caliber pistol, now duly stored and catalogued. Indeed, the biggest news to come out of the Nixon papers recently was that Presley asked to become a federal agent-at-large for the Bureau of Narcotics and Dangerous Drugs. The appointment was never made.

Again, another surprise and an effective understatement at the end. Get off stage. The job is done.

Try this yourself. Pick the best story you've written recently and figure out, paragraph by paragraph, how you did it.

Chapter 6

DRAFT: Write for Surprise

Write what you don't know.

This command appears to contradict what we were all taught in school and in the city room, but it is at the center of the writing process. When I run workshops for journalists, business writers, students, or teachers, the one thing I want to accomplish is to have them write for surprise—what they didn't know they knew. Donald Barthelme said, ". . . we are looking for the as-yet-unspeakable, the as-yet-unspoken. Writing is a process of dealing with not-knowing . . ."

Early in my writing life, I was taught the opposite: "Know what you want to say before you say it." I believed this maxim and learned to accomplish it on command. I loved the precis and the topic sentence in school, the stair-step outlines with all those Roman numerals and large and small letters. On rewrite at the paper, I learned the formulas of the hard-news lead and the news pyramid.

But I didn't become a writer until I began to write what I didn't know, what I had no plan to write, sometimes even the opposite of what I knew or felt about a subject. At first this made me feel uncomfortable. And it made my editors uncomfortable. They did not want surprise. They wanted what they expected.

My teachers had been angry when they found I was traitor to their assignments, for which I wrote first and made the outline afterward; when I liked the book the teacher expected me to criticize; or when I criticized the book the teacher expected me to praise; when I wrote about Thanksgiving from the point of view of the Indians, not the Pilgrims.

But I learned what was expected of me. I had to pass the class; I had to get published. The traditions had reason on their side. They were often appropriate for the situation. Traditions in writing have worked to solve writing problems in certain situations. As much as I may have resented and fought the conventions, I am now glad I learned them. They are the firm underpinnings of my craft.

Once I had the control of the conventions of my craft, I began to push their edges from the inside. The writing kept twisting and changing under my pen. My drafts betrayed my intent. I didn't really become a writer until I achieved faith that the draft would instruct. This doesn't mean I lied. It does mean that I learned to respect the draft, to pay attention to what appeared a failure and *might* be a hint, a clue. Even an insight.

Inviting Surprise

The art of writing is the craft of becoming, of knowing, of exploring, of learning, of discovering, of thinking itself. Language records and extends meaning, revealing—if the writer is lucky—an unexpected significance, a surprise.

An Exercise in Surprise

This is a writing game that will show you how to surprise yourself with your writing. Use a few three-by-five cards or a small pad of paper and work fast, spending only five minutes or less on each point. I will play along to demonstrate what I mean.

1. List several significant events in your life.

   My list:

   father left home

   teenage appendicitis operation

   first parachute jump

   daughter's death

   my heart bypass

   Uncle Will's oil heat

2. Pick the one that surprises you.

   My surprise was "Uncle Will's oil heat" since it seemed such a small issue compared to the others, all of which I've written about. Why did it come to mind? Why is my subconscious telling me to pay attention?

3. Write a few lines about the topic you pick. Write fast. Don't worry about grammar or spelling. If there is a name or fact you can't remember, leave a blank.

I was impressed when I first saw Uncle Will's new house on Chesterfield Road in East Milton more than sixty years ago. I remember the lawn, the distance from neighbors, the big rooms and the new furniture but most of all the small, round dial on the wall. Turn it right and the heat came on. I could hear it. I could feel it.

4. Stop. Turn the card over and write something different on the same subject.

I hated the furnace, burning my finger opening the door, jumping back from the sudden heat, shaking the grate, cleaning out the ashes and the clinkers, the great lumps of whatever it was that did not burn and piling it in the ash can.

5. Stop. Take another card and write about it again.

I could never do it—or much else—right. It was a man's job but it was Mother who corrected me or my father, did the job over, cleaned the ashes out her way and piled in the coal her way, always different, it seemed, always right.

6. Do one other card.

Mother piled the ashes to the top of the ash cans. Dad and I did not because we could not carry a full barrel up the half flight of stairs and out to the street. Mother could. She had to lift grandma in her bed a hundred times a day and she was stronger than either of the men in the house.

7. Now you can decide to write on or not, but I hope that you have written what you did not intend to write, that this brief exercise has taken you to the center of the writing process of exploration and discovery.

In my case, it has given me a column and, potentially, several other pieces of writing. Here's the column as it was published in the *Globe* on April 27, 1999:

More mornings than not, I start the day with an appropriate grump followed by a bit of glum. Then celebration. I turn on the faucet and, just like that, hot water. No kettle to heat on the gas stove, no wax taper to ignite the explosive gas heater under the curled pipes of the water heater. Just a turn of the faucet—and hot water.

I clump downstairs and feel the heat rising. Not only do I have thermostats on the wall, I have new automated ones. I do not even have to turn the dial.

I travel back to my first visit to the new house on Chesterfield Road in East Milton that Uncle Will bought more than 60 years ago. No coal to shovel, no clinkers to fish out of the furnace, no heavy barrel of ashes to haul up the cellar steps and roll to the curb. Just a dial on a wall.

My dreams became clear. When I grew up I would some day live in a single-family home with oil heat. I didn't know if I would own it. We had always had a landlord and rent that we often paid late, the landlord himself at the door.

I have exceeded my dreams. Like so many over 60s, I can't quite believe my good fortune. I live higher on the hog than I ever imagined.

The house is paid for and so is the car that sits in the attached garage. My father never owned a car. He and mother never drove.

Of course, all this is crass materialism, and I realize that materialism has its limitations. I love to read—if not live—my Thoreau.

In fact, many of my most critical thoughts about my neighbors' materialism come while I revel in a hot shower rather than a few kettles of lukewarm water in a tub. I had taken showers at high school but never expected to have my own private shower next to my bedroom.

I delight in the refrigerator, which I still call the ice box. But there is no dwindling chunk of ice and no tricky tray of melt water to balance down stairs from our upstairs flat and dump out back.

We even own a freezer of our own. I can still remember the first package of frozen peas sold to us by Birds Eye, how green they were and how much better they tasted than the gray-green mush of tinned peas, a staple of the Scot's diet.

In summer we have air conditioning. I hate heat and think there should be a law banning temperatures above 72 degrees. I miss the lazy rhythm of my grandmother fanning herself on the porch after chores were done, but love the brisk cold of air conditioning. So would she if she had lived to experience it. I know air-conditioned air is unnatural and uses up valuable resources, but it keeps me cool and I glory in that.

What wonderful things so quickly become ordinary. At this moment I finish listening to the complex interplay of the Bach double violin concertos and slide Daniel Smith into the tray of my computer's DVD player and the swirling melodies from his bassoon fill my office.

I have what only crown princes had a couple of hundred years ago, private orchestras to serenade them on command. I have a wall of private orchestras, soloists, choruses, trios, quartets, quintets, even octets—more than 1,500 CDs, more than 90,000 minutes of music waiting for my invitation to perform.

I remember lifting the heavy 78 disk of John McCormack singing and placing it on the Victrola, cranking the arm until I could crank no more, releasing the brake, bending the hinge of the arm so the cactus needle I had sharpened by hand rode the first groove of the record, and the wonderful sound that poured out.

I have not lost the wonder at the quality of sound from my CD player. I have not lost the wonder at the clothes washer and dryer, the vacuum cleaner and dishwasher, garbage disposal and single-party telephone line (with answering machine), FM radio, TV, computer, and all the technical devices that have become commonplace in a life that seems at once so long and so very short.

This column was a nostalgic piece but it did run counter to my intent. I was going to write a piece against today's materialism, but the draft celebrated materialism. And in my card exercise may be a complicated Mother's Day column—my mother was a complex person and my relationship with her complicated. This material, of course, could be a short story, a poem, a novel, an article, a memoir. The possibility of surprise is unlimited.

And the technique works just as well when I write a less personal piece of writing. It reveals the possibility of meaning and approach in objective as well as subjective material.

Cultivating Surprise

Writing for surprise can become a way of life. You write to record what you know and extend it by writing; you write what you know and go beyond it by exploring your response to what you know. Writing will become a major tool of your reporting. You will write, first of all, to define and describe your story.

Attitudes That Encourage Surprise

- *Know and respect yourself.* Pay attention to your individual world and to your personal response to your own experience.
- *Welcome difference.* Do not fear doubt, contradiction, challenge, questions, problems, opposition. They are all opportunities to learn.
- *Connect.* E. M. Forster wrote, "Only connect." Connect yourself with the story, connect the elements in the story.
- *Play.* Writing is one of the highest forms of play. Put together, take apart, make believe.
- *Confront your fears.* Donald Barthelme advised, "Write about what you're most afraid of." Use writing against your ghosts, prejudices, worries.

Techniques That Stimulate Surprise

- Write with velocity so that you race beyond your censors, beyond what you have written before, beyond the way you have written before.
- Steal a technique from a movie, a poem, a play, a novel, a painting and use it to tell a conventional story. Use genre as a lens.
- Fail. Try a way of writing that you can't do, that you have never seen done.

- Switch the point of view from which the story is told.
- Empathize. Write your way into the skin of people in the story to discover their stories.
- Listen to the voices of the people in the story; listen to your voice as you tell the story. Voice will instruct, revealing thinking and feeling.

Tricks of the Writing Trade

One day I made a list of what I wish I'd known before I showed up for my first job on a newspaper. Perhaps knowing these things will help you.

Ask the Reader's Questions

Ask yourself the questions the reader will ask before you even start reporting—not the questions you'd *like* them to ask, but the questions they *will* ask. Most stories can be told by answering five questions, give or take a question. Keep revising the questions as you discover new information.

Collect Abundant Detail

Writing is a constant process of selection. The effective story can be told by the amount of good material you toss in the wastebasket. Use all your senses—sight, hearing, smell, taste, touch—to pack your notebook, and your memory, with specifics you may need when writing.

View Each Story from Different Points of View

Most journalists are predictable; they see every story the way every other journalist sees it. We've already talked about ways to view a story from different points of view. Practice these.

Enter the Skin of Your Sources

Yes, you will have to become detached (though not unconcerned) to write well, but you will not get the most important stories unless you develop the ability to empathize, to understand what the story is doing to the participants. This doesn't mean you approve or disapprove; it does mean that you understand. Note that this can dovetail with seeing the story from different points of view.

Rehearse

While you are reporting, and after you finish reporting and head back to the office, write the story in your head. Play with words, phrases, and lines—listen to the music of the stories that may be written, because music nearly as often as facts can tell you what the story means.

Listen for the Initiating Line

Good writing usually begins with a line. It may be a sentence, but often it is not. The line is a series of words that contain tension, or conflict, and music. The forces in the story are coiled within that line, just for a moment, eager to be released by the writing of the story. I will not write until I find that line, which may sound ordinary to others but has energy and resonance for me. Sometimes it is the lead—often it is not—but it ignites the draft.

Say One Thing

Effective stories have one dominant message. You may have to write a first draft to discover the message, but there should be a single meaning that has priority over all the other meanings in the story. If you can't tell the message in a sentence or less after you have written the final draft, you haven't written the final draft.

Write Many Leads to Find the Lead

Most reporters are hired on papers of the level of the *Globe* because they have written the best first-draft leads wherever they have worked. If they work and continue to improve they will learn that first-draft leads are not good enough. The breakthrough to top writer may come when the reporter writes many leads—ten, fifteen, twenty, or more—taking three minutes or less for each draft lead during this essential play.

Write Without Notes

Put your notes aside and write the first draft from memory. Follow the instinctive flow of the story so that you can make unexpected connections as well as expected ones. Check your notes afterward for accuracy, but you will find that what you forget probably is best forgotten, and what you remembered in the flow of writing is what needs to be remembered.

Write Easily

Forced writing usually sounds like forced writing. Good writing should have the ease of good conversation. Find your way to tell the story without forcing it, letting it appear naturally. To do this you may have to write fast so that you can outrace the censors who live within us all.

To produce writing worth criticism, remember William Stafford's counsel:

> I believe that the so-called "writing block" is a product of some kind of disproportion between your standards and your performance. . . . One should lower his standards until there is no felt threshold to go over in writing. It's easy to write. You just shouldn't have standards that inhibit you from writing.
>
> I can imagine a person beginning to feel he's not able to write up to that standard he imagines the world has set for him. But to me that's surrealistic. The only standard I can rationally have is the standard I'm meeting right now. . . . You should be more willing to forgive yourself. It doesn't make any difference if you are good or bad today. The assessment of the product is something that happens after you've done it.

Write with Your Ear

Writing that is read and remembered has the illusion of a speaking voice—an individual, human voice is heard. Put the heard quality into the writing by listening for the voice of the text. This is not the eccentric, self-indulgent voice of the writer or the traditional voice of the institution, but a mixture of many elements brought together in a voice that supports and illuminates the meaning of a story.

Write with Information

Writing that is full of meaning is not written with language, but information—specific, accurate, significant information. The reader wants to become an authority who can quote the concrete details, the statistics, the quotations you have delivered.

Reveal

"Show, don't tell" is the fiction writer's counsel. It's not bad advice for the journalist. Show *and* tell. Put the reader in the story and then, when the reader asks, "What's it mean?" tell the reader. It is our job to reveal the story to the reader, to make the reader experience the story, to cause the reader to think and feel.

Vary the Documentation

Make the reader believe by giving the reader evidence at each point in the story. Most writers fall into the trap of using one form of documentation with which they have become comfortable. The documentation shouldn't fit the writer, rather, it should be appropriate to the point being made. Choose a quote, an anecdote, a statistic, a citation from a report, a description, or other evidence because it supports the point effectively.

Answer the Reader's Questions

Yes, point one again. You anticipated those questions before and during your reporting: now answer them in a draft. The most effective way to organize a story is to put those questions in the order the reader will ask them. A well-written, and well-read, story answers the reader's questions when they are asked.

Cut Anything That Doesn't Move the Story Forward

No interesting detail, no significant action, no great quote, no brilliant phrase belongs in the story if it doesn't advance the principal message of the story. All the stories within the story that give it depth and texture must relate to the main meaning of the story.

Stop in Mid-Sentence When Interrupted

It is important to maintain the voice and flow of the story. The best way to do this is to interrupt your draft when you know what is coming next, what you are saying, and how it may be said. That way, when you sit back down to write, you'll be able to pick up where you left off.

Be Accurate in Detail and Context

If one fact is wrong, the reader will not believe the whole story; however, accuracy is not just a matter of facts, but facts in context. Writing is a matter of selection, and we have the responsibility to make sure that our facts are accurate in relation to other facts and to the context of the story.

Be Your Own Editor

You know the context of the story better than any editor can. You have a professional obligation to your reader, your paper, and yourself to be your own editor. Stand back and role-play a specific reader—see and hear your story as that reader will. It may be efficient to do three quick readings.

1. *Read for meaning.* If you don't have one, there's no reason to go on. Find the meaning.
2. *Read for structure.* If the story isn't ordered so that the principal meaning is developed (the reader's questions answered in the sequence they will be asked), there's no reason to go on. Find the structure.
3. *Read for language.* Make sure each word communicates the meaning of the story. Break the traditions of language only when it is essential to clarify meaning.

Write for Yourself

Of course you must listen to editors, to colleagues (especially those who make you want to write), and to readers. We all need test readers to see if we are communicating and editor-protectors to keep us from playing the unintentional fool; but writing is fundamentally a lonely business. Ironically, we are motivated as writers by a hunger for applause, for praise, for love, and yet we grow as writers by going our lonely way.

Editors and readers do not know what they want until they read it. Doris Lessing says, "You have to create your own demand." Exceptional writing cannot be commanded. It has to come from within the writer, surprising the writer as much as it may surprise the reader. Be realistic, do what you have to do to get published, but march to your own command.

Revealing People on the Page

Our challenge is to make people come alive on the page in realistic dimension. Newswriters have the same challenge as the novelist, biographer, or dramatist: to bring order to disorder, to give fair meaning to apparent meaninglessness, to reveal a sequence of actions and reactions that rarely was apparent at the time they occurred. We must accept the fact that we distort and simplify; our responsibility is to do it fairly, to place the lives of subjects in a significant context, and to reveal them as completely as possible to our readers. The stories that attempt biography in the newspaper usually fall into two categories: the interview and the profile.

The Interview

The interview normally has one principal source, the subject. The purpose of the interview is to allow the reader to hear and see an individual in the news as that person describes the issues from the source's point of view. What the person says is of primary importance, not who he or she is or what he or she is like.

The reader should hear what the subject says and how the subject says it. The interview should reproduce the music of the subject's language, which reveals the person behind the words. If possible, the reader should see the subject physically, ideally in actions that reveal the subject to the reader.

The interview may be on a limited topic or range over many subjects, but the story should carry a single, dominant impression. Why just one? A well-developed story has texture—there are many things going on within the story—but only one theme or meaning should dominate. The story should have a single focus and each element should be connected to and advance that meaning. This dominant impression doesn't need to be simplistic; it can encompass tension, conflict, and confusion. A story's focus may be on a conflict, a contradiction, or an inaction as well as an action, but the story should give a clear message. There should be a clarification and simplification that is fair and in an appropriate context when the story is finished.

The Profile

The profile goes beyond the interview to reveal the subject with more complexity. The subject is a source, not the source and, in fact, may not even be the principal source.

The reader does not usually see the world from the point of view of the subject (although that may be a way to write a profile), but stands back and sees the subject from one or more perspectives. The reader is shown the subject from the point of view of others as well as the subject's own point of view; the writer organizes complication and contradiction into a dominant impression that is fair and significant.

We can continue to learn how to make people come alive on the page through the study of other newspaper interviews and subjects; through reading magazines, biographies, short stories, and novels; through studying plays, movies, and television; through reflecting on our own experience; and through interviewing our colleagues.

Tricks of the Trade for Interviews and Profiles

I have found some tricks of the trade helpful as I have developed my own interviews and profiles.

Preparing for an Interview or Profile

- Write down the five questions the reader will ask.
- List as many sources as possible, past and present, friend and enemy, including people who do not know the subject but who are affected by the subject.
- Imagine you are the subject. View the world from the subject's point of view.
- Read clips, but remember you are doing your own story. Look for details (chronology and sources) but do not overreact to the stories others have written by following the pack or rebelling against the pack.

Reporting an Interview or Profile

- Pay attention to what is surprising you, to what you are learning that you did not expect.
- Consider the distance you stand from the subject. How much of yourself should you reveal? How empathetic should you be? Be consistent and natural in your style.
- Listen to what the subject and the sources are saying and *how* they are saying it. Try to capture the how as well as the what—the gesture, the actions, the pauses and pacing—so you can re-create that in the writing.
- Observe the subject's world and the subject in that world before interviewing the subject if possible.
- Take notes as well as tape, not only to protect yourself if the tape doesn't work, but to capture your observations that will not be recorded on the tape. Work to create a natural manner that puts the subject at ease.
- Keep track of lines that are evolving; repeated events, images, or metaphors; and problems or concerns expressed by the subject or those around the subject.
- Interview the subject in conditions in which the subject is comfortable, and remember such environments are significant. Or confront the subject in a place where he or she is exposed under stress—the surgeon in the operating room, the surgeon telling the family that the patient has died.
- Observe the subject at work if possible. Note how people react to the subject and how the subject reacts to people.
- Consider three interviews if you have time: one to get to know each other, another to get most of the information, and a third to develop points and resolve inconsistencies.

- Ask the subject to describe himself or herself and the essential work the subject does. Invite the subject to reflect. Many subjects are doers and have not reflected upon their lives as neurotic reporters have.
- Ask the subject and others for additional sources.

Preparing to Write the Interview or Profile

- You may have to type up your notes—I always mean to—but if you do, do not confuse stenography with writing. Step back. Put the notes away. Take out a pad of paper, think about the story. Tell it to yourself or a trusted editor or colleague. What surprised you, what did you learn, what one thing above everything else?
- Give the meaning of the story in one sentence.
- Write the head or the billboard for the story.
- Quickly draft many leads that will first reveal the direction, pace, and voice of the story and then refine it. The leads you do not use will often be turning points in the story or the end.
- Quickly draft a dozen endings for the story. Pick one.
- List three to five specific pieces of information that will carry you from the lead to the end.
- Visualize, perhaps even draw, the shape of the story.
- Decide on the length with the editor and then decide how you can work within it. Realize that, indeed, less may be more.

Writing the Interview or Profile

- Write the story fast, in one sitting, so that you can run ahead of the internal censor, encourage insightful accident, and spin out a coherent tone and sequence.
- Use dialogue as well as quotations.
- Reveal the person physically in significant action.
- Put the subject in a place. Use specific details that reveal the subject.
- Write a lead that helps you and the reader to understand the essential issue of the story.
- Listen for a voice that is consistent and appropriate to the meaning of the story.
- Answer the reader's questions when they will be asked.
- Construct the dominant impression using a sequential body of evidence that does not so much tell the reader how to react, but invites the reader to react.
- Vary the documentation so that you are using the form of documentation that best supports the point being made.

- Consider anecdotes—little stories with character, action and reaction, dialogue, and setting—that make a significant and fair point. Make sure they advance the meaning of the story.
- Give the reader a trail to follow through the story, such as narrative, chronology, cause and effect, problem and solution, process, or a walk with the subject.
- Do what works for you. If nothing is working, go back and re-create the conditions that worked on a similar story in the past. Remember that we can learn from others, but we have our own working style as well as our own writing style. Keep them evolving.
- Write to reveal the subject to you and then to the reader; write to satisfy yourself, then the reader, and possibly an editor.

The Craft of Description

Too often, we think of description as a way to decorate a story when it may actually be the story. Visualization is a way of thought—we see to understand—and the craft of description serves us in many ways.

Description makes the meaning of the story concrete; it makes the story, and its significance, accessible to the reader. Before that stage, the act of writing perceptive description may reveal the importance of the story to the writer. Published writers report that they observe the story with their mind's eye, and then record it. This is certainly my experience whether I am writing fiction, poetry, or nonfiction.

Description (accurate, clear, precise) reveals the story to the reader. It allows the reader to observe the mayor in action, to observe the process by which a law is passed, or to see the implication of the law on a taxpayer.

Readers deserve more than our opinion of what has happened. Yes, stories written as if they were cleansed of all opinion are just that—the writer's view of what the Massachusetts House, the Red Sox, or the MIT researchers have done. Our "opinion" of what has happened will only be believed if we deliver supporting evidence, and description can be an effective way of providing convincing documentation.

Many stories in newspapers float like balloons that have escaped from wailing five-year-olds. (That quick descriptive simile may help you to see an idea: stories that have no context.) One way to bring the floating story down to earth is with description that puts the story in context. Description makes the medical theory visit the ward and the economic theory operate the register in the supermarket checkout lane.

Readers usually need a sense of place to experience and understand the story. They need to ride the subway, to sit with the jury, and to be in the laboratory or the project apartment. The responsible reporter/writer puts the reader there with well-crafted description based on careful, observant reporting.

Often we have to prepare the reader for the story we must deliver, to establish the mood, to set the scene: description again.

Readers want to read about people, and description populates the story. The legislature becomes a working collection of individuals, the police force becomes a cop alone on a beat, and taxpayers become a couple with a fixed income facing a zooming real estate tax.

Description can add texture and depth to a story, allowing the reader to see significant complexity: The welfare mother has a rented television, a rented VCR, a rented stereo, and a video game being purchased on time; the reader is shown these "luxuries" and then the addicts in the project stairwell, the gangs strutting in the yard outside, the thirteen-year-old pimping for his eleven-year-old sister. The reader discovers the luxuries are an electronic moat one mother is trying to build around her children so they will never go out to play in the projects. Description is too often considered passive; it can, and should, provide energy and deliver information that drives the story forward.

Techniques of Description

In school, description is often taught as a genre, separate from other forms of writing, as if it were a chunk of prose shoehorned into the text; and this misconception remains in too many writers' minds. Description should be woven through the text.

To explore some of the possibilities of description, I am going to take a flat description and show the effects of different descriptive techniques. I am doing this exercise to learn more than to teach. Try it yourself to discover and sharpen your writing tools.

1. Flat description.

> The body was found in the kitchen of the Dorchester Street house.

2. Make one word more active.

> The body was *discovered* in the kitchen of the Dorchester Street house.

3. Use a word with a different connotation.

> The body was discovered in the kitchen of the Dorchester Street *home.*

4. Add a word or two to make the sentence more descriptive.

> The *mother's* body was discovered in the kitchen of the Dorchester Street home.

5. Add a specific piece of information such as age, title, etcetera.

The *twenty-three-year-old* mother's body was discovered in the kitchen of *her* Dorchester Street home.

6. Add a revealing detail.

The twenty-three-year-old mother's body was discovered in the kitchen of her Dorchester Street home. *Hamburger for homemade spaghetti sauce simmered on the stove.*

7. Give the reader an image. Move a detail to the beginning or end of the paragraph for emphasis.

Steam still rose from the hamburger simmering for homemade spaghetti sauce when the twenty-three-year-old mother's body was discovered in the kitchen of her Dorchester Street home.

8. Add a quotation.

"Maria was always in the kitchen," her mother said, "making homemade bread, listening to other people's problems, doing for the kids, writing her poems at the kitchen table."

9. Work from or toward a dominant impression. Use a phrase to focus the description.

The spiral notebook open, the pen uncapped, the last line of poetry halfwritten, the meat for spaghetti sauce simmering on the stove—the entire kitchen revealed evidence of an unfinished life.

or

The kitchen revealed evidence of an unfinished life: the spiral notebook open, the pen uncapped, the last line of poetry half-written, the meat for the spaghetti sauce simmering on the stove.

10. Describe a process.

Her mother turned off the stove, capped the pen, read the unfinished poetry line, and closed the notebook.

11. Use a natural order: a walk through a room, or the way the eye moves, from one item to another in a normal sequence.

Maria's mother ran right to the kitchen, stopped, *looking directly at the police and the reporters, then down to her daughter, to the stove, to the notebook on the table, finally to her daughter again.*

12. Appeal to a sense other than sight whenever possible.

Even after her mother had turned off the stove, *the kitchen was filled with the spicy smell of a meal* that would never be served.

13. Use the distance most effective for what you are trying to say. Start far away and move in close, or reverse the process.

> *Through the window,* it looked like a family kitchen, filled with friends, *but inside there was silence and the body of a young mother* sprawled, face up, on the floor.

14. Describe by comparison or analogy.

> The old car in the driveway had bumper stickers over bumper stickers, each against war, but *the scene in the kitchen looked like a clip of a terrorist attack in another country.*

Fitting More News into Less Space

Through the years, writers have stared with horror, looking over the edge, as the news hole has shrunk. Some papers have carried this too far and declared across-the-board mandates about story length. I think there should be a diversity of lengths, but that each story should earn its space. In my own experience, however, shorter is usually better.

Here are some of the problems writers have faced when required to shrink their story length.

I tend to look for the big story in all that I do, and then have enormous problems wrestling it down to newspaper size. Any advice?

- Look for the single, most revealing anecdote, quote, statistic, detail, or fact. Focus in close.
- Recognize that each story must have one dominant message. Kurt Vonnegut once said, "Don't put anything in a story that does not reveal character or advance the action." That's superb fiction writing advice that should be applied to our trade. Everything in the story should move the story forward toward its final meaning.
- John Steinbeck put on a three-by-five card a sentence or two that encapsulated the meaning of each book he was writing. Try that. I've found it invaluable.
- Each story should answer the reader's questions. Usually there are four or five questions the reader must have answered. Ask them, and answer them.
- Draft a dozen leads, or two dozen. Just the first line or so. Do it quickly—a matter of minutes for each one—until you find the lead that focuses the story. Then develop that lead.

- Outline. Make a note of the lead, then the ending. Put down the three to five main points in between and then number them so that they take you from the lead to the end.
- Decide on the form of the story. It may be inverted pyramid, narrative, profile, problem/solution, exposition, analysis, question and answer, scene and exposition, walk through, or whatever; but each form has its own discipline, qualities that drive it forward and those that get in the way.
- Choose the voice. Each story has its voice, that speaking quality of style, tone, and tempo that holds the story together. Knowing (naming and testing) the voice is a great help in selecting what belongs in the story and what should be left out.
- Write the first draft fast without your notes. What you remember will probably be what you should remember, and what is forgotten probably should be forgotten. Check your notes after you finish the draft to make sure that's true.
- Write for one reader. Imagine a person you know and write to that person. A story that includes too much and lacks focus is often written to satisfy the chorus of editors and censors who haunt us all.

How do you write the forty- to fifty-line story with humor or punch? Accept limitation as an artistic challenge. Brevity can clarify and concentrate the mind the way combat or being rolled into an operating room can. All art involves restrictions, and the size of a canvas, the duration of a symphony, and the length of a story are essential parts of the artistic process.

Art is also a matter of selection. The trick in the short article is to select the essential part of the story and then to develop it fully. Most writers, when ordered to write short, make the mistake of writing the garbage-compactor story, compressing everything that is in the notebook into a hard, indigestible pellet of news.

Stories of any length should have one dominant meaning. Effective short stories must have one dominant meaning. Everything in the story should lead toward or away from that meaning. The pace of the story, its form, its order, and its tone should all support that single meaning. And the story should be developed with all the information to satisfy the reader and to give the story appropriate texture.

Too many long stories are filled with information that the reporter includes in case someone (usually an editor) says, "Why didn't you include *x, y,* or *z*?" The brief story requires hard decisions and trust. Interesting information will be left out. There is no way that you can write a short save-your-ass story. Such stories require teamwork between writer and editor. But the result is worth the effort. Most stories get better as they get shorter.

What are some tips for keeping any story to eighty lines?

- Write the ending first so that you have a clear sense of direction as you write the draft. Don't worry, you'll still be able to write for discovery.
- Write a headline or a billboard that will concentrate the focus of the story.
- Ask yourself the most essential question the reader will ask. Answer it.
- Write fast without your notes, remembering what you should remember, forgetting what should be forgotten.
- Make a list of all the interesting information, all the potential stories within the story that do not advance the dominant message to the reader. Leave them all out.

❖ Journalist at Work ❖ KEVIN CULLEN Interview

Globe writers and editors repeatedly express their respect for the traditional skills displayed by Kevin Cullen, now European bureau chief, as he produces hard news stories on deadline that have his own special touch. He works within precise limitations of time and space, and is a master of selection.

Q: *How do you spot and cultivate a good source?*

A: Spotting a good source is being able to see through the trees and recognize the person most capable in any given field. In law enforcement, or any form of government, for that matter, it is seldom the person of highest rank.

There's no easy way to recognize these people, except to listen to what people say: who's respected, and who's considered a bozo by the vast majority. You have to follow your instincts.

Keeping a source is easy. Once you get him or her talking you've got to show results. You've got to get stories in the paper. And, despite the urge to tilt things the source's way, you've got to resist and play it as fairly as possible.

Q: *How do you get people to talk and capture the way they speak?*

A: When I interview a longshoreman, my Boston accent is much thicker. I *pahk my cah* and *tawk to da guy*. When I interview criminals, I swear a lot, because they swear a lot. When I talk to priests, my parochial-school deference comes through. *Fahtha this* and *Fahtha that*. When I talk to lawyers, I use as much legal jargon as possible, to demonstrate I'm not the usual dolt layperson. When I talk to old ladies in South Boston, I'm polite. When I talk to a cop whose partner has been gunned down in front of him, I'm sympathetic. A reporter shouldn't be an actor, but creating an atmosphere in which the interview subject is most natural and comfortable usually cuts through the crap and gets the subject talking freely.

Q: *How do you take notes?*

A: Not nearly as well as I should. I find it hard not to look at the person I'm talking to, and I find it hard to look at them and take legible, good notes. A tape recorder is a pain, except if you have the luxury of time. Besides, a recorder can sometimes make people ill at ease and kill that free exchange you're trying to promote.

The most important thing to do is to guard against stopping an interview simply because you think you've got all you need for a forty- or sixty-line story. I find some of the best quotes come out much later in the interview, which stands to reason, because that is usually when the person loosens up and some kind of rapport has developed between interviewer and interviewee.

Q: *How do you make use of notes?*

A: The most essential thing is to read them. Very often, I find if I don't read my notes over carefully, I'll miss a key quote or piece of color, simply because I've forgotten that it came up in the interview.

Q: *What do you try to do in a lead?*

A: A hard news lead should be as short as possible. This is Journalism School 101 stuff. I think it's pretty hard to explain anything to anyone at our level about writing a hard news lead. You either hit the right things or you don't.

The softer lead is a different matter, much more subjective. My own feeling is that, whenever you have the material to support it, a soft lead can be used to lure in more readers than a hard news lead ever could.

A soft lead, which is a misnomer if it is done well, should be striking. It should make people read a line and say, "Hmm, this looks interesting. That sounds wild." It should read like the first line of a Frank O'Connor short story: striking for its simplicity, but immediately conveying to the reader that the author knows his stuff. The lead should carry the confidence of the author.

I think leads should set the tone for the rest of the story. If it's a bizarre story, use a bizarre lead; if a sad story, a sad lead, if funny, funny.

Q: *What process do you use in going through the draft?*

A: I don't use outlines. I write stream of (somewhat) consciousness. I usually try to get the lead down first. If the kicker is the next to come to mind, that goes down at the bottom. If a nice transition pops into my head, even if it will eventually find its way to the next-to-last paragraph, that goes down. The key is to keep writing, keep the juices flowing. My biggest problem is getting sidetracked—getting phone calls or working on something else even while I'm writing.

Q: *How do you hear and tune a strong voice?*

A: You listen. If you listen, you hear. Don't be afraid to include a "Jesus Christ" or an "I mean" if they say it, as that's how may people begin their sentences in conversation. That creates a strong, credible voice.

Q: *How do you get a strong sense of the people you're reporting on, and the places where they live and work into your notebook and ultimately your stories?*

A: Being from the Boston area, I have a lifelong knowledge of the area that cannot be replaced by books or anything short of total immersion, like a Tony Lukas in *Common Ground*, but who has the time for that?

When I went to Northern Ireland on assignment, I drew on past experience, including living in Dublin for a year and in Belfast for several months. I also drew on past reading. But, remembering all that, I listened to what people said and tried to report that faithfully. No big secret.

Q: *How do you pace your stories?*

A: As I mentioned before, I think, except for a straight, hard news story, they should read like short stories. There should be a beginning, a middle, and an end, with catchy, well-turned transitions in between. Quotes are great transitional vehicles. Mechanically speaking, it's good to remember that a long sentence should be followed by a short one or two. That creates a pace for the reader.

Q: *Problems?*

A: My stories are late too often. Sometimes it's because I dwell on transitions and things like that too much. Often it's because I try to make too many phone calls late in the afternoon.

That problem seems to be getting worse, not better, as I get older and become more conscious of the importance of writing. My previous tabloid mentality was: Screw it, if you have it first, you did your job, the hell with presentation. Now I want to have it first but write it well. Hopefully it will solve itself as I become more confident in my own ability.

There's a mental roadblock in that. I feel if I put less time into my work down the road, I'm not doing as thorough a job.

Q: *Do you have any writers whom you use as models or guides? Any books you would suggest other reporters read?*

A: Probably the greatest influence on me has been the work of Frank O'Connor, the Irish short-story writer. I admired Ray Fitzgerald, the late *Globe* sportswriter, growing up, and I always thought that Mike Barnicle could tell a story because he knows how people, all people, feel.

I would recommend that anyone interested in writing better news stories under deadline pressure read O'Connor's collected works, which I stole from Diana Altera two years ago and haven't returned.

❖ Journalist at Work ❖
Analysis of a RICHARD KNOX Story

It seems appropriate to perform an autopsy on the work of a medical writer. I think we can learn by taking apart stories we admire or stories we have written (whether we have admired them or not) to see what works and how.

Richard Knox's "How luck, high-tech foiled 'sudden death'," starting on page one of the January 16, 1989, *Globe*, is worthy of careful examination. The topic is highly technical and so, to make the reader read and to dramatize the story, Knox decided to tell it through a narrative case history. He had to tune the story so that it was dramatic but not melodramatic, technical but not too technical:

Francis Jefferson, known as "Rindge" by his wide circle of friends, was having the time of his life on the evening of Dec. 5. Just retired from a satisfying 30-year career dealing with juvenile delinquents, Jefferson was master of ceremonies at a reunion of people who grew up in the Humbolt Avenue area of Roxbury in the early 1940s.

Knox takes two paragraphs to introduce you to the victim of the heart attack, convince you he is worth your concern, and set the scene for the always-unexpected "sudden death" attack.

It was a great occasion, drawing 600 people to the Prince Masonic Hall in the Grove Hall section of Dorchester. The program went off without a hitch. The music began. Jefferson started to dance with an old friend.

Today he remembers none of it. At 9:45 that evening, Jefferson's scarred, 62-year-old heart, overstimulated by the excitement, suddenly fell into a wild, often-fatal dance of its own, known medically as ventricular fibrillation.

Now the pace changes. Notice how much more specific information Knox gives the reader. And the information is in context; it is delivered when the reader needs it. I was particularly impressed by the description of the beat as a dance (ironic since the victim was dancing) and the fact that the writer delivered the medical name after the definition.

It's sometimes called a "sudden death" heart attack, and it kills about 315,000 Americans each year—one every 100 seconds.

Now the incident is put in a larger, more meaningful perspective. And there is the message: This could be you.

Jefferson didn't die, and he almost certainly won't die the next time his heart goes haywire.

Knox is in a conversation with the reader, which is just the right place to be. The reader finishes this paragraph and asks, "Why?" Knox will now tell the reader.

The reasons why combine equal measure of luck and high-technology medicine. Jefferson's story tells a good deal about sudden cardiac death in Boston, and why the great majority who suffer cardiac arrest don't survive.

Here is an interesting organizational device, important in all sorts of complex political, environmental, business, and budget stories. Knox lays out the topics he will deal with in the order he will deal with them.

First, the luck. Among the crowd was a nurse, Gloria Browne, who recognized what was going on and knew how to do cardiopulmonary resuscitation, as only a tiny fraction of citizens in this region do. Meanwhile, someone fetched help for the Engine 24-Ladder 32 station of the Boston Fire Department next door. Someone else called 911 at 9:45 p.m. The ambulance arrived 9 minutes later, an unusually fast response time for Boston, according to Boston emergency services officials.

The writer is very specific and specificity brings with it authority. Knox weaves in the fact that few local people know CPR, a theme that will emerge later in the article.

Knox is also fair in pointing out that the ambulance response time that may seem slow to the reader is unusually fast "for Boston," another topic to be dealt with later. He is weaving a number of threads through this story.

Next the technology came into play. Since last September, Boston's municipal ambulances have been equipped with portable defibrillators, programmed to recognize ventricular fibrillation and to shock a quivering heart back into normal rhythm.

Now he moves on to the next topic. Note the grace with which he works in definitions and the energy of such words as "quivering."

That's just what emergency medical technicians Paul Hughes and James Rattigan did. A few minutes behind them came the advanced life-support team of John Doyle and Brendan Kearney, paramedics trained to start intravenous lines, administer heart-quieting drugs and stabilize cardiac arrest victims en route to the hospital.

Neat, effective narrative that easily carries information to the reader.

By the time Jefferson arrived at Boston City Hospital, at 10:24 p.m., his pulse was normal and he was breathing on his own.

Jefferson is one of 104 cardiac arrests in Boston since the portable defibrillator came into use on September 20. Of those, only 33 were reached in time to try shocking the heart back to normal rhythm. The attempt was successful in 12 patients, but six died anyway before they got to the hospital.

Again, Knox puts the story in perspective, albeit a pretty discouraging perspective. I wondered why the story was written if the figures were so bad, then remembered that Jefferson was a special case. Okay, Knox, tell me how special and why I should know it.

Of the remaining six, only Jefferson has survived to be discharged from the hospital.

But that's not the end of the tale. The most dramatic application of technology—the one that makes Jefferson's rescue more than just a temporary victory—was yet to come.

Now a transition paragraph and a promise to the reader.

On Christmas Day, Jefferson had another close brush with death. His 81-year-old mother, his sister and his brother-in-law had just arrived at Boston City Hospital to visit when he suddenly felt dizzy and blacked out. Doctors and nurses shooed the horrified family away as they once again shocked Jefferson back to life.

Another dramatic scene, and readers like scenes. This one reinforces the importance of what is going to happen to Jefferson.

Clearly, the drugs he was taking to block another episode of ventricular fibrillation were not working. Jefferson, who had survived a serious heart attack and two separate open-heart operations in the 1970s to bypass clogged coronary arteries, would almost certainly suffer another cardiac arrest after he left the hospital. And next time he might not be so lucky.

The writer gives me the case history when I need it.

Without effective medication, about one-third of all sudden death survivors will have another episode within a year, studies have shown. Within two years half are dead.

More on how serious a condition Jefferson and others with his condition find themselves in.

Cardiologist Rodney H. Falk proposed another alternative, one that Jefferson had never heard of: implanting a miniaturized automatic defibrillator in his abdomen with wires leading to the heart. The next time ventricular fibrillation struck, the $15,000 machine would recognize the change in rhythm within six seconds, draw an electric charge from its batteries within another six seconds, and deliver a jolt of electricity powerful enough to quell the abnormal rhythm.

Now to the center of the story, just when we are impatient for it—and understand its significance.

Knox does an expert job of making technical detail clear to the average reader.

The shock is only about one-tenth as powerful as that delivered externally by a conventional defibrillator.

But it's enough to make its owners feel as though they've been kicked in the chest.

"It's as though you had an ambulance squad sitting in your chest," Falk told Jefferson. "You will do extremely well. Three years ago I couldn't tell you that. This device has revolutionized the care of patients in your situation."

The writer anticipates and answers the reader's questions: What's it feel like?

"I was convinced this would make sense," Jefferson said Friday as he was preparing to go home from the hospital. "Partly because of the confidence Dr. Falk had in it. I had confidence in him."

I like hearing from the patient and seeing the decision from his perspective.

Surgeons implanted the automatic device in Jefferson 11 days ago in a lengthy operation during which they deliberately provoked his heart into fibrillation to test the system. Falk tested it again last Thursday, pushing Jefferson's heart over the brink, then watching tensely as the defibrillator jolted him back to life.

We are taken into the operating room to see and feel the tension in such an experimental technique. And this happens after we are concerned about the patient and understand the seriousness of his condition.

"He went out like a light," the cardiologist said. "Then suddenly he was awake again." Jefferson retains no memory of the life-saving shocks.

Later Friday, as he relaxed in his three-decker, Jefferson said his emotion was gratitude for "All the people who did something to save me. The system saved me. The system worked."

Unfortunately, the system that worked for Jefferson fails for most "sudden death" victims.

A nice turn here that allows Knox to go beyond his case history to the larger issues in the story.

As Boston City Hospital doctors and emergency services personnel pointed out last week, implantable fibrillators are no good if people don't survive long enough to get to the hospital, or if they die at the hospital because their brains were devastated by lack of oxygen due to inadequate and sluggish care on the way there. And portable fibrillators on every ambulance are not enough if ambulances are too few, response times too slow and if too few ordinary citizens are trained to resuscitate cardiac arrest victims while waiting for emergency personnel to arrive.

Knox is responsible. He doesn't just write a melodramatic, everything-is-wonderful story. He always keeps the story in an appropriate context.

"Mr. Jefferson had a lot of things going for him, but not everybody has," said David M. Ladd, director of training and special operations for Boston Emergency Medical Services. "The point needs to be made. We have the technology and the ability to save a lot of lives. The problem is we don't have enough of it. And somebody has to train the public."

Falk agreed. "The crucial message is to get medical care to cardiac arrest victims, not cardiac arrest victims to medical care," the cardiologist said.

"Citizens can do a far greater job then physicians can in reducing the toll of sudden death. We can only deal with the survivors, but the public can ensure there are more survivors for us to work on."

Richard Knox gets out of the way and lets authorities make his point for him.

The story was accompanied by a sidebar going into greater technical detail for those readers who were interested. The craft in this story is appropriate to the increasing number of complex stories that must be reported in a responsible newspaper. We all can learn from it.

Chapter 7

DEVELOP: Work on What Works

From toilet training on, we are taught by error. "You made another mistake!" Most teachers follow the same instructional model: Find and correct what is wrong. Then we graduate and find that most editors teach by error.

This is the way I was taught until I started teaching myself. When I was writing magazine articles, I photocopied a draft on large paper and wrote in the margins what I was actually doing when I revised. I made a startling discovery. I was not so much correcting error as expanding success, identifying what worked and extending it. When I focused on the strengths of the draft, most of the weaknesses disappeared and if errors remained, they were edited.

Write What's Right

My writing took huge leaps forward when I didn't read my first drafts looking for what was wrong, but what was right. I asked myself two questions *in this order*:

One: What Works?

I read the draft to see which sections work. It may be the beginning or the end, the middle or part of the middle. I also look to discover which elements work. These may include the voice, the sequence or order, the documentation, the genre or form, the point of view, the pace, proportion, distance, any of the many elements that make the engine of writing go.

I work to make the good parts better, focusing on developing what is working rather than what is not working. This is not a Pollyanna avoidance of what is wrong but a craftsperson's assessment of what is right, what is already working that could be made even better.

There is excitement and discovery in this process. I am not writing with a sense of failure and guilt, but a sense of accomplishment and discovery. I find that as I work on what has worked, my writing gets better than I have imagined. I am thinking and feeling and making, the draft carries me beyond the ordinary, beyond expectation. In many cases the draft leads me or I take instruction from the draft. It is the draft that not only tells me what to say but how to say it.

Revision is not punishment for failure, but opportunity. It is, indeed, reseeing, a new thinking, a new making, the exploration of thought and feeling that writing should be for the writer that becomes, for readers, published writing that not only informs but ignites their own thinking and feeling.

Two: What Needs Work?

Then, when I have developed what works, I turn to what still does not work. Most of the problems of the first drafts have been solved by the development of what works but, of course, problems often remain and they have to be solved. Usually this is easy because of the development of what worked.

The solution to language problems lies in the now-developed strong voice; problems of order, pace, proportion can be solved by the strong line of logic that runs through the developed article. What works clarifies and defines what does not work and with that clarification comes solutions—and one of the most frequent is to cut what does not work. Usually what was a problem is no longer needed.

How to Develop a Draft

Many news stories are first-draft stories; that is the discipline we all share. We can deliver on deadline, usually by resorting to the stereotypes and clichés of journalism. But if newspapers are going to provide the reader with stories that are not broadcast in radio-news flashes or caught in a few moments on the television evening news, we need to develop our first-draft stories.

When I first became a writing coach on a newspaper, I found reporters underwrote. They did not fill their stories with direct quotes with clear attributions but paraphrased with a general attribution. They did not deliver facts. They did not report with all their senses. They either did not observe and record information or they left it in their notebooks when they wrote.

My first drafts are almost always far shorter than the final one. First I get a sketch of the territory and then as I write to make myself understand, then my reader understand, I have documented, attributed, defined, and answered the reader's questions.

Context

I often refer to the paragraph or paragraphs after the lead that are often called the *nut graf* or the billboard as the context draft. This is especially true when the lead focuses on one incident—a fire, political speech, accident, murder, school-bond vote, medical breakthrough. In every case, to understand the story, it has to be put in context. The context may be a series of arson fires, an election in which abortion has become an issue, a road that has caused many accidents, a school bond that has been turned down many times causing the school to lose its accreditation, a treatment for a little-known but spreading disease that is killing children.

The facts, quotations, anecdotes, actions, reported in the story need to be part of a larger significance, to be seen in perspective of other information if the reader is to understand and care.

Documentation

Articles should be developed with a variety of evidence. As writers, we fall into habits of supporting what we have to say with quotations or anecdotes, citing government reports or university studies, statistics or maps, description or exposition, but the reader needs a form of documentation that is appropriate to the information being supported. It is also important to vary the documentation to produce lively copy that will keep the reader turning the page.

And don't forget that "Who sez?" is a healthy, normal reader's reaction. The reader needs accurate, believable attributions for quotations and facts.

Faces

People want to read about people. *Time* started a whole new trend in magazines by putting a face on the news each week and following it inside with a profile that incorporated the information in the story woven through biography. And Time Inc. owns *People* magazine.

Populating the news, telling what is happening in terms of people, is one of the great strengths—and one of the great weaknesses—of journalism. We have become a nation of celebrity worshippers rather than a nation of ideas but people will read stories if people walk, talk, act, and react on the page.

Voice and Voices

It is the voice of the text—the author's voice tuned to the topic and the audience—that attracts and holds the reader's interest. Voice produces trust. Voice creates the illusion of conversation, an individual writer speaking—and listening—to an individual reader and responding to that reader in a personal way.

Another important way to develop a piece of writing is to bring other voices to the page, allowing the reader to hear those who are causing the event, opposing it, being affected by it.

Distance

As we develop an article, we often remain at one distance. Some of us are comfortable moving in close to the story, walking right into the kitchen, sharing a cup of coffee with the victim, perhaps even attempt to slither into the skin of the subject. Others always stand at a great distance, viewing the board dimensions of the story, avoiding the immediate for the past, the impersonal for the personal.

In most stories the writer should do both, using a zoom lens that brings the reader in close when that is the best was to communicate, then backing off when that is appropriate.

First Person

It is print journalist tradition to avoid the first person (in fact, the capital letter *I* had been filed off all the Royal typewriters in the old *Boston Herald* city room when I arrived in 1948). Since I write a first-person column, I do think there is a place for the reporter to speak directly of his or her own experiences, observations, knowledge to the reader.

I also think that in developing a story, it is all right to move into the first person and out, if you have a special authority, experience, or reaction that is the best way to reveal the story and its meaning to the reader.

Setting

In developing a story, it may be very helpful for the reader to see the crowded floor of the Senate or the row upon row of empty seats while an important issue was debated. They may need to ride in a squad car, patrol the front lines, be in the operating room, see the walls topped by prison wire around the Asian factory where American-made products are being produced, hunker in the baseball-catcher's squat. The reader needs to know that most stories take place in a world that influences the story.

Action

Too many news stories are passive. They tell about the story when it could be better revealed with the reader taken through the legislative or judicial process. The debate or interrogation might be recorded. The reader might be taken along on the scientific, manufacturing, or police investigation method; the conditions at the state psychiatric hospital might be shown dramatically by a walk through the wards.

Chronology

The reader will read on if the clock is ticking and the story is developed with the clock counting off the seconds for the last plays of the game or the hours running out on the boat rescue from the winter seas.

Connect

It is important, in developing a story, to connect the subject that may be unfamiliar to the reader with a subject that is familiar to the reader. This can be dangerous, even patronizing. The reader has to know the reader and the reader's world to connect the story to the reader's experience.

Answer the Reader's Questions

And one more time, a good way to develop a story is to anticipate and answer the reader's questions at the moment they are asked.

Layering

One of the best ways to develop a draft, giving it increasing depth and texture, is to write by layering, as I have done when oil painting, adding layer upon layer until I achieve the colors that capture the subject. It's been fascinating to see what happens.

On long or difficult pieces of writing, I begin each day at the beginning and write over what I have written before. Some days I'll find myself improving one section of the story or one element that runs through the story, another day a different one. Layering is especially helpful for journalists who have the time to work on the long piece in which tone and texture are important. Many news stories are written over a series of days, and writing through the piece each day for several days helps develop and deepen a draft.

It also helps me deal with the destructive pressure to produce perfect copy every day. As playwright and screenwriter David Mamet reminds us:

> As a writer, I've tried to train myself to go one achievable step at a time: To say, for example, "Today I don't have to be particularly inventive, all I have to be is careful," and make up an outline of the actual physical things the character does in act one. And then, the following day to say, "Today I don't have to be careful. I already have this careful, literal outline, and all I have to do is be a little inventive," etcetera, etcetera.

The act of layering can be forgiving. We don't have to get it all right today, we just have to do a decent job on one element in the text.

Here is an example of how I might build up a draft in a book I am writing on aging, writing something then writing over it again and again.

1. Aging is an adventure.
2. Aging is an adventure we take if we are lucky.
3. Aging is an expedition into the unknown and in preparing for an expedition of exploration one packs what may be needed in the trip ahead.
4. Preparing for my expedition into the unknown world of aging, I realize I packed by father's example of working right up to the day he died.
5. Preparing for my expedition into the unknown world of aging, I realize I packed by father's habit of working right up to the day he died. He had always wanted to be a minister but my grandfather took him out of school when he was fourteen and he became a sometimes good and often bad businessman, but in retirement he worked for his church directing a ministry for the elderly and I have followed his example doing the work I love—writing—as my exploration into growing old moves forward morning by morning.

We should always remember that there is no one way to write anything. I've published more than twenty books and each one seems to have been written differently. We have a tendency to limit ourselves to one way to approach each project as if all the writing tasks are the same. Eudora Welty reminds us:

> The writer himself studies intensely how to do it while he is in the thick of doing it; then when the particular novel or story is done, he is likely to forget how; he does well to. Each work is new. Mercifully,

the question of how abides less in the abstract, and less in the past, than in the specific, in the work at hand.

Notes on Narrative

We talk a lot about stories in newspapers, but we do not seem to understand the importance of story—that is, narrative—and to appreciate it and find ways to adapt it for the newspaper.

Story is the mother of all forms of writing. Despite some intellectuals' lack of respect for traditional narrative, it is the principal way we all, intellectuals included, explore, understand, and explain our world to each other. We live and believe the narratives we have woven from our past and our experience. More than we realize, we see the world through story.

As one who has published novels and short stories as well as nonfiction narrative, I thought it might be interesting to make some notes on the craft of writing narrative so that you might see ways to make use of these skills in your stories.

Character

Story begins best with character. We read because we become involved with characters, we remember stories because of characters. As writers we need to develop characters that are believable as well as physically and psychologically complex; characters that writer and readers feel strongly about, in a compassionate way. We report what characters do and how they do it so that the characters reveal themselves to us and to our readers. We need to see the characters physically, in action.

Dramatic Action

The evolving, natural interaction between the characters and their world makes the story move forward. Plot or ideas do not manipulate character, but characters reacting to each other reveal ideas and create the plot, or chain of action and reaction.

The action and reaction must be significant to the characters. Significance or importance may be measured by the fact that the actor and reactor are changed by the action, which can rarely be reversed.

Conflict is central to story. The characters' actions have an affect on one another: action and reaction. The action and reaction of the characters moves the story toward an actual or implied resolution.

The writer does not tell the reader how to feel, what to think. The writer gets out of the way and gives the reader the experience of the story, and that causes the reader to think and feel.

External Dialogue

Dialogue is action. "Get thee to a nunnery" is not just chatter, not to the woman involved. Dialogue is what characters do to one another. Characters speak to each other in a shared world. They speak from a ground of common knowledge.

Dialogue has the illusion of oral language. It should be written out loud, with your ear. It may consist of fragments, incomplete statements, or interruptions. Characters do not always listen to each other and respond directly to what is said.

The dialogue must express its own emotion and its own meaning. Don't rely on the qualities, "he said angrily," to convey your speaker's anger. Most times it should be obvious who is speaking. "He said" should pace the dialogue, provide a beat, and reinforce the meaning. The characters should sound different from the writer or narrator and from each other.

Internal Dialogue

The characters' thoughts are revealed through internal dialogue. The characters' thoughts are limited to each character's background and experience within the story and all the other restrictions of dialogue. The character does not reflect the knowledge and thinking of the author. The voice of internal dialogue must be appropriate to the character and the character's world.

Place

The story takes place in a world. The reader should discover and experience that world as it is important to the actions of the characters.

Description does not usually stand by itself, despite the teacher's instruction to write a descriptive paragraph. It is woven in. Description should be built of specific, revealing details, details that support the action and meaning of the story. Description should not move from left to right or top to bottom but convey a dominant impression from a focal point significant to the story.

A character's action is a very efficient form of description. He sits down and the chair breaks; the reader discovers the character is as portly as a writing coach.

Person

Stories are usually best told in the third person. The reader identifies most easily with third-person characters and they are most easily revealed in action.

First person seems easy, but it is actually hard to carry off. How do you reveal the narrator's appearance, for example? The focus is limited to what the narrator can see, hear, know, or do.

The second person (you) often doesn't work.

Point of View

Where the camera is placed. The reader can only see what the camera lens can see.

The camera zooms back and in close. The closer in, the less the camera lens can see but the intensity increases; the farther back, the larger the context and the greater the detachment.

The reader stands beside the camera and can only see, hear, and know what the camera reveals.

Narrative Voice

The voice or music of the story is as important as character and dramatic action. It reveals and supports the meaning of the story. It is the soundtrack and more.

Reading is an individual act. The reader hears the story and likes to hear an individual voice speaking to an individual reader. The narrative voice is the natural voice of the writer tuned to the story. It is the way that this particular story must be told. The voice must be appropriate to the time, place, and nature of the story. A voice that delights the reader is consistent but has a series of small, appropriate, revealing surprises.

Exposition

The trick is to use as little exposition as possible. Exposition is the material unimportant to the characters but that must be told to the reader so that the reader will understand the story. Exposition, if necessary, is buried in the action of the story, including the actions or internal and external dialogue.

Scene

Scene is the basic unit of narrative. It is the place where characters meet and interact in a setting. Stories, novels, plays, and movies move forward through a series of scenes in which an action takes place and its effect is felt, which causes a new action or scene.

Chronology

Time in a story does not move forward equally. I find it helpful to think of a necklace with various-size beads on it. Time moves quickly between scenes that are developed in details. Years may be a blank space between scenes; a moment may take pages to develop and be revealed. The reader needs a sense of time moving forward, a clock ticking. A good rule is to have a story start as near the end as possible.

A story does not need an introduction; the reader should be placed immediately in the story. The information the reader needs to understand the story should come as the reader needs it.

A story should not end with a conclusion that tells the reader what it means. It's too late for that. The story should end with an action that causes the reader to come to his or her own conclusion.

A flashback in time may be necessary, but this signals a failure of your chronology. Background information should be woven into the story and given to the reader as the reader needs it.

Theme

Theme is the narrative in its entirety. To paraphrase Archibald MacLeish, a story should not mean, but be. The story is the statement of the theme or meaning of the story. The theme is usually discovered by the writer through the writing. The writer usually feels no need to articulate or reduce the story to a meaning.

Each reader will find a different theme or meaning in the story depending on the background, the knowledge, the experience, and the psychological need of the individual reader.

These notes reflect the attitudes of one writer who is working on fiction. More news stories could be told as narratives, but it will be up to individual newswriters working on specific stories to teach us how that can best be done.

❖ Journalist at Work ❖ RENEE GRAHAM Interview

I talked to Renee Graham soon after she arrived at the *Globe*, and was immediately impressed by her attitude and her talent. She majored in newspaper journalism at Syracuse University, graduating in 1984. She worked as an intern for the *Syracuse Herald Journal* during her senior year and stayed on for two years after college. Desperate for a warmer climate, Graham moved south and worked at the *Miami Herald* for two years as a general-assignment reporter, then as the social-services reporter. She has been at the *Globe* since March 1988 and has become a columnist for the living section.

Q: *How do you prepare for an interview?*

A: It's always annoyed me when some talk-show host or interviewer says, "Well, I haven't read your book, but I've heard . . ." My interest usually fades at that point because I don't think the interviewer is properly equipped. You have to do your homework. You have to know your topic and subject, otherwise you stumble through the interview and never really accomplish what you want to do. Before an interview, I read up on a subject as much as possible. I use back clips, magazine articles, or even transcripts from news shows such as *60 Minutes* and *20/20*, if available. I don't believe you can over prepare for an interview. Each bit of background information helps you ask better questions. I also think it impresses your subject if you walk into their home or office with some basic knowledge of their topic or situation.

Q: *Do you have any special techniques for telephone interviews?*

A: Obviously, you miss a lot with telephone interviews and it's difficult to put a person immediately at ease since they can't see you; however, that can work to your advantage. When I was in college I worked for a crisis hotline and it never ceased to amaze me how open people would be with someone they couldn't see. Some people seem to find it easier to be interviewed over the telephone.

Q: *Do you have any special techniques for face-to-face interviews?*

A: I try to maintain eye contact and keep my own fidgeting to a minimum. It's distracting if the interviewer is rattling papers, crossing and uncrossing his or her legs, playing with loose threads, or staring out the window. If someone has taken the time to talk with me, the least I can do is act like I'm giving them my undivided attention.

Q: *How do you get people to answer questions they don't want to answer?*

A: My techniques vary depending on the person. Most of the time, it's give-and-take. I let them talk about something they want to talk about, then I ask them the hard questions. Sometimes, if the person is particularly skittish, I'll ask a tough question right off. That way they think the worst is over and the rest of the interview will be a breeze. If necessary, I'll bury parts of difficult questions in other questions.

Q: *How do you collect the revealing details that make your stories clear and lively? What do you look for when reporting a story?*

A: I try to pay special attention to small details: mannerisms, vocal inflections, pauses in speech, and so on. I also look for other revealing things: pictures, wall hangings, anything that can tell a little bit more about a person or topic.

Q: *Some writers say they have had a breakthrough piece that has given them confidence. Do you have such a piece? What was it? What was the breakthrough?*

A: I see my magazine story on the teenage father as my "breakthrough" piece. I'd never written a magazine story before and was quite excited by the opportunity to try something new. The magazine format allowed me to lay aside some of the tenets of newswriting. I could use large chunks of narrative or dialogue in ways that few news editors would allow. I didn't have to worry about a *nut graf* in the first ten lines. As a writer, I found the experience exhilarating and liberating.

Q: *When you have a complicated story, do you have any techniques that help you understand and communicate it?*

A: When I'm writing complicated stories, I make sure I ask the simple questions, the types of questions the average *Globe* reader might have. I don't approach stories merely as a newspaper writer, but as a newspaper reader, always keeping in mind small questions that sometimes go unanswered in complicated stories.

Q: *What other kinds of writing have you done? How do they help your newswriting?*

A: When I was in college, I concentrated on fiction, short stories, and poetry—and did some freelance work. Although I find little time for writing other than my newspaper work, I still try to employ the same techniques I began to develop as a writer of fiction. The best pieces are those that really tell a story—instead of merely spewing out facts. Investigative stories should have all the tension of a good mystery. With human-interest stories, the reader should come away with more than just a vague idea of what the subject is all about. In the same way I tried to develop characters in short stories, I now try to give a full picture of those I interview.

Q: *Will you describe the process you normally go through in writing a story?*

A: Often, I will try to find the "rhythm" of a story. I approach my writing much the way I approach dance or music. I can't plan how my body will respond to a certain type of music any more than I can predict what will happen when I sit in front of my computer. I find it helpful to read a few passages or the entire story aloud so I can hear how they sound. In a spoken voice, I know if a passage rings true or not. Of course, this is sometimes difficult to do in the newsroom without annoying coworkers, but it's the only process that I consistently use while writing.

Q: *Do you outline, organize your notes, and so forth?*

A: For most interviews, I use a tape recorder, which allows me to make notes to myself about other things: what a person is wearing, something intriguing that may be happening around them, the way they respond to certain questions.

Q: *What are the three problems you face most frequently in writing? How do you solve them?*

A: I'm constantly battling clichés. Sometimes, especially when I'm on deadline, I want to do something different, but those clichés are just sitting there, calling my name, begging me to take the easy way out. To avoid that, I constantly try to look at conventional things in different, unusual ways. Of course, there's the oldest nemesis, writer's block, but my natural aversion to overtime helps me get past that most of the time. The biggest problem, which really isn't a problem at all, is the perpetual challenge to improve. One of the best things about working here is the willingness of coworkers to bestow compliments. It's nice to know my work is appreciated, but I can't ever allow that knowledge to make me think that I've reached my high point as a writer. As a constant reminder, I keep a small sticker with the title of a Public Enemy song affixed to my desk: "Don't Believe the Hype."

Q: *Do you have a clear and individual voice you can tune to a particular story? How do you hear and tune your voice?*

A: As I mentioned before, I read my stories aloud to hear their rhythm. As a writer, I adapt myself to the story's mood, using my "voice" to tell that story best. When I began to read John Cheever's short stories in high school, I found myself trying to write with his dry wit and flair for irony. It didn't work. Cheever's voice isn't my voice, whatever that may be. It's difficult to describe it, but I just know what sounds right for me as a writer.

Q: *What is your process of revision and editing? Do you have your own private checklist?*

A: I prefer to edit my stories on a printout. After staring at a computer screen for several hours, everything starts to blur together and it's more likely that I'll overlook mistakes or changes that need to be made. First, I check names, addresses, titles of organizations, etcetera. Then I recheck each quote and attribution to make sure I've got the right people saying the right things.

Q: *What advice do you have for beginning writers?*

A: Be creative. Don't be afraid to try something your journalism professors distinctly told you to avoid. Be experimental, say a prayer, and send it to your editor. The worst they can do is send it back.

Q: *What books, authors, or publications have you found helpful as a writer that you would recommend to other people?*

A: I've always been an admirer of Zora Neale Hurston, John Cheever, Toni Morrison, and, recently, Armistead Maupin. Although each has a very distinct style, they all have an impeccable command of character development, dialogue, and setting. I've also learned a great deal about story development from filmmakers and screenwriters such as Billy Wilder and Paddy Chayefsky. And I'm still a big fan of Dr. Theodor Geisel, better known as Dr. Seuss. The man practically invented literary minimalism.

Q: *What can a writer do to develop an effective relationship with an editor?*

A: You have to cultivate editors to your writing style, leaving room for thoughtful criticism. An acrimonious relationship with an editor benefits no one, especially the writer. Don't be afraid to fight for your work; after all, your name is the only one that appears on the story—but remember nothing you write is carved in stone. At this stage in my career, I'm still developing my style and voice as a writer and welcome the advice of those interested in helping me hone my craft.

❖ Journalist at Work ❖
SALLY JACOBS Interview

I keep clipping Sally Jacobs's stories. Her work, now for the *Globe Magazine*, is marked for me by a mastery of the professional skills we should all have with an ability to push the limits of those skills, so that her stories have a special impact that doesn't draw attention to her, but to the story.

Q: *How do you get a reader to read?*

A: Every time I start a story I think of that picture of the middle-aged couple sitting at the breakfast table. The man, reading the paper, suddenly drops his coffee cup, nearly collapses into his wheat germ, and exclaims to his wife, "Good God, Martha! Did you read this?"

I would, of course, like everybody to react to my stories that way and then refuse to budge until they have read to the bitter end. In the real world, to get them involved in the first few paragraphs, I try to create as powerful and vivid a picture as I can, something that promises of what to come without promising more than it can deliver.

A "soft lead" is wrong for many spot stories, but the alternative is not always the five *W*s capped by a "he said." I try hard to avoid that kind of lead—instead, I come up with a line or two that tells readers just as much as a conventional lead but with more electricity.

There's really no way to describe how to do that, but if there is, I wish someone would tell me. Generally, I find that what strikes me personally as funny or curious works well as a lead.

Q: *What do you try to do, and not do, when drafting a story?*

A: I keep thinking about George and Martha. I figure I've got to make up for the coffee he spilled and try hard to keep the action going in the story.

With a really great tale, the story stays alive on its own. More often, you've got to work, to alternate form, to gradually unleash your information and color, to keep it going. Although you've told the reader pretty much what to expect up high in the story, you've got to hold back in order to keep the tension alive. How to do that well, of course, is the trick.

Q: *How do you get ideas for stories?*

A: I find the problem is not so much getting ideas for stories as it is choosing from among the many stories I'd like to do. Some of the best stories, of course, are not the great exposé of wrongdoing or badness but the simple event, the person or weird happening that often doesn't appear to be a story at first glance.

I try to talk regularly with people who are familiar with the areas I'm interested in, like criminal justice and social services, and usually those conversations generate at least a few ideas. Inmates and people on the receiving end of state services usually know of situations even stranger than their own.

Q: *What are the elements of a story idea that make it worthwhile for you to pursue it?*

A: I have a keen interest in oddballs and weirdos, which, as any reporter knows, includes just about everybody This is an appetite that grows sharper with the years and means I know not what.

I like stories with distinct, colorful characters, which I think not only help to order a story, but make it more fun for readers. The fact that they have come to my or the *Globe's* attention often means that they are at odds with society or one of its symptoms, which generally constitutes the tension in the story.

Q: *How do you get people to talk to you?*

A: There are sprinkled among humanity some people who consider reporters a step on the evolutionary scale below roaches and wouldn't tell you if your back was on fire. But I find that most people want to talk and, in fact, am constantly amazed at the emotions and intimacies that people gab about to the media.

With people less inclined, I try to offer something of myself, to show a knowledge and understanding of their situation that may make them more willing. Most important, I try to be patient. Deadlines can make one impatient with a reluctant interviewee, but I find that usually people just need a little time and conversation before they are willing to talk.

Q: *Which note-taking techniques are most valuable to you?*

A: Writing legibly is a continual challenge. I confess, there have been times in the past when I have gone to write a story several weeks after an interview and have been convinced that I, or the person being interviewed, must have been on drugs. For years I have made myself go quickly over my notes soon after taking them in order to clarify in readable writing important quotes or comments.

I stress that I only do this with portions of the interview that I'm fairly confident I will use in the story—which is generally less than I expect. I find that the best way to capture a story on paper is to write quickly and largely from memory so as not to lose the pace, which does not allow for much time to leaf through a notebook. But I always try to skim my notes before and after writing to make sure I haven't missed something particularly colorful or revealing. Usually I have.

Tape recorders are even more problematic simply because they take too much time. By the time I've nailed down the phrase I thought I wanted, I've thought of a better way.

Q: *How can an editor best help you?*

A: I came from a newspaper where editors could not rest easy at night unless they had rewritten a good part of your story and reporters made voodoo dolls of those able to sleep the soundest. Here, I find precisely the opposite problem.

To me, a good editor is not always the one who does the least, who waits for the story to show up and then keeps it at arm's length. I think editors need to be involved, to take time to talk to a reporter about an approach, about ideas, and the like, without dictating The Way. A lot of times I get my best ideas, or find out where I have holes in my thinking, in talking with an editor.

Too, when writing under pressure, any reporter may unintentionally make mistakes or take a shortcut. Although I write my stories the way I think they should run, I would far rather have someone tighten my copy if it needs it than have it run sloppy.

Chapter 8

CLARIFY: Represent the Reader

Effective writers turn traitor to their own copy, reading what they have written through the eyes of an enemy reader who has no loyalty to the writer, little interest in the subject, no concern with form or style, but with an aggressive skepticism, and an eagerness to turn the page. Writers must detach themselves from intent, not reading what is *supposed* to be on the page but what is *on* the page.

Some writers fall in love with what they have written. They cannot stand back and read what the reader will read—or what the reader needs to read that is not on the page. When I was not proud of my first draft, I was paralyzed by it. I could not see an alternative. Once drafted, the pages were unchangeable.

Then I fell into despair. Everything I wrote seemed best described by the Old English word *dung*. I was saved from permanent literary constipation by economic necessity: I liked to eat, my wife liked to eat, my daughters liked to eat. I submitted drafts I thought were terrible and enough got published—often after revision and editing—to bring food to the kitchen.

Love and despair, confidence and terror, are necessary. The professional writer has to have enough ego and skill to produce a draft, then enough critical ability to separate from the draft and become the draft's first reader.

Eventually rewriting and editing stops feeling like failure and becomes a central satisfaction of our craft. "What makes me happy is rewriting," says columnist Ellen Goodman. "In the first draft you get your ideas and your theme clear, if you are using some kind of metaphor you get that established, and certainly you have to know where you're coming out. But the next time through it's like cleaning house, getting rid of all the junk, getting things in the right order, tightening things up. I like the process of making writing neat." Bernard Malamud adds, "I love the flowers of afterthought."

Editing Your Own Copy

John Ciardi once said that writing is "a schizophrenic process. To begin passionately and to end critically—to begin hot and to end cold—and, more important, to try to be passion-hot and critic-cold at the same time."

It doesn't get any easier. The longer we write, the more alternatives we see: There are a hundred ways to tell the story, a thousand ways to turn the sentence on the lathe of experience. The longer we write, the more experience we have with our craft, the more critical we become—at least those who take pride in their craft and want to grow better at its execution. The writer is continually engaged in a civil war between freedom and discipline, a war that must never be won or lost but must always continue, providing the tension that is essential to our craft.

Before writing, we have to be aware of what has been written previously and how it has been written, but we have to be open to the unexpected, ready to welcome surprise in content and in approach.

During writing, we have to employ all the lessons of our craft but push against them, encouraging those accidents of insight and style that produce significant, lively writing.

After writing, we have to understand what we have written and make sure others understand it. The critic within us takes over as we make sure that what we say is accurate in detail and context; that what we say is graceful and clear.

For years I found it most efficient to read the draft at least three times:

1. I read as fast as I could to see if there is a single dominant meaning.
2. I read at half-speed to see if the draft is ordered and developed and that each important point is supported by evidence.
3. I read slowly—word by word, line by line—to hear and tune the language so that the text has accuracy, clarity, and grace.

I used to think I wrote and then I edited (or was edited), but I have come to realize that my editors, internal and external, are always with me from idea through final draft. And the editorial role changes as I move through the writing process. In the beginning the critic is important, but has to be resisted, or at least kept under control; in the middle of producing the text, critic and creator have to work in harmony; at the end, the critic takes over.

Experienced writers read by ear as much as by eye, hearing the draft paragraph by paragraph, sentence by sentence, phrase by phrase, word by word. The best writers become their own first editors, reading the draft as it will most certainly be read by a reader—in haste and with skepticism. Newswriters have to make their copy lively, compelling, accurate, clear, and as short as possible, adding and taking away, reading and writing to be read.

Editing Before Writing

Effective writers—if they know it or not—begin editing long before they attempt the first lead. The editing starts as they catch a story idea out of the corner of the eye or as they receive an assignment and begin to make it their own. They begin an internal dialogue.

What's new? Where is the surprise in the story? It may be something as obvious as a new treatment for diabetes or a new context for an old story—young love in a nursing home. The writer keeps looking for change before and as it happens.

Where is the revealing tension in the story? Each good story unwinds as a tension within it is released. The reader confronts new information that affects a previously believed truth, two—or more—forces headed for a collision, a conflict between issues or persons, a question, an unexpected problem, a solution to an old problem, a contradiction, or a story behind a story and is compelled to read on. Before writing, the writer should find the central tension that will release this story.

Why should anyone read the story? I used to have an agent who snapped a cruel, "So what?" to most of my story ideas. Good question. Who would be interested? Who would read the story? How would it attract and serve a reader? To begin reporting a story it helps to identify a reader who needs the information the story provides or will enjoy discovering that information. Will the reader read from fear, because of curiosity, because the information is of practical value, because it is funny, because it makes the reader mad, sad, laugh, or identify with the victim, because it makes the reader think or escape or feel, or because it changes the reader's vision of the world? There are many reasons but the effective writer identifies at least one that will connect this paper's readers with this story.

Which form will carry the meaning to the reader? Form is meaning. When we use narrative, we say that the information we need to communicate has a beginning, a middle, and an end, organized by time. A profile says that people control, or powerfully influence, events; an interview says that someone has something important to say. We must make sure that the form we choose supports the meaning we have to communicate.

What voice will be most effective for the story? Voice is the magic in writing: an individual human voice is recorded in silent symbols on the page and then, hours or years later, is heard in the reader's ears. It is that individual quality of voice that attracts and holds readers, communicates an attitude toward the story, and makes the meaning of the story clear and believed. The trick is to tune your voice so that it calls attention not to the writer but to the meaning of the story.

What length and shape do I expect the story to develop? When I first taught, I resented the students' question, "How long do you want my paper to be?" I thought it an indication of laziness or excessive concern with grades. But it is a profound question. The size of the canvas affects the picture. Give me a blank wall and I will do something different than I will on an eight-by-ten canvas. The entire conceiving of the story, the reporting as well as the writing, depends on a concept of length and shape. Of course, stories will change (grow or shrink) during the reporting or the writing, and then the writer has to consult with the editor to adjust their shared vision of how the story will appear.

Editing During Writing

It is important to write as dumbly as possible, a talent with which I was born and which I have developed through the years, despite teachers and editors. The writer has to give himself or herself over to the story, writing with natural instinct and with the instinct of craft (those skills that have been absorbed into our "natural" writing process). Yet the head intrudes. We stand back from the canvas during the making process, and during those moments we may consider some of the following questions—or hold them until the draft is done.

What's the promise of the lead? It must be fulfilled. Each lead is a contract with the reader. Significance or help or enjoyment or understanding or something else is offered to the reader who stays with the story. We must make sure we can deliver on our promise, or we must go back and write a lead with a promise on which we can deliver.

Does the voice of the story support its meaning? Clever writing or dull writing draws the reader away from the meaning of the story. We must tune our language to the voice appropriate to this story and to our readers. We must never forget that the music of the story is communicating meaning as much as information, organization, documentation, or form—perhaps more.

How does this paragraph move the story forward? When I first started doing magazine pieces, another writer, the late Hannah Lees, gave me a gift. She told me to write one paragraph to a page—and for years I cut paper into half sheets and followed her counsel. I had been writing all over the place, spreading under—and over—developed paragraphs through my drafts (I averaged about thirty per magazine piece).

When I wrote a paragraph to a page, I began to learn the importance of the paragraph and how to develop one idea in a paragraph so that it moved the reader's understanding of the story forward.

Does the pace keep moving the reader forward but allow the reader time to absorb each point? Timing is rarely talked about in writing, but the writer, like the comic, has to pace the delivery so that the reader is not allowed to escape but is allowed time to absorb each point before moving on to the next one. Reading aloud helps the writer to hear and judge the pace.

What would make the reader believe what I'm saying? Most of us grow lazy in documenting our pieces. We grab whatever is handy or what we're comfortable with using, sprinkling our stories with quotes or statistics, anecdotes or references, instead of choosing the appropriate form of evidence to support the point being made.

How can I make the reader care about what I'm saying? Should we appeal to emotions? Yes, if it is appropriate. It is important that we make our readers feel as well as think. They need to meet the people in the story, see the effect of the event on those people, and observe the impact of the story. We should not tell the reader how to feel with summary words (*sad, beautiful, tragic, happy*) but give the reader an experience that will make the reader feel. As Mark Twain said, "Don't say the old lady screamed—bring her on and let her scream."

Does each point answer a reader's question and ask a new one? Remember that each story is a conversation with the reader. The reader isn't passive, but is asking questions. It is your job to anticipate those questions and to answer them.

Editing After Writing

Now the writer steps back and assumes the role of reader. I often role-play a specific person, putting myself in that person's head, and then read the story from their point of view. I pick someone who is intelligent but who does not know or care about the story I have written.

There is a sequence to editing from larger to smaller questions. If you do not know, for example, what the story means, then there is no point in moving forward to fix the language. In fact, since language can only be fixed in relation to meaning it is impossible to revise or edit a story without first knowing what it is supposed to mean.

What does the story say? An effective story has a single, dominant message that can be said in a simple sentence. The meaning of the story should have evolved during the reporting and the writing, but now it is set and that meaning becomes the North Star that guides the writer through all the decisions of rewriting and editing.

Is the message worth saying? If not, what would make it worth saying? Unlike political candidates, we should say something that will serve our readers. If you don't know the significance of the story, you won't be able to make intelligent editorial decisions. Look at the context of the story, the world in which the story exists, to see how the events you are reporting affect that world or the world of your readers.

Is the information in the story accurate in detail and in context? Reading is an act of trust. When you fail to be trustworthy, you lose a reader—usually for good. At *Time*, we were very good at the accuracy of detail and would call an Arab prince at 3:00 A.M. to ask if it was his third or fourth wife and was she wearing real lace, but we were not very good at placing the accurate detail in a proper context. Our task is selection; we choose the fragment to represent the whole. The challenge is to make that representation fair.

Does the form of the story communicate its meaning? We should not forget that form is meaning. How we design the story—on the basis of chronology, personality, or event—supports what we have to say.

Is the voice of the text appropriate, attractive, and consistent? We think of voice as belonging to the writer, but it really belongs to the text. We must make sure that the voice of the text is tuned so that it clarifies, supports, and communicates the meaning.

Does the story deliver an adequate amount of documented information to the reader? Does the form of the documentation vary according to what is being documented? The reader has a hunger for information that will transform him or her into an authority on the subject. Readers read pages that allow them to say to their friends, "Hey, did you know that . . . ?"

Is the pace of the story appropriate to the meaning and effective in keeping the reader reading? Each good piece of writing has its own beat, which speeds up or slows down according to what is being said and how it will be heard by the reader.

Are the reader's questions answered when they are asked? Does the story move logically from lead to end? The effective writer knows where the reader is and what the reader needs to know at any point in the story.

What needs to be added? Most stories are underdeveloped. They do not give the reader a satisfying serving of specific information.

What needs to be cut? To get room for that satisfying information, cut and focus. A focused story has room for depth.

Is each section of the story complete? Does it grow from the previous section and lead the reader to the next section? Longer stories are constructed from units of meaning that satisfy the reader's need to understand part of the story so that they will be able to understand the next part. It may be helpful to check this by asking how each section answers one question and asks a new one that leads the reader to the next section.

Does each paragraph say one thing and develop and document that meaning? Each paragraph should deliver information essential to the development of the section.

Does each sentence contain a meaning that is delivered clearly, simply, accurately, and musically? The sentence is the basic writing unit. Vary your sentences, but build on the sentence-verb-object sentence. The declarative sentence is the cornerstone of a clear style. Read your sentences aloud. They should flow with music that supports and communicates the meaning of the sentence.

Does the length of paragraphs and sentences vary according to the meaning being communicated? Length is usually short for the points of emphasis or complication, longer for material in between. If not, consider their length in terms of their meaning.

Is it possible for the reader to see, hear, touch, smell, and taste the story? When you can alert a reader's senses, the reader will be drawn into the story.

Do the verbs provide energy to the sentences? Active verbs are the engines that drive meaning forward.

Are the nouns specific? The reader's hunger for the specific is rarely satisfied.

Are the adjectives and adverbs necessary? Of course I use both, but never without feeling a tiny sense of failure that I have not found the right noun or verb.

Can the jargon be eliminated? If not, can it be defined immediately, right in the middle of the sentence? As writers, we have an ear for language. It is easy for us to pick up the jargon and clichés of the people we interview. Watch out.

Is each word the right word? A word must be right in terms of meaning—it carries its load of information by connotation and denotation.

Are the traditions of our language broken only to clarify meaning? Language changes under our hands. We accept new forms of language when they communicate meaning with more clarity and grace than traditional usage. Break traditions when it increases communication.

Does the story follow the publication's style book? Most newspapers have a style book—either their own or a general one, such as *Chicago Manual of Style*. Use it.

Have you read the story aloud? Does the story read as if a person were talking with the reader or does it read as if it were made by machine? The ear is the best editor. Read and listen and revise until the text sounds right.

Tuning Your Voice

Listen to writers talk about voice, the music that carries the text to the reader.

Raymond Carver

> I think that a writer's signature should be on his work, just like a composer's signature should be on his work. If you hear a few bars of Mozart, you don't need to hear too much to know who wrote that music, and I'd like to think that you could pick up a story by me and read a few sentences or a paragraph, without seeing the name, and know it was my story.

John Fowles

The most difficult task for a writer is to get the right "voice" for his material. By voice I mean the overall impression one has of the creator behind what he creates.

Michael Harper

You have to shape the word, sing in dimensions, and layer the harmonies and jurisdictions implicit in design. It's a great discovery, the voicing of meaning.

Eudora Welty

Ever since I was first read to, then started reading to myself, there has never been a line read that I didn't hear. As my eyes followed the sentence, a voice was saying it silently to me. It isn't my mother's voice, or the voice of any person I can identify, certainly not my own. It is human, but inward, and it is inwardly that I listen to it. It is to me the voice of the story or the poem itself.

Voice is the most important element in newspaper writing. Reporting produces the accurate, specific, revealing material that is the raw material of good writing, but it is voice that makes the reader understand and care.

Voice illuminates fact; voice makes confusing information clear; voice makes what appears insignificant significant; voice attracts and holds readers, compels readers to think and to feel.

Voice is an individual human voice tuned to the purpose of its message and the ear of the reader. The tuned voice is the voice of the text. That is what the writer listens to while drafting and revising.

Tuning the voice of the text is the most complex writing activity. We must deal with layer upon layer of concern:

- Is this the right word?
- Is this the right word for the words just before it and just after it? Is this the right group of words in a sentence?
- Is this the right sentence for the paragraph?
- Is this the right paragraph for the draft?

We learn to read, write, reread, and rewrite simultaneously just before we start to put words on the page, while we draft or while we revise and edit, working in split seconds between the particular and the whole. And if we are to keep improving as writers we need, from time to time, to go back and consider what we are doing so that we can develop and improve our writing instinct.

The Elements of Voice

It is as difficult to capture voice as it is to bottle the perfume of spring, but I think there are four basic elements in an effective voice:

- *Angle of vision:* where the writer stands in relation to the subject
- *Precision of language:* the right word in relation to the words surrounding it
- *Position of information through language:* to provide emphasis, pace, and flow
- *Music of the text:* carries and supports what is being said

Tuning for angle of vision. Voice begins with the way the writer views the subject. The writer's biography, experience, knowledge of the subject, and attitude toward the subject all affect the writer's voice.

Vantage point
The place where the writer stands will be the place from which the reader views the subject. That place is usually influenced by personal and professional concerns.

Personal
Each of us sees the world in his or her own way. I have a special understanding of the feelings of soldiers in combat since I was in combat fifty years ago. Each of us would use language a bit differently to take advantage of personal vantage points.

Professional
We also see the world as journalists, we know how to view events so that we can run the stream of confusion into a coherent news story, on deadline. We always stand a bit apart, reporting what is going on with some degree of professional detachment, and our voice reflects that attitude.

Focus
Voice selects. The words we use and their setting in phrase, sentence, and paragraph limits the subject and forces the reader to concentrate on significant elements in the story. Voice is framed by our language.

Distance
The writer's voice establishes the distance that the writer, and therefore the reader, stands from the subject; the voice may bring the reader in close and move the reader back in a pattern calculated to reveal meaning.

Tuning for precision. We begin tuning the voice of the text by seeking the right word, the right phrase, the right sentence, the right paragraph.

Accuracy. The reader will not listen to the writer for long if the reader does not trust the writer, and trust is earned by the accuracy of the material the reader knows. If the reader finds the writer making errors of fact, then the reader will not trust anything the writer says. The word—and the evolving combinations of words—that make up the voice must be accurate. Red hair must be red. But truth is not a matter of checking each fact in isolation. When I was at *Time*, a fact checker put a dot over every word. The details were accurate but they were not always (some would say not often) accurate in context. The voice of the text must be tuned so that it can be trusted.

Specificity. A lively voice depends on specific, revealing details. In tuning my voice, I find that one of the elements I concentrate on the most is making the text increasingly specific.

Emphasis. Voice tells the reader what is important, and there are some positions that emphasize information more than others. In a paragraph, for example, the point of the greatest emphasis is at the end, the next greatest in the beginning, the least in the middle. As we tune the voice of the text we move words that emphasize the meaning of the material to those points.

Sequence. The voice of the text moves the reader through the story in a logical manner so that the full meaning of the draft becomes clear under the reader's eye.

Pace. Pace establishes the speed that the reader will move through the text, slowing down, for example, when a complex idea needs to be understood and speeding up during the chase. Voice adjusts the varying speed of the text so that it clarifies meaning.

Flow. Pace is closely allied to flow, the energy that moves the reader through the text in a pleasing and compelling manner.

Readers. Voice anticipates the reader's need for information, the reader's questions, and responds to them. The text is tuned to the reader's ear so that it will be heard in the way the writer desires.

Tuning for Music

Each piece of writing has music, it has melody, it has a beat, it has a sound that the reader hears. It is the challenge of the hearing writer to tune the music in the text's voice so that it clarifies and communicates the meaning of the text.

How you can encourage voice in your writing. Voice is the most personal quality in writing; the writer's voice reveals the writer. To hear your voice, you have to write with your own language, in your own way. That means you have to accept yourself and write in the way that is right for you. Your voice is composed of your ethnic heritage, your family and neighborhood experience, your education, your personality and your professional training. You have to hear your own voice, your natural way of writing so that you know the raw material you have to develop.

Then you have to adapt, or tune, your voice to the text, developing a text voice that expresses the meaning of the draft within all the professional limitations of time, space, tradition, and audience.

How you can encourage voice in others. We tend to try to make everyone the same, to concentrate on a beginning writer's failure to write in the language we expect. If we want to develop voice, we have to look positively at difference, to see what is unusual and specific in the writer's individual way of writing. Then, by respecting that voice, we can teach the writer to respect his or her own voice, to hear it, and then to tune it to the traditions of the writing task. If we are lucky, the writer's individual voice will remain strong and we can encourage the writer to use it to extend those traditions.

Writers Working with Editors

Although I've been married twice, I find the marriage relationship easier than the one between writer and editor. Writers and editors depend on each other; without the writer there is no copy and without the editor there is no publication. But dependency does not necessarily bring respect or affection, in foreign or personal affairs. In fact, need may cause resentment, suspicion, even combat. Yet there is no divorce during the creation of a story for the next edition—writer and editor have to work together.

Entering the Editor's World

To work well with an editor, it is important to practice the reporter's skill of empathy and enter the editor's world. Most writers remind me of a tenor who was listening to the tape playback at an opera recording session. He turned to me and started talking as soon as his last solo was finished. The other performers tried to shush him, but he paid no attention. He told me, "The opera is finished." And it was, for him.

The geography of the editor's world includes:

- Many stories will arrive on deadline or after
- Fear of blankness—an edition that will be published without anything between the advertisements
- A superior editor, or editors, who will second-guess every editorial decision
- An obsession (and an appropriate one) with accuracy in and out of context
- A personal loyalty to journalism's and the publication's traditions
- A belief that the writer gets more attention than he or she deserves while the editor labors in obscurity, salvaging the creative attempts of writers
- A belief that the editor wrote better than these reporters when he or she was a reporter—this belief increases the longer it is since the editor was a reporter

Each editor's geography will change, but most will have these elements and more. It is important for the writer to know each editor's world and to recognize its landmarks. If you can imagine how your editor views the world, you may be able to make better use of that editor, understanding when to stand clear, when to make contact, and how.

Developing the Editor You Need

Every writer needs at least one editor, most of us need two. One is an assigning or developing editor with whom we can consult before and during the writing. Another is a copyeditor who can read with detachment, representing the reader and making sure that the story is clear, graceful, and accurate.

Working out a relationship with an editor is tricky. It is often a matter of personality, and the best way to get around conflicts of personality is to focus on the task at hand: the editing of the text. Few of us can change our personalities, but all of us in this profession have had to learn to work together to produce a daily paper. If we focus on the task, very different personalities can work effectively together.

Once we have established that the text is the focus, then it seems to me that it is the responsibility of the writer to request the editing the writer needs. The editor, of course, has the power to decide if that form of editing is appropriate. But most editors are grateful for clues from the writer as to what the writer needs. An editor, naturally, will handle each story in the manner to which he or she is accustomed. This may lead to problems. The writer is concerned about organization, and the editor focuses on usage. Neither will communicate effectively with the other in such a case.

The range of editing a writer needs is extensive. It varies from writer to writer and task to task.

Idea editing. The writer asks himself or herself, then asks the story editor: "What's the focus of the story? What's the dominant idea? What is the one thing the reader will take from the story? How is the story different from the others we've run on the same subject? Why should anyone read this story? What do you expect the reader to think or feel or do after reading the story? What do you think you (and therefore the reader) may learn from the story?"

Reporting editing. The writer asks himself or herself, then asks the story editor: "What are the sources I need for this story? What written records are available? Whom should I talk to? Who is responsible for the story? Who is affected by the story? Who is for it? Who is against it? What is the face on the story? Who or what is the force behind the scenes? What is the place of the story? How does the place affect the story?"

Structural editing. The writer asks himself or herself, then asks the story editor: "What is the length of the story? What is its form or genre—profile, straight news, reconstruction, analysis? What are the potential leads on the story? What are possible endings? Which main points will get the reader from a lead to an end? Which questions will the reader ask, and in what order will they be asked? What are the proportions of the story from quotation to paraphrase, anecdote to factual analysis, description to narrative?"

Language editing. The writer asks himself or herself, then asks the story editor: "What is the voice that will communicate the meaning of the story most effectively? What is the effect of balance between long and short sentences and paragraphs? What is the pace of the story and how should it change within the story? What can be cut? What needs to be added? What should be put in a different place? What needs to be clarified? What needs to be documented? What needs to be checked for accuracy?"

Each of us should make up our own checklist for our own editing, and each of us should be able to find an editor from whom we can receive the help we need. Often there is a sequence or timing that is required on each story. This may extend over weeks, or take place in three-minute conferences during an afternoon.

Most editors will appreciate such input from the writer. And if they see other problems, they can decide whether to mention them now or wait and see if they get solved along the way. The editor, of course, can also make suggestions in the same tone of consultation and professional respect.

Proposing a Story

I learned the hard way—by bitter misunderstandings, failed stories, and envelopes without checks—when I was freelancing full-time for magazines to write a written proposal on a story idea and, as a newspaper writing coach, I have found this procedure just as important when a reporter is suggesting a major story or series. It was also my habit to write a formal proposal even if the story has been assigned in a face-to-face or telephone conversation. It is also what I do when I have a new editor—a few years ago, because of mergers, I had four editors on one book project!

Here's my formula:

- Include the headline that *may* appear on the story. I want the editor to see the story as it will be seen by the reader.
- Write the lead that *may* appear in the story. I may have to make up an anecdote, or quote, or scene, even some facts, but I am not writing a contract. I am writing a proposal. I want to see the story as a reader may see it, and I want the editor to see that potential story. And I find that a lead, which includes the focus, the tone, and, by implication, the whole shape and length of the story, is the best way to do it.
- Indent and use bullets as I have here, to indicate the three to five main points of the story. I keep them short, tight, and specific. As in the lead, I am not tentative, and I reveal each point in a few lines as it may be revealed to the reader. In the case of a book, I use a chapter title and about five lines under it to show the editor the dimensions and the sequence of the material in the book.
- Write a final paragraph that tells the editor what the editor needs to know. If I have access to the sources in the story, if there is a special history of the publication with the subject of the story, if there is a special audience for the story, if there is a possibility for special art, or whatever. I do *not* lecture the editor, explaining why this story should be published. I try to make those reasons obvious through the information that I have presented to the editor.

I type these proposals single spaced and try to keep them on one page, except when I am proposing a book. I find that the written proposal is far more effective than an oral one. When I talk an idea through, the chance is that the editor hears something different from what I thought the editor heard, and I hear something different from the editor's response than the editor intended. When I create a written text, it forces me to be much clearer in my proposal. I have to anticipate and solve problems. This procedure allows the editor to respond in a much more disciplined way, to propose alternatives, to identify problems, and to make productive suggestions.

The editor who has received such a written proposal may become a supporter of a radically different story from what the writer originally expected. The editor may see, for example, that this story needs to be a narrative, or that it has to be written entirely in dialogue, or that it is appropriate to see the story from only one point of view. If the story is a surprise—a topic or an approach—that is not usually done by the publication, the written proposal allows the editor to consult with her or his superiors.

Thanking Editors

When I first started writing, I thought editors were my enemy, but eventually I learned that I needed editors. Editors allowed me to be more daring, to attempt to write what I have not written before in ways that might not work and I learned that few writers ever thank editors, instead taking their byline and dancing alone in front of the reader. When assigning or copyeditors help me, I thank them after we talk or in a note—and when they help me frequently, a note goes to their editors.

Editors Working with Writers

Editors should also work to have good working relationships with writers. Remember that the more talented the writer, the more insecure the writer. Good writers care about what they have written and need a response. The tendency is for the editor to spend all the time with the problem writers, not realizing that the good writers usually don't know they are good. The confident writers who "know" they are good rarely are. Here are some of the ways editors can cultivate effective and loyal writers.

Invite the Writer to Collaborate

The writer knows the story firsthand. When the story needs to be fixed, resist the instinct to fix it yourself. Suggest the writer collaborate, recommending ways the story may be fixed, and let the writer do the fixing. In this way, the writer learns and the editor may learn as well.

Respond Quickly

At least acknowledge your receipt of the piece, and if it can't be edited promptly, explain why. Silence is always interpreted as rejection by the caring writer.

Describe What Works

Writers need to build on their strengths and they often do not know what those strengths are. They need *specific* praise that points out what works and why.

Describe What Needs Work

Writers need an honest, candid response to their work, but again it must be specific so the writer knows what needs to be edited, and how.

Don't Fear Praise

Many editors fear that praise will produce a prima donna. They don't realize that the best writers need support and encouragement. They will always be humbled by the blank page.

❖ Journalist at Work ❖ EVELYNNE KRAMER Interview

I need editing and I've learned to cultivate editors. I have my horror stories, but they have been rare. On the other hand, working with editors who can get inside my writing and really help me has been equally rare.

Mort Howell, adviser to the newspaper I edited my freshman year in college, could do that. He didn't make me write *his* text, but helped me realize my own. Eddie Devin, assistant city editor on the old *Boston Herald*, was another. Bob Johnson, for whom I wrote my first articles for *The Saturday Evening Post*, and Walter Ross of *Coronet* were others. Linda Buchanan Allen, now a writer but formerly an editor at Houghton Mifflin, was another editor who taught me. Laurie Runion of Harcourt, now a freelance editor, and Tom Newkirk, editor for this book and others of mine, have all been collaborators in my work. I am fortunate to have Jim Concannon as the editor of my *Globe* column, a task Evelynne Kramer had for years before she moved on to edit the *Globe Magazine* and then take early retirement.

Evelynne Kramer was a professional. She was graduated from Syracuse University and worked at the *Syracuse Herald-Journal*, the *Binghamton Evening Press*, the *Daily Hampshire Gazette*, and the *Springfield Union* before joining *The Boston Globe*, where she has held many jobs including city editor, State House editor, city hall editor, regional editor, and an editor of the focus section before coming to the living arts section.

Q: *What do you know about editing now that you wish you had known when you began editing?*

A: I think editing requires patience and that editors need to think about long-term goals with a writer—not just working with the story that's on the screen. We can all get better at what we do, but improvement sometimes takes a lot of time and more often than not, in fits and starts. Patience, alas, has never been my long suit; it's something I've had to work on.

I have also learned that nobody wants to hear what's wrong with a story before he or she hears what's right with it. It's sometimes easy for editors to forget that under the pressure of deadlines, but I think learning to focus on what works in a story is critical to building an effective relationship with a writer.

Q: *I depend on hearing that you think a column or a feature works before you go through the copy with me. I smile because I know the pattern, but I confess that I need it. I know what may be wrong better than I know what works. Will you describe how the editor's role changes as you move from giving an assignment to editing final copy? What is the most important editing skill at each stage?*

A: During the assignment, an editor needs to be able to communicate the premise of a story, but that's only half of it. The editor also needs to listen to the writer's ideas, to sort out what the writer thinks the story might be, and even to be prepared to change the direction of a story totally.

Figuring out how an assignment is proceeding also calls on the editor to listen, concentrate, and respond with confidence to new information. What surprises the editor can be a clue to how to structure the story or how to write the lead.

The final editing of a story takes what we used to call pencil skills, the ability to see what the writer is up to and to help the writer achieve that on his or her own terms. It all has to make sense to the reader, of course, or it's all for naught.

Q: *Once you suggested that I toss out a column and start over. It was done so gracefully that I got all excited about writing a new draft. How do you deliver bad news so the writer isn't discouraged and will be motivated to revise or do better next time?*

A: As an editor, that's one of the hardest things to learn to do, and many times I have not done it as gracefully as I should.

The first step is to reassure the writer that it is all going to turn out all right, that you are an ally in the process, and that you are not going to leave the writer hanging out to dry, even if—as was the case in your column—you think a complete rewrite is needed. Writers also need to know that you have confidence in their ability, and that you and the writer are in it together.

I have learned a lot about giving feedback from my music teacher. First, you have to understand that I have no musical talent even though I have enjoyed fooling around with the piano for years. Bruce, my teacher, somehow encourages me to keep going, to try again even when I have screwed up badly. Part of his technique is to find something I did right and comment on it. Then, he can launch into a discussion, usually long, of what I did wrong.

Q: *I've talked about the attitudes I try to bring to the editor/writer relationship. What attitudes do you hope the editor will bring to the editor/writer encounter?*

A: I think it is important for the editor to respect the writer and to communicate that respect honestly and clearly. Respect is independent of whether you agree or disagree about an approach to a story.

Q: *And what attitudes do you hope the writer will bring to the editor/writer encounter?*

A: Ditto. I think it is important for writers to respect their editors. I don't know as much about the subject matter as any of the writers I work with, but I hope I know something about editing, and that can help the writer and ultimately the reader.

Q: *All my writing life I have suffered from editors who bring preconceptions to the reading of my copy that make the editing a nightmare. You are just the opposite. You are able to read my copy on its own terms and make suggestions within my context and voice. How do you do this?*

A: Accepting a writer's voice has a lot to do with accepting a writer. It's really about accepting people for who they are, not what you want them to be. What more can I say about this? When it comes right down to it, this has a lot to do with learning to accept yourself, and that's a lifelong task. I'm better at it now than I used to be.

Q: *What response do you think editors need from writers?*

A: I think editors need to hear when they have done something right, when they've improved a story, come up with a good idea, or helped a writer get better. Editors need encouragement almost as much as writers;

if writers want their editors to be there for them, they need to tell them when they've done something right.

Q: *You've been responsible for many lively stories in* Food, At Home, *and* Living. *What are the elements of a good story idea? What techniques do you have for fitting writer to idea or vice versa? How do you encourage ideas from writers?*

A: A good story surprises the reader. A good story idea surprises me. It's been a lot of fun to encourage some new thinking about the kind of story that belongs in Food and At Home. I like to think most of us can write from our own lives from time to time, and I like to encourage writers to think about their own experiences as a starting point. Some of the most talked-about stories we've done in these sections (Nick King's piece on single dads comes to mind) were born over a casual conversation about ordinary activities.

Our readers need to laugh and they need to see themselves in the newspaper. I would like to think they can do both in these sections.

Q: *Let's talk about leads: What do you like in a lead? Dislike? What's often missing? How can an editor or writer sharpen a lead?*

A: A lead is an invitation to read on. Sometimes, the story calls for a clearly written hard-news approach, sometimes, a more leisurely pace. It's hard to generalize, but I thing an effective lead makes me want to know more. Taking a second look at a lead minutes, or hours, later can help you see something that was missing or help you fix a phrase that falls flat. It's that second reading that's really helpful.

Q: *How have you trained yourself to read with such care? Do you read aloud? What do you do so you can hear the draft?*

A: I think most editors develop an ear with practice. If I sense a problem with a sentence, I read it over several times very slowly, sometimes aloud, to try to figure out where it breaks down. Interestingly, many writers are not surprised when you point to a paragraph that is a clunker. They already may have had a sense that something wasn't working.

Q: *What do you do when you read a draft that has serious organizational problems? What tricks of your trade have you developed to bring order to chaos or to help the writer bring order to chaos?*

A: If I sense a problem, I usually try to break the story down into an outline—to see the parts of a whole. Then I try to figure out whether there is a logical progression of ideas—whether my questions get answered as they come to me. If they don't I am likely to suggest a refiguring of the piece.

Q: *I hate to admit it, but I live for your praise. I'm not proud of being a dancing bear, but I am. Will you say something about the importance of telling a writer what works as well as what doesn't work and how an editor can do it?*

A: There is always something that works with a story and that is a good starting point, as I've said. It's important for an editor to be honest about this, though, because false praise serves neither the writer nor editor. Writers can see right through it, and that can damage your credibility pretty quickly. You've got to focus on something that really does distinguish the piece and go from there.

❖ Journalist at Work ❖ Case History of a DONALD M. MURRAY Column

My weekly "Over 60" columns for the *Globe* usually begin with the ordinary. My eye catches a glint from an insignificant element in my life or the lives of those around me, and I see it suddenly with humor, anger, sadness, amusement, nostalgia, or concern. Emotion gives it significance.

Right here my writing of the case history was justified: I had never before fully understood the role emotion plays in making me see a story where I had not seen a story before. I wrote the last sentence and found it true when I read it. It reminds me to pay attention to how emotion focuses my attention. I may see more stories I have overlooked.

When I got home on Wednesday night recently I discovered I had left my daybook and date book at the *Globe*. Total panic. I didn't know what I had to do the next day, who to see, what to write. I called Tom Mulvoy and he understood! They were found and sent overnight. I noticed how dependent I, and my wife, had become on our notes to ourselves, our lists, our calendars.

I recommend having a special notebook or file cards or using your reporter's notebook to write down fragments that may become the germ of future stories. Writing them helps you remember them and often a special twist is added in the transcription.

As should happen to all of us on all stories, the material around us begins to organize itself into a pattern. I made a note in my daybook Thursday morning: "you can tell the old ones—we leave a trail of notes." That's enough to hold the idea in place. I might write about it this week or next August.

The next morning my eye caught that line, and I took about five or six minutes to draft the following on the word processor:

You can always find those of us who are Over Sixty. We leave a trail of paper.

We make notes in planners, on calendars, on 3 by 5 cards, in memo books, on the backs of envelopes, on the edges of paper torn from newspapers and magazines, on the backs of other notes, on re-recycled paper, on small colored pads of paper and on large white pads of paper.

We stick yellow notes, small medium and large, to the door where we will see them when we go out; to the door where we will see them on the way in. We put them on telephones, the refrigerator we still call the ice-box, on books, on the TV screen, on kitchen cabinets, on headboards and bureau, on chairs, cabinet doors, chair backs, on the auto dashboard.

[My wife added, in piles on the floor.]

But we never find the right note . . .

The three dots are a signal to myself that I may develop this or drop it or leave it.

And if we find an interesting one, it blurs. I wear tri-focals (which should be called try focals).

Try-focals *was a typo. I liked it. Some of my best writing comes from typos. I wonder if I would write as well as I do if I couldn't type.*

My neck clicks as I try one focal, then another and another, finally take them off and focus by placing the tip of my nose at the edge of the note.

Fifteen minutes later when I walk into the coffee table I try to find where I have put my glasses but that is another column.

When I do get the notes in range, I face problems in translation. Here are some recent examples from our home:

"Jfpx called. Pls call back at 779-8py8."

[278 – 25 = 253 of 800]

I always try to stop a draft at a point where I have a pretty good idea of what I'm going to do next if I am interrupted. That makes it easier to get back into the text.

The cryptic note at the end indicates I'm trying to satisfy my editor's request for 800 words, or more.

This came easily. It was ripe. If it hadn't come easily, I would have dumped it. If the idea has validity, it will come again. If I had to write on assignment and the lead didn't come easily, I would draft a dozen, fifteen, two-dozen leads as fast as possible, about three minutes each, until I got one I could go with. The time spent on leads speeds up the rest of the writing for me. What I was looking for was a voice for this text. I think I found it—and my first reader, my wife, agrees—but I will not know until I write it and my editor reads and responds.

Here is my first draft, warts and all:

> You can always find those of use who are Over Sixty. We leave a trail of paper.
>
> We make notes in planners; on calendars; on 3 by 5 cards; in memo books; on the backs of envelopes, sales slips, doctors' appointment cards; on the edges of paper torn from newspapers and magazines; on the back of other notes; on re-recycled paper; on small colored pads of paper; on long, yellow legal pads; on the telephone message, stationery, pads of paper we were "given" by our employer in the years before we retired.
>
> We stick yellow notes, small medium and large, to the door where we will see them when we go out; to the door where we will see them on the way in. We put them on telephones, use magnets to attach them to the refrigerator we still call the ice-box, on books, on the TV screen, on kitchen cabinets, on headboard and bureau, on chairs, cabinet doors, chair backs, on the auto dashboard, in piles on the floor where we may see them as we step around the other stuff we've left on the floor so that we will see it.

But if we find a note that looks interesting, it blurs. I wear tri-focals [which should be called try focals]. My neck clicks as I try one focal, then another and another, finally taking them off and focus by placing the top of my nose at the edge of the note.

Fifteen minutes later when I walk into the coffee table I realize I'm unglassed and try to remember where I have put my spectacles but that is another column.

When I do get the notes in range, I face problems in translation. Here are some recent examples from our home:

- "Jfpx called. Pls call back 779-8py8."
- "Ripe shoes."
- "Car needs introspection. Lube loys torque."
- "Frg773x's birthday. Hurry anniversary. Gift?"
- "Bk. Monster cd. py due."
- "A peel tx asses 4 pm. Bring s5ttly fl."
- "Bnans. Oat mgrp. chp wne. rgyt juc."
- "Call frd abt slumba prty."
- "Put inbgyttr in mal. tdy."
- "Wagratater!!!!!"

My wife starts laughing to herself in the car. That's less worrisome than when she laughs in her sleep and can't remember why. "Why are you laughing?"

"Do you remember the Palmer Method?"

"Hours upon hours of making circles on the ball of your forearm."

"Your what?"

"That's what I used to ask but every teacher in our school knew what it meant."

"Could you read what they wrote on the board?"

"Sometimes."

And we both laughed. But it isn't funny when you are Over Sixty and can't remember if you keep a cat.

At our age, forgetting why you are standing in the hardware store or who you promised to call on the phone or the name of your best friend, brings terror.

Is it the first sign of what is it, that terrible disease we used to call sen something. Oh yes, senility. What's the other one? Al something, Alzheimer's? That's it.

I hear my self laughing nervously. Talking to yourself is one thing. Laughing out loud in an empty room is . . . Well, black humor worked in combat, I'll try in the Golden Years. There is absolutely nothing funny about Alzheimer's, but if I don't laugh, I'll whimper.

Still I need more comfort and I think back when I was young and my mind drifted off in class, how the coach would find me staring through a window he couldn't see during practice (sometimes in a game), how many times mother had to remind me to take out the garbage, how my sergeants used their own gentle forms of persuasion to get my attention when I forgot I was involved in participatory patriotism.

But returning to who I was as a teenager when I walked around gap-mouthed trying to find out where to put my hands and how the world worked wasn't very comforting.

Then I was saved by a news story. A California professor, Lofti A. Zadeh, has developed a computer theory called fuzzy logic. He has been scorned in the U.S. but Japan is using his fuzzy logic computer program to run trains, and they have just established a Laboratory for International Fuzzy Engineering Research with 36 million dollars.

I've got it. Mature memory is a higher form of thinking made necessary by a brain filled to capacity with wisdom. The resulting fuzzy memory leads directly to fuzzy thinking and we'll find out what that means when I get the Center for Fuzzy Thinking funded. No one under sixty need apply.

[752 words]

Now I'll read it through, run the spell check program, and have my wife read it. I made only a few changes, just a touch of fine tuning here and there for clarification and a bit more to make sure the reader doesn't think I think Alzheimer's is funny.

Here I did something unusual. I submitted the column in draft to several of the seminars of *Globe* writers and editors and received several suggestions. I wish I had the time to have a panel of writers and editors read everything I write. Books these days sometimes get so little editing; I have to exploit my friends to help me see my draft anew.

Here are what my readers said:

- Some thought the lead was especially good. One said it wasn't only Over Sixty who leave trails of paper. True, but I'm writing the "Over Sixty" column and focusing on the impact at that age.
- Many liked the way I let the detail pile up. They though I paced that well, that it needed such length to have an impact. Several liked *ice-box* and *auto dashboard,* terms no young writer would use. One said too much, too much. I had wondered if it was too much myself and I had thought of new things to add. I read it carefully and made changes.
- The list got a lot of attention. Everyone liked it but some were confused and I had to make sure they got the joke. Will cut *slumba party*. It takes the reader off on an imaginary trip, as it suggests an orgy of old-timers in Doctor Denton's. My editor, who was part of the seminar, wanted four items, others wanted six, but most wanted fewer than my ten.
- Most of the *Globe* seminar members were too young to remember the Palmer Method. ALL people over sixty will remember, but I have young readers, too. Can I sneak in a definition? Is it worth saving or should I cut it all?

- We had an interesting discussion at the point when I said that we oldies fear forgetting because it seems a symptom of Alzheimer's. Some thought I should set up the terror of memory loss when you are over sixty more dramatically. I thought that was a given in my audience and I could play on terror they have. No need to dramatize it. I promised to read it through carefully to decide who's right.
- One writer thought I could cut the last line of the paragraph beginning "Is it the first sign . . ." and the last sentence of the column. I agreed.
- I worried that I might offend somebody who has Alzheimer's in their family. No one thought I would. It was very important for me to hear that. Many times someone else will catch a tone or a hidden insensitivity of which I am not aware.
- A couple of readers thought I could cut the teenage stuff. Another writer pointed out that the sentence beginning "But returning . . ." made the reader take a long trip between subject and verb. I agreed instantly, knowing if I kept it, I'd clean it up. One editor strongly urged me to include a note on the research that explains why we lose memory as we age. I considered both suggestions seriously, knowing I could not make the decision on the teenager stuff until I had done the research on the other issue. If I include that research, it may affect the tone, length, proportion, and pace of the column.

I edited the column, accepting, adapting, or discarding their comments. Discarding after careful consideration. If one person misreads what I've read, I don't get defensive. If one person misses the point, others may.

I thought I was done with the column and moved it into the appropriate file directory on my computer. Here's the column after my editing.

> You can always find those of use who are Over Sixty. We leave a trail of paper.
>
> We make notes in planners; on calendars; on 3 by 5 cards; in memo books; on the backs of envelopes, sales slips, doctors' appointment cards; on the edges of paper torn from newspapers and magazines; on the back of other notes; on re-recycled paper; on small colored pads of paper; on long, yellow legal pads; on the office stationery we "borrowed" before retiring.
>
> We stick yellow notes, small medium and large, to the door where we will see them when we go out; to the door where we will see them on the way in. We put them on telephones, use magnets to attach them to the refrigerator we still call the ice-box, on bookmarks, on the TV screen, on kitchen cabinets, on headboard and bureau, on chairs, cabinet doors, chair backs, on the auto dashboard, in piles on

the floor where we may see them as we step around the other stuff we've left on the floor so that we will see it.

But if we find a note that looks interesting, it blurs. I wear tri-focals (which should be called try focals). My neck clicks as I try one focal, then another and another, finally taking them off and focus by placing the tip of my nose at the edge of the note.

Fifteen minutes later when I walk into the coffee table I realize I'm unglassed and try to remember where I have put my spectacles but that is another column.

When I do get the notes in range, I face problems in translation. Here are some recent examples from our home:

- "Jfpx called. Pls call back 779-8py8."
- "Ripe shoes."
- "Car needs introspection. Lube loys torque."
- "Mail cat. Rtrn old stmach. Nude dinr tnite."

My wife starts laughing to herself in the car. That's less worrisome than when she laughs in her sleep and can't remember why. "Why are you laughing?"

"Do you remember the Palmer Method of penmanship?"

"Hours upon hours of making circles on the ball of your forearm."

"Your what?"

"That's what I used to ask but every teacher in our school knew that it meant your forearm muscle."

"Could you read what they wrote on the board?"

"Sometimes."

And we both laughed. But it isn't funny when you are over sixty and can't remember if you keep a cat.

At our age, forgetting why you are standing in the hardware store or who you promised to call on the phone or the name of your best friend, brings terror.

Is it the first sign of what is it, that terrible disease we used to call sen something. Oh yes, senility. What's the other one? Al something?

I hear myself laughing nervously. Talking to yourself is one thing. Laughing out loud in an empty room is . . . Well, black humor worked in combat, I'll try it in the Golden Years. There is absolutely nothing funny about Alzheimer's, but if I don't laugh, I'll whimper.

Still I need more comfort and I think back when I was young and my mind drifted off in class, how the coach would find me staring through a window he couldn't see during practice (sometimes in a game), how many times mother had to remind me to take out the garbage, how my sergeants used their own gentle forms of persuasion to get my attention when I forgot I was involved in participatory patriotism.

But returning to who I was as a teenager when I walked around gap-mouthed trying to find out where to put my hands and how the world worked wasn't very comforting.

Authorities say that memory loss is normal and that it shouldn't cause panic. When you relax the names will come to you. They may be right. I remember them at 3 the next morning when I no longer remember what I wanted to do with the name.

B. F. Skinner, now 85, says that we oldies forget names "because names have so little going for them by way of context."

I have a different theory. A California professor, Lofti A. Zadeh, has developed a computer theory called fuzzy logic. He has been scorned in the U.S. but Japan is using his fuzzy logic computer program to run trains, and they have just established a Laboratory for International Fuzzy Engineering Research with 36 million dollars.

I've got it. Mature memory is a higher form of thinking made necessary by a brain filled to capacity with wisdom. The resulting fuzzy memory leads directly to fuzzy thinking and we'll find out what that means when I get the Center for Fuzzy Thinking funded. No one under sixty need apply.

Then I read it over. I started making little changes, a comma here, a dash; then I came to the word *translation* and in fixing that I began to play with the text.

A reading by a colleague or an editor will often make me return to the text to see new possibilities in it. My editor liked the column, but in "fixing" it, the text started in a new direction and I followed. I always follow the text when it moves under my hand. I may not go where it goes, but I have to follow to see where it wants to take me. More often than not, the text knows where I should go better than I do.

I was having fun and what I sent in was changed—for the better, I think. My editor was surprised but pleased. She said, "This proves good writing is rewriting." We made a few minor changes and this is how it was published April 11, 1989. The revision only took about half an hour, but it was fun to do and I think the result was a better column.

I can't remember when my own rewriting of an article, poem, or book (fiction or nonfiction) didn't make it better. (I need editors to question my drafts and make suggestions, but editors' revisions of what I thought was my final draft haven't always been successful in my opinion.) I don't do as much rewriting now as I did when I was freelancing magazine articles and went through each one thirty times. Much of my writing is first draft these days. After fifty years of rewriting, and being rewritten, I should be able to produce a good first draft once in awhile.

Chapter 9

How to Remain an Apprentice

The danger is accomplishment. Once we learn how to do something, the tendency is to keep doing it. We lose the terror of early days and become content. We no longer fail and therefore escape the essential instruction of failure. We take no risks.

I remember my first months in the city room, where every reporting and writing task seemed a mystery, a task beyond my grasp. Then I feared failure and did not realize how valuable it was. I was beaten into shape by a hard-eyed gang of critical editors who pointed out what was wrong, usually in shouts hurled from city desk to copy desk, a teaching by public humiliation.

I expected this sort of instruction and it bothered me but I could take it. I'd been writing since I could remember. I'd flunked out of high school and gotten into a junior college partly on the basis of football where the coach's yells were better than his cleats in my rear. I'd survived the subtle encouragement of paratroop training and had real Germans fire real ammunition at me. What surprised me was how short my newspaper apprenticeship was. In less than a year, I became one of the boys—a sexist but accurate term—then, took no risks and received no criticism.

Then I became truly scared. I was an old-timer and I was only twenty-five years old. Some fortunate instinct, perhaps a stubborn Scots gene, made me realize that I had to keep teaching myself, that I had both to meet and to exceed the standards of my editors. I reverted to the apprenticeship that has lasted into my mid-seventies and now know will continue as long as I can breathe. I am forever grateful that I will never learn to write but that I will keep on learning.

Rejecting Rejection

When someone tells me she or he wants to become a published writer, I tell them: "Remember that all the acceptances are as irrational as the rejections." Writing is not a rational business.

For decades I tried to decode rejections for lessons in writing. There are none—or damned few. When Max Ways at *Time* made a glider out of a short piece of mine and sailed it out the twenty-eighth floor window in Rockefeller Center saying, "Why, Murray, do you always give me first-draft shit?" I had no answer. I wasn't going to tell him it was my fourteenth draft! I learned some things about Max as an editor but nothing about writing.

The reasons my pieces were rejected—and there were periods when I was a full-time freelance magazine writer that two out of three *assigned* articles were rejected—were rarely a matter of talent, most often a matter of inventory, a change in editors, a merger of publications, a new policy, a news break, something not directly connected with my draft.

Of course I didn't know this for years—for decades—and kept looking for lessons in the notes or rejection conversations I had with editors. Most were polite but dishonest. When I was a teenager or dating between marriages, young women did not say no by saying, "You look funny"; "You have horrible breath"; "You are borrrrrring." They said they were busy, were moving to New York, or were not yet ready—for what I never knew. Editors read a draft, don't want a particular manuscript and make up a polite reason that will allow the writer to submit again.

I kept thinking my problem was lack of talent but then one day, I realized that much of my best work was being turned down and my worst was being published and praised. One magazine said I couldn't write medical articles and another said I could *only* write medical stories. A novel in which the hero became a quadriplegic in the first chapter was rejected at lunch by an editor who couldn't stand illness, and accepted that same afternoon by an editor who was a hypochondriac and loved illness. The book that launched me into writing more than sixteen editions of a dozen or more books—this one included—on writing and the teaching of writing was rejected *and* accepted by the same publishing house! I won the Pulitzer Prize once but similar work was submitted the year before and other work has been submitted four times since.

If the editor, however, says, "I'll publish this if . . ." then you must pay attention to the editor—and to yourself—to see if you can discover the piece you can and want to write that the editor will want to accept and publish. I now know the rejection does not mean that I am without talent, that I cannot write, that I have nothing worth saying on the subject. It only means that this particular editor didn't think this particular draft worked at this particular time for this particular publisher. Will I try another draft? I will *try* to discover another draft by writing one, but accepted or rejected, it will not prove whether or not I am a writer. I am a writer. I write—and writing is the answer to rejection. Write what you have to write and send it out knowing that "all the acceptances are as irrational as the rejections."

Learning from Others

As we continue our lifelong apprenticeship to writing, we should keep an eye on the others at the workbench. Their way of working, their failures and accomplishments, their materials and their ideas should all stimulate our craft now and in the future. Sometimes, in working on a solution in writing I will realize that I have been influenced by something I read years ago. It may be a form, a voice, a pattern of print on a page, a character, a point of view, all sorts of things that come to me in another form to solve a different problem. We acquire this knowledge of our craft in many ways and store it away unconsciously more than consciously.

Reading Writing

The journalist is experienced at skimming through newspapers, magazines, online publications, books and then like a cormorant, diving suddenly down into the text, surfacing with a wiggling mouthful of fish. In college, I studied with literature teachers who demanded slow reading. I never thought Mort Howell would let us escape Egdon Heath in Hardy's *Return of the Native*. I marked that book up in his class fifty-seven years ago and I can see its green cover on my shelf as I type this sentence.

Journalists are scavengers who haunt magazine stores, buy newspapers while traveling, browse in libraries and bookstores and the bookshelves in friends' houses for what they do not know, something that catches their eye or mind, a subject they are writing about, or a way of writing that seems different, interesting, perhaps useful someday.

We need to read the old masters—Montaigne and Orwell—and the new masters—Dillard and Didion. We need to read what is popular and unpopular, traditional and untraditional, what puts us off as well as what pulls us in.

The following three books should also be on the desks of all of us who are apprenticed to this craft:

- *The Art of the Personal Essay—An Anthology from the Classical Era to the Present,* edited by Phillip Lopate, A Teachers and Writers Collaborative Book, Anchor Books/Doubleday, 1994.

- *The Art of Fact—A Historical Anthology of Literary Journalism*, edited by Kevin Kerrane and Ben Yagoda, Scribner, 1997.
- *Telling Stories Taking Risks: Journalism Writing at the Century's Edge*, editor by Alice M. Klement and Carolyn Matalene, Wadsworth, 1998.

Recently two journals have begun publishing, to which working journalists should subscribe:

- *Creative Nonfiction*, edited by Lee Gutkind: available through the Creative Nonfiction Foundation, 5501 Walnut Street, Suite 202, Pittsburgh, Pennsylvania 15232
- *Fourth Genre*, edited by Michael Steinberg: available through Michigan State University Press, 1405 South Harrison Road, 25 Manly Miles Building, East Lansing, Michigan 48823

I am always surprised by how much I can learn from bad writing. Nothing is hidden. The backstage pulleys and sets are all on view. Bad books can often teach what—obviously—we should do and—more obviously—what we should not do. And we should read great writing, writing that we will never be able to equal because, in some strange way we do not understand, all the writers I know are inspired by writing that is better than theirs. Perhaps they should read and quit, but instead they read and go to their computers.

Reading About Writing

There is a vast literature about our craft that many journalists do not know of and explore. Each good bookstore has a section of books on the writer's craft and it is true that the majority of these books are purchased by those who want to become writers but to remain an apprentice writer, I maintain and read a large library of books about the writing craft.

Some of the best books about writing as a journalist are:

1. *Reporting and Writing: Basics for the 21st Century*, by Christopher Scanlan, Harcourt, 2000. This basic textbook written by a practicing journalist and teacher of professional journalists covers all the important aspects of journalism today. I have learned from reading this book as will both beginners and experienced professionals.
2. *Best Newspaper Writing*, a series of annual books that began in 1979, edited in different years by Roy Peter Clark, Don Fry, Karen F. Brown, and Christopher Scanlan, is available through The Poynter Institute for Media Studies, 801 Third Street South, St. Petersburg, Florida 33701 and Bonus Books, Inc., 160 East Illinois Street, Chicago, Illinois 60611. This series should be on the shelf of every

serious journalist. It reprints the stories of the annual reporting and writing winners of the American Association of Newspaper Editors together with craft interviews that discuss the making of the stories with instructive detail.

3. *On Writing Well: The Classic Guide to Writing Nonfiction*, sixth edition, by William Zinsser, Harper, 1998. William Zinsser is a master journalist and his book is one that instructs me each time I read one of the several editions I have in my library.
4. *The Writing Trade—A Year in the Life of a Writer* by John Jerome, Lyons & Burford, 1992. I have enormous respect for the craft of John Jerome and learn from it each time I reread one of his books. Here he tells what it is like to be a nonfiction writer, good, bad, and in between, which I find authoritative and helpful.
5. *How to Write* by Richard Rhodes, William Morrow, 1995; and *Follow the Story: How to Write Successful Nonfiction* by James B. Stewart, A Touchstone Book, 1998. In these two books, two of the most prolific and respected nonfiction writers—both have won the Pulitzer Prize—allow us to follow them as they report and write. We are taken behind the scenes by two master journalists and allowed to see them at work in commentary that is never patronizing and always instructive.
6. *Bird by Bird—Some Instructions on Writing* and Life by Anne Lamott, Pantheon, 1994; and *The Writing Life* by Annie Dillard, HarperCollins, 1998. These two books by exceptionally skilled writers extend the limits of traditional journalism and are filled with wise, inspiring counsel.
7. *Working at Writing: Columnists and Critics Composing* by Robert L. Root, Jr., Southern Illinois University Press, 1991. The author studies working columnists and critics using the academic discipline of case study. Although the work is done for the academy, it is never academic and is constantly helpful to the lifelong apprentice.
8. *http://www.projo.com/words.* There has been an explosion of Web sites concerned with writing that lead to other Web sites. One of the best on journalistic reporting and writing is this one run by the *Providence Journal.*

Reading the Other Arts

Journalists should not restrict themselves to reading journalism, but explore the worlds of poetry, fiction, drama, biography, memoir, autobiography, history, and science. Journalists also should read film, television, and radio. I believe I have learned a great deal about writing by studying art and listening to music. The techniques of one art are increasingly being utilized in another.

Writing Colleagues

I write alone but I am not alone. As I writer, I am aware of my writing colleagues and how they may have solved a similar problem or how they would smile or shake their heads in despair at what I have just done on the page.

These are the people with whom I share the victories and defeats of the writing life, people to whom I can talk in professional jargon—voice, what works, kicker and *nut graf*—about what I have to write and how I may write it. E-mail has been a blessing for me. I live in New Hampshire but my colleagues write in Florida, Utah, Ohio, New York, Idaho, Texas, Arizona, Maine, Michigan, Nova Scotia, Australia, and Massachusetts as well as my home state.

I am, however, increasingly careful about who I ask to read my drafts. Chip Scanlan, the person I ask most frequently, lives in Florida. I have discovered it is important for the writer to request the reading the writer needs—for voice, order, development, pace, proportion, or line-by-line editing.

Writing Communities

I have belonged to a number of writing groups during my professional career. Last year I left a poetry group with whom I had written for years and I have just joined a fiction group.

Advantages. The advantages for me is that the group deadline makes me write more than I would without it. I enjoy the companionship of other writers with whom I can share my particular—and often peculiar—little victories: a line that works, a word that surprises, a phrase that turns me in a new direction. The group understands.

I find most of the criticism—including my own comments on the writings of others—less helpful. We are trained by school to be critics and so we fire away. Much of it, in my case, is off-target because the critic does not understand—or agree with—the context of the piece, its purpose, history, prospective audience, stage in the development of the writer.

I do find, however, that I am often helped by what seems to work for the group members. I usually know what isn't working but often do not know what is.

Dangers. Since writers are by nature insecure and writing is by nature individual, the writing group member may take incompetent, irrelevant, ignorant, even mean and competitive criticism seriously and be silenced or made to write in a way that does not fit the writer.

Rules. There are a few rules that I have found helpful:

- Everyone writes. Those who write least or not at all become the harshest critics.
- The writer runs the session, setting the agenda and telling the group what kind of reading the writer needs.
- The group members note what works before what doesn't work.
- Drafts are distributed before the meeting.

Test. The test for me always is whether I feel like writing when I leave the meeting. If I do, I return; if I do not, I do not return.

Learning from Yourself

To maintain your essential apprenticeship you have to be both teacher and learner. You have to lose yourself in the draft—and then step back and see it as an observer. You need to be aware of yourself as a maker, constantly recording what you are doing and how you are doing it.

What Works

We learn best by first developing our strengths. We should take note of what we do well and how we do it. We should have a remembered or written history that extends from the moment we had the idea or were given an assignment to the final editing. We should also be aware of all that surrounds the writing: our tools, where and when we wrote, the nature of our discussions with editors or test-reader colleagues, the pace of work, the length of work sessions, the time of day, everything that influenced our writing task or our feelings about the evolving task.

What Needs Work

We should also be aware of what needs work and select at least one problem in each project to work on: how we use statistics, attribution, quotations, scenes, exposition, documentation, liveliness.

Risk

I try to take an identifiable risk on each project. These may be small, technical challenges such as using stronger verbs than usual or a larger one—writing an entire column in dialogue. My colleague, the late novelist and short story writer Thomas Williams, said that you should have one technical problem to solve—one thing to try or to learn in each piece of writing. I try to remember his counsel.

Daybooks, Notebooks, and Journals

I am in my 106th daybook. This is where I talk to myself about writing, begin drafts, make notes and outlines, put down observations, store ideas. I am too well married to keep a diary and I grow unbearably pompous when I try to keep a journal. My eight-by-ten spiral bound, eighty-page National notebook with narrow ruled "Eye-Ease" paper is a field book, a log, a lab book that helps me learn from what I am doing.

Exploring the Interior Landscape

I have also taught myself by exploring the interior landscape. I left the battlefield in 1945, but I still walk that battlefield in my pages more than half a century later. I go further back in time to my childhood and school to discover what I need to write. I keep exploring my craft and now I not only age, but write a column and a book about my own aging and my reaction to it.

Making Writing Easy

Many writers whimper and whine about how hard it is to write. They should go into real estate. Writing—and any other craft that presumes to be art—should be play more than work.

I've worked hard to make writing easy, to be fluent, to let the draft flow toward its own meaning, to make writing a process of discovery of content and of craft.

nulla dies sine linea

The first lesson in making writing easy is to write every day. Habit is far more important than talent. If it is your habit to write—usually at the same time and place—then you will write.

Break Down Long Projects into Short Ones

Books are written one page at a time. One of the most productive writers of our time tries for three pages a day. "I set that quota for myself many years ago," Updike explains, "and it seems to be about right. It's not so much that you're overwhelmed by it, and it's not so little that you don't begin to accumulate a manuscript."

Know Tomorrow's Task Today

I don't know what I will say when I write tomorrow, but when I leave my writing desk I know tomorrow's writing task and my subconscious grinds away so that when I return to my writing desk and turn on the faucet, words pour out.

Scheduled Time

I write best in the morning and since an hour and a half is about my most effective period, I try to schedule three hours so the writing period is insulated.

Fragmentary Time

Much of my most important writing, however, is done away from the writing desk in my daybook, on the three-by-five cards I carry in my shirt pocket and in my mind, in slivers of distraction when I do not see the TV screen, look up from the book I am reading, stare across the restaurant, turn down the wrong road. I accomplish a lot of writing because I make good use of three, seven, two, ten minutes.

Let the Writing Instruct

Writing solves my writing problems. My writing improves my writing. I sit down not knowing what to say or how to say it and the writing, draft after draft, tells me what I know and how to share it with those who do not have the good fortune of spending a life apprenticed to the writer's craft.

❖ Journalist at Work ❖ MARY SIT Interview

I admired Mary Sit, who is now a business writer with *The Houston Chronicle*, for her ability to do a range of complex stories in a manner that enticed me into reading them and allowed me to understand them. When she was interviewed, Mary was a new member of the *Globe* staff and looked at her job from that perspective.

Sit is a native Texan who grew up in Houston, Japan, Hong Kong, Taiwan, and England. She was graduated from the University of Houston, majoring in journalism, and had a fellowship at the Institute of Journalism Education, University of California, Berkeley. She worked as a television producer and reporter at an ABC affiliate in Austin, Texas and, before coming to the *Globe*, worked one year at *The Day* in New London, Connecticut. Sit came to the *Globe* through a one-year minority internship program in September 1987 and became a staff reporter a year later.

Q: *Will you tell us the reporting and writing attitudes and techniques you use to bring clarity to complexity?*

A: I never did business reporting before I came to the *Globe*. My first week was like trying to report the news in a foreign language without knowing how to count to ten in that language.

My basic rule of thumb is: If I can't understand the concept, then I can't explain it to readers or write about it intelligently.

I ask my sources tons of questions, including "dumb" questions, and force them to explain things on a level I can understand. Since business news is new to me, that can be a pretty basic level.

I don't make any assumptions in reporting. I over-report to make sure I've covered all the bases.

Q: *What homework do you do as a business writer?*

A: When I first interviewed for a job here, Lincoln Millstein, the business editor, asked me: "How much business writing have you done?"

I replied, "Not much."

He said, "Don't worry about it. Just read the *Wall Street Journal* every day." And then he pointed out exactly what columns and stories to read.

Every night I take home a stack of papers: the *Wall Street Journal, The New York Times,* and *Herald*. Of course, I read the *Globe* every morning.

Q: *What note-taking methods have you developed that work especially well on complex stories?*

A: I took Gregg shorthand in high school because I knew back then I wanted to be a reporter. It helps tremendously out in the field.

In the office on phone interviews, I open a new file for each source and type notes directly into the computer. Immediately after the interview, I organize the notes, moving some paragraphs around and adding subheads in all caps.

I always put every source's name, title, and phone number at the top of the page. Nothing's more frustrating than scrambling through scraps of paper and scribbles when you have to call back a source.

Q: *Will you describe the kinds of questions that produce the most information?*

A: I think sometimes a certain attitude, rather than a proscribed list of questions, can produce the most information. By that, I mean if you're naturally very curious and genuinely interested in what a person has to say, projecting an "I care, I really want to know" attitude, a person is more apt to open up and go beyond the thirty-second soundbite.

Q: *How do you check complicated and contradictory information?*

A: Ask the same questions to three or four experts in the same field. Pretty soon a certain theme emerges or a common thread appears that clarifies the picture. As a former teacher advised: "Report the hell out of your stories!"

Q: *Will you tell us how you organize a complicated story?*

A: I use yellow highlighter pens and Post-it notes. Since I'm not comfortable using split screens and electronic files to write from, I make a printout of every interview, staple the pages, and spread them out on my desk.

I separate the stacks with Post-it notes: pro sources, anti sources, the experts, etcetera.

Q: *Will you describe how you write the draft of a complex story?*

A: Before I write, I thoroughly read everything I've reported. I'll scan the supplemental, secondary material—the stuff the public-relations people send, old clips. If I haven't gotten an idea out in the field for my lead, this thorough rereading usually triggers an idea. Sometimes, I'll jot down topics in rough outline form just to make sure I don't forget to include them in the story.

In the back of my mind, I'm always asking myself, "What's the simplest way to say this? Would Mom understand this?" (Mom is a concert pianist who learned to speak English at age fourteen and is now a businesswoman who subscribes to the *Wall Street Journal*.)

Q: *What are your most difficult reporting problems? How do you solve them?*

A: Knowing when to stop reporting is hard for me. Especially when I'm excited about a topic, I tend to jump from one aspect to another to another, it's all so fascinating. But then it's difficult to narrow the focus again.

Deadline pressure solves this one. I stop because I have to start writing.

Q: *What are your most difficult writing problems? How do you solve them?*

A: Creating metaphors or images that work in business stories is tough. I try to read lots of other people's business stories to see what they do. It's sometimes hard to paint pictures of business concepts that are still fuzzy to me.

Q: *Do you have reporters or writers who have been models for you?*

A: I've observed and absorbed from the reporters around me. I admire Charlie Stein for the way he can take the most complicated economic story and explain it in a very clear, readable style, with wit and humor, too. Desiree French works nonstop and has the fastest turnaround from assignment to final copy. Teresa Hanafin is never too busy or too pressured to answer questions, be a verbal thesaurus, or listen to me "talk out" my story so I can figure out what I'm doing. David Mehegan writes business stories that don't sound like business stories. Some of Bruce Butterfield's stories read like the beginning of a bestseller.

Q: *What had you learned before you came to the* Globe *that has been especially valuable here?*

A: I worked at a small paper where we were expected to turn out two stories a day and three on Friday so I learned to work fast and meet deadlines.

I also learned to be selective in picking my battles.

Q: *What did you have to learn at the* Globe?

A: I learned that we tell stories at the *Globe*. Don't just throw a bunch of facts at the reader—tell it in a compelling, dramatic fashion.

Q: *Who taught it to you and how? Or did you teach yourself?*

A: My editors taught me—Lincoln Millstein, Steve Bailey, and Mary Jane Wilkinson. I came to the *Globe* through a one-year internship program that requires editors to evaluate you monthly. Lincoln would spend about an hour with me. He pointed out reporters I should observe. He demonstrated reporting techniques by acting out scenes.

Lincoln said the most important thing to learn is to write with confidence. Experiment with your writing and take chances. Steve did a lot of daily editing and would show me how to shape business news into interesting tales. Mary Jane would patiently listen to all my questions and concerns about a story and help me focus on a theme and the way to approach that. She was generous with positive feedback, which, of course, motivated me even more.

My editors were smart; by throwing a lot of stories at me they boosted my self-confidence.

Q: *What was the most surprising difference between the* Globe *and where you had worked previously?*

A: The resources and pockets were deeper here. I could dial 2940 and a librarian would research clips for me. There were more tools available here to support the reporter.

Q: *How does the* Globe *treat a beginning staff member? What could the* Globe *do better?*

A: I felt like my editors treated me like any other staff member. They needed me in business. I got real stories, not just wire stuff to rewrite. I tried not to think of myself as "the minority intern" but as a regular part of the team who was going to be around after twelve months.

The *Globe* could do a better job of introducing new reporters to the staff. And although I got a lot of support, I think some of the new reporters don't get the support and direction they need to excel.

Q: *What advice do you have for a young, beginning writer at the* Globe?

A: Don't be afraid to ask questions. Walk into your editor's office and get his or her attention. Ask your colleagues for help. Since you're a so-called "young beginner," most will not feel threatened by you and are glad to answer questions.

Find out what your editor values in a reporter, really listen to what he or she is telling you, then follow that advice. Do it their way first—later, once you know you've won their respect, trust your own instincts.

❖ Journalist at Work ❖ FAMOUS WRITERS Living and Dead

When I was in North Quincy Junior High I abandoned the branch library in Wollaston and discovered the open stacks at the main Quincy Library. While searching, mostly unsuccessfully, for books on *s-e-x* I found books on writing; books about writers, foreign correspondents, and journalists; books by writers. I started a commonplace book, years before I ever heard that term, writing down quotations by writers about writing. Now I have published a collection of quotations on writing called *Shoptalk: Learning to Write with Writers.* It was developed from the thousands of quotations I had collected through the years and this "interview" will be with some of those writers from whom I have learned writing.

Q: *What are you looking for when you go out on a story?*

The writer is looking for the informing material. (Maxine Kumin)

Q: *Have you had any assignments when there was no story?*

I blame myself for not often enough seeing the extraordinary in the ordinary. Somewhere in his journals Dostoyevsky remarks that a writer can begin anywhere, at the most commonplace thing, scratch around in it long enough, pry and dig away long enough, and, lo!, soon he will hit upon the marvelous. (Saul Bellow)

Q: *What do you think has made you an effective reporter?*

Curiosity urges you on—the driving force. (John Dos Passos)

Q: *Will you describe how you work as a reporter?*

The writer . . . sees what he did not expect to see. . . . Inattentive learner in the schoolroom of life, he keeps some faculty free to hear and wonder. His is the roving eye. By that roving eye is his subject found. The glance, at first only vaguely caught, goes on to concentrate, deepen, becomes the vision. (Elizabeth Bowen)

Q: *What advice do you have for a beginning reporter?*

Try to be one of the people on whom nothing is lost. (Henry James)

Q: *What about your relationship with your sources?*

Isn't disloyalty as much the writer's virtue as loyalty is the soldier's? (Graham Greene)

Q: *Why did you become a writer in the first place?*

I began to write because I was too shy to talk, and too lonely not to send messages. (Heather McHugh)

Q: *You can write fast stories on deadline when you have to, but the stories that have won awards are different. Can you describe it?*

I strive for imperfection, for that rawness, clumsiness, an awkwardness—which retains an energy—so hard to do. Perfection is the death of energy. (Walter Abish)

Q: *Could you describe that again?*

To write well, one needs a natural facility and an acquired difficulty. (Joubert)

Q: *One editor mentioned your ability at rewrite. What do you do?*

The greatest artist is the simplifier. (Henri Frederic Amiel)

Q: *I'm impressed at how you can take an ordinary police story or a hearing at city hall and give it a special quality. How do you do that?*

A sentence is born both good and bad at the same time. The whole secret lies in a barely perceptible twist. The control handle must be warm in your hand. You must turn it only once, never twice. (Isaac Babel)

Q: *But it doesn't seem tricky, what you do. How do you keep from getting between the reader and the story, from getting in the way?*

The hardest thing about writing, in a sense, is not writing. I mean, the sentence is not designed to show you off, you know. It is not supposed to be "look at me! Look, no hands!" It's supposed to be a pipeline between the reader and you. One condition of the sentence is to write so well that no one notices that you're writing. (James Baldwin)

Q: *Your writing seems so, well, natural.*

It takes a great deal of experience to become natural. (Willa Cather)

Q: *Did you study style?*

I never study style; all that I do is try to get the subject as clear as I can in my own head, and express it in the commonest language which occurs to me. (Charles Darwin)

Q: *How would you describe the writing you like?*

A good style in literature, if closely examined, will be seen to consist in a constant succession of tiny surprises. (Ford Maddox Ford)

Q: *What other qualities do you see in the best writing in the* Globe*?*

Vigorous writing is concise. A sentence should contain no unnecessary words, a paragraph no unnecessary sentences, for the same reason that a drawing should have no unnecessary lines and a machine no unnecessary parts. This requires not that the writer make all his sentences short, or that he avoid all detail and treat his subjects only in outline, but that every word tell. (William Strunk, as reported by E. B. White)

Q: *As a reporter, you seem to be able to find the revealing detail and build your stories from those significant specifics. How do you accomplish this?*

The more particular, the more specific you are, the more universal you are. (Nancy Hale)

Q: *When I read your writing, I seem to hear it. How do you get that quality in your articles?*

I still read everything aloud. I have a fundamental conviction that if a sentence cannot be read aloud with sincerity, conviction, and communicable emphasis, it is not a good sentence. Good writing requires good rhythms and good words. You cannot know whether the rhythms and the words are good unless you read them aloud. Reading aloud is also the easiest way to see that prose tracks, that it runs on smoothly from sentence to sentence, idea to idea, section to section within the larger whole. Reading aloud also makes the mind consider connotations of words and perhaps above all their relations to each other. (Richard Marius)

Q: *How do you proceed to write a story?*

I don't write a word of the article until I have the lead. It just sets the whole tone—the whole point of view. I know exactly where I'm going as soon as I have the lead. (Nora Ephron)

Q: *Sometimes, I can't get started writing immediately. Does that ever happen to you?*

Delay is natural to a writer. He is like a surfer—he bides his time, waits for the perfect wave on which to ride in. Delay is instinctive with him. He waits for the surge (of emotion? of strength? of courage?) that will carry him along. (E. B. White)

Q: *Is that writer's block?*

There is no such thing as writer's block. My father drove a truck for forty years. And never once did he wake up in the morning and say: "I have truck-driver's block today I am not going to work." (Roger Simon)

Q: *What rituals do you have to get started?*

Rituals? Ridiculous! My only ritual is to sit close enough to the typewriter so that my fingers touch the keys. (Isaac Asimov)

Q: *Let's go back to when you've finished your reporting and are on deadline.*

I try to write without consulting my material; this avoids interruption and prevents me from overloading my text with quotations. In this way I establish a comfortable distance from the mass and pressure of data. It helps the narrative flow. It is a guard against irrelevancies. (Leon Edel)

Q: *Any other tricks while writing on deadline?*

Too often I wait for the sentence to finish taking shape in my mind before setting it down. It is better to seize it by the end that first offers itself, head and foot, though not knowing the rest, then pull: The rest will follow along. (André Gide)

Q: *Do you organize your stories?*

I want to get the structural problems out of the way first, so I can get to what matters more. After they're solved, the only thing left for me to do is tell the story as well as possible. At that point, there is no escape. I'm just dealing with words on paper. (John McPhee)

Q: *What about organizing a complicated story?*

If in the first chapter you say that a gun hung on the wall, in the second or third chapter it must without fail be discharged. (Anton Chekhov)

Q: *Do you follow your plan?*

Follow the accident, fear the fixed plan—that is the rule. (John Fowles)

Q: *How do you document your stories so readers will keep reading?*

The writer makes his living by anecdotes. He searches them out and carves them as the raw materials of his profession. No hunter stalking his prey is more alert to the presence of his quarry than a writer looking for small incidents that cast a strong light on human behavior . . . very little has meaning to the writer except as it is tied to the reality of a single person, and except as that reality can illustrate a larger lesson or principle. (Norman Cousins)

Q: *Don't you get tired of fiddling with your language?*

Working at sentences and rhythms is probably the most satisfying thing I do as a writer. I think after a while a writer can begin to know himself through his language. He sees someone or something reflected back at him from these constructions. Over the years it's possible for a writer to shape himself as a human being through the language he uses. I think written language, fiction, goes that deep. He not only sees himself but begins to make himself or remake himself. (Don Delillo)

Q: *Then you care about grammar?*

What I know about grammar is its infinite power. To shift the structure of a sentence alters the meaning of that sentence, as definitely and inflexibly as the position of a camera alters the meaning of the object photographed. Many people know about camera angles now, but not so many know about sentences. (Joan Didion)

Q: *Any rules you have found that are particularly helpful?*

Writing simply means no dependent clauses, no dangling things, no flashbacks, and keeping the subject near the predicate. We throw in as many fresh words as we can get away with. Simple, short sentences don't always work. You have to do tricks with pacing, alternate long sentences with short, to keep it vital and alive. Virtually every page is a cliffhanger and you've got to force them to turn it. (Theodor Geisel, a.k.a. Dr Seuss)

Q: *That's all?*

The adjective is the enemy of the noun. (Voltaire)

Q: *How do you know the writing is going well?*

When I see a paragraph shrinking under my eyes like a strip of bacon in a skillet, I know I'm on the right track. (Peter DeVries)

Q: *That doesn't sound very spontaneous, yet your writing has that spontaneous quality.*

In my own case there are days when the result is so bad that no fewer than five revisions are required. However, when I'm greatly inspired, only four revisions are needed before, as I've often said, I put in that note of spontaneity which even my meanest critics concede. (John Kenneth Galbraith)

Q: *Have you had any difficulty with editors?*

No passion in the world is equal to the passion to alter someone else's draft. (H. G. Wells)

Q: *What's the most difficult problem you've had?*

A poet can survive anything but a misprint. (Oscar Wilde)

Q: *Is writing easy for you?*

A writer is a person for whom writing is more difficult than it is for other people. (Thomas Mann)

Q: *Still you keep writing?*

As late as 1806 I was waiting for genius to descend upon me so that I might write . . . If I had spoken around 1795 of my plan to write, some sensible man would have told me "to write every day for an hour or two." Genius or no genius. That advice would have made me use ten years of my life that I spent stupidly waiting for genius. (Stendhal)

Q: *You must be very disciplined.*

Writing a book is like rearing children—willpower has very little to do with it. If you have a little baby crying in the middle of the night, and if you depend only on willpower to get you out of bed to feed the baby, that baby will starve. You do it out of love. (Annie Dillard)

Q: *What advice do you have to young writers on the* Globe*?*

There is no mystery about art. Do the things that you can see, they will show you those that you cannot see. By doing what you can you will gradually get to know what it is that you want to do and cannot do, and so be able to do it. (Samuel Butler)

Q: *But we said a writer should learn to be natural. How do you find out what is natural for you?*

To be nobody but yourself in a world which is doing its best, night and day, to make you everybody else—means to fight the hardest battle which any human being can fight—and never stop fighting. (e. e. cummings)

Q: *But what if the editors don't like natural?*

You have to remember that nobody every wants a new writer. You have to create your own demand. (Doris Lessing)

Q: *What do you think of that writer on the staff—you know the one—who calls attention to himself by his style?*

His overpowering impulse is to gyrate before his fellow man, flapping his wings and emitting defiant yells. This being forbidden by the police of all civilized countries, he takes it out by putting his yells on paper. Such is the thing called self-expression. (H. L. Mencken)

Q: *How do you think the* Globe *could improve its writing?*

Let the speech be short, comprehending much in few words. (Ecclesiastes)

Recommended Reading

Berg, Elizabeth. 1999. *Escaping Into the Open: The Art of Writing True.* New York: HarperCollins.

Blundell, William E. 1988. *The Art and Craft of Feature Writing.* New York: New American Library.

Clark, Roy Peter, and Scanlan, Christopher. 2000. *America's Best Newspaper Writing: ASNE's Prizewinning Beats, Features, Opinions and Classics.* New York: St. Martin's Press.

Franklin, Jon. 1986. *Writing for Story: Craft Secrets of Dramatic Nonfiction by a Two-time Pulitzer Prize Winner.* New York: Athenaeum.

Graff, Henry and Barzun, Jacques. 1992. Fifth edition. *The Modern Researcher.* Fort Worth: Harcourt Brace.

Harrigan, Jane. 1993. *The Editorial Eye.* New York: St. Martin's Press.

Jerome, John. 1992. *Writing Trade: A Year in the Life.* New York: Viking.

Lamott, Anne. 1994. *Bird by Bird: Some Instructions on Writing and Life.* New York: Pantheon.

Miller, Lisa C. 1998. *Power Journalism: Computer-assisted Reporting.* Ft. Worth: Harcourt Brace.

Murray, Donald M. 1989. Second edition. *Learning by Teaching.* Portsmouth: Heinemann.

———. 1989. *Expecting the Unexpected.* Portsmouth: Heinemann.

———. 1990. *Shoptalk, Learning to Write With Writers.* Portsmouth: Heinemann.

———. 1993. Third edition. *Read to Write.* Fort Worth: Harcourt Brace.

———. 1996. *Writer in the Newsroom.* St. Petersburg: The Poynter Institute.

———. 1996. *Crafting a Life in Essay, Story, Poem.* Portsmouth: Heinemann.

———. 1998. Sixth edition. *Write to Learn.* Fort Worth: Harcourt Brace.

———. 2000. Fourth edition. *The Craft of Revision.* Fort Worth: Harcourt Brace.

Perry, Susan K. 1999. *Writing in Flow: Keys to Enhanced Creativity.* Cincinnati: Writer's Digest Books.

Plimpton, George, editor. 1998. *The Writer's Chapbook: A Compendium of Fact, Opinion, Wit, and Advice from the 20th Century's Preeminent Writers* [edited from The Paris Review Interviews]. New York: Modern Library.

Rhodes, Richard. 1995. *How to Write: Advice And Reflections.* New York: Morrow.

Scanlan, Christopher. 2000. *Reporting and Writing: Basics for the 21st century.* Fort Worth: Harcourt Brace.

Stewart, James B. 1998. *Follow the Story: How to Write Successful Nonfiction.* New York: Simon and Schuster.

Zinsser, William. 1998. Sixth edition. *On Writing Well: The Classic Guide to Writing Nonfiction.* New York: HarperCollins.

Index

Q

R

S

T